CM01082484

THE
QUANTIFIED
SCHOLAR

HOW RESEARCH EVALUATIONS
TRANSFORMED THE BRITISH
SOCIAL SCIENCES

JUAN PABLO
PARDO-GUERRA

Columbia University Press   *New York*

Columbia University Press
Publishers Since 1893
New York   Chichester, West Sussex
cup.columbia.edu

Library of Congress Cataloging-in-Publication Data
Names: Pardo-Guerra, Juan Pablo, author.
Title: The quantified scholar : how research evaluations transformed
the British social sciences / Juan Pablo Pardo-Guerra, UC San Diego.
Description: New York : Columbia University Press, [2022] |
Includes bibliographical references and index.
Identifiers: LCCN 2021062717 (print) | LCCN 2021062718 (ebook) |
ISBN 9780231197809 (Hardback : acid-free paper) |
ISBN 9780231197816 (Trade Paperback : acid-free paper) |
ISBN 9780231552356 (eBook)
Subjects: LCSH: Educational evaluation—
Great Britain—Management. | Social sciences—Study and
teaching (Higher)—Great Britain—Research. | Higher education
and state—Great Britain.
Classification: LCC LB2822.75 .P36 2022 (print) |
LCC LB2822.75 (ebook) | DDC 379.41—dc23/eng/20220425
LC record available at https://lccn.loc.gov/2021062717
LC ebook record available at https://lccn.loc.gov/2021062718

Columbia University Press books are printed on permanent
and durable acid-free paper.
Printed and bound by CPI Group (UK) Ltd, Croydon, CR0 4YY

Cover design: Elliott S. Cairns
Cover image: SCOTTCHAN/Shutterstock.com

A Lupe y Juan Pablo

CONTENTS

ACKNOWLEDGMENTS

Austrian philosopher Ludwig Wittgenstein famously argued that there is no such thing as a private language. In science and technology studies, the field where I trained, this claim was taken to hold that knowledge can only exist as the product of community. Knowledge is present only as a collective realization, not as an individual project.

Acknowledgment sections like the one you are reading now are a relatively recent addition to books that reflect this collective character of knowledge. References matter, of course, but the shoulders of giants we stand on go beyond the books and articles we have read and include, necessarily, the contributions of those who have created the conditions for our work. To them, I offer my most sincere gratitude.

A book like this would have been impossible without the direct input and labor of two groups of people. My interviewees kindly gifted me their time and confidence. I can only hope to have fully captured the texture of their experiences. Here I include the many colleagues and friends with whom I have held ongoing conversations about research evaluations for more than a decade. Their insights and observations were decidedly formative, and their friendship and support a source of constant respite.

My two research assistants—Renan Sallai Iwayama and Prithviraj Pahwa—provided their time, skills, expertise, and patience with my sometimes disorganized style in setting up the computational models that informed this work. Though I am a computational social scientist, I code slowly and fear that, had I been unaided in this project, it would have never come to fruition. Renan's and Prithviraj's work was simply essential, and I am forever in their debt.

Early support for this project from friends and colleagues was also critical. Abigail Andrews and Vanesa Ribas provided generous and focused comments on an early outline of the proposal for this book. I am ever grateful for their friendship. Kerry McKenzie's interest was always a fuel for thinking about the evaluative experience of British academia. Marion Fourcade's insightful and exceedingly kind comments and conversations were central to rethinking the project as it evolved. Feedback received at various events, including the 2020 meeting of the American Sociological Association, the 2020 and 2021 meetings of the Society for the Advancement of Socio-Economics, and generous seminars/workshops at Columbia University, the University of Virginia, and the University of California at Los Angeles contributed much to shaping the argument of this book.

As the book was written during a time of lockdowns, part of the intellectual community behind it was discovered online. This project was an opportunity to reengage with some classical work in sociology (the contributions of Wendy Espeland, Michael Sauder, and Michèle Lamont were indisputable inspirations), but it was also a chance to create bridges with a new generation of higher education scholars and students of rankings and quantification. The exceptional Jelena Branković provided particularly impressive support, with detailed suggestions on a draft of the manuscript. Her comments certainly made this a better book, and I am forever thankful.

Of course, this book was only possible because of the detailed and assiduous editorial work of Eric Schwartz, Lowell Frye, and the staff at Columbia University Press. I thank them for the opportunity to publish this work under their guidance and care, and for arranging exceptional reviewers who provided constrictive criticisms of earlier drafts of the manuscript—one reviewer was particularly commendable for providing several pages of excellent, detailed comments. My thanks extend also to my editor, Letta Page, whose expertise, suggestions, and labor of care and dedication made this a better book. Letta's work was infinitely kind, detailed, and supportive, and I am in her debt. I also thank Ben Kolstad for his thoughtful editorial comments and corrections.

Finally, I thank Nara and Samuel for enduring and tolerating with love and kindness my absences and distractions.

THE
QUANTIFIED
SCHOLAR

1

CHAINS OF KNOWLEDGE

I t was, as a matter of fact, a sunny day in 2014. I probably should remember this with greater clarity—such days are rarities in late-winter London—but my memory has imposed a drizzle that Google denies. Apparently, I was too captivated, too distracted, by what unfolded as we gathered in the newly remodeled common room for our routine departmental meeting, the smell of recently installed linoleum still fresh in the air.

At the time, I was a lecturer[1] in the Department of Sociology of the London School of Economics and Political Science. As in most other institutions, being a full-time academic at LSE involved occasional faculty meetings with colleagues. We would discuss matters relevant to our teaching programs and internal administration, the hiring of new faculty, the intellectual direction of our department, and our views on our institution's constantly changing initiatives and policies. Bureaucracy, some would grumble, or, more generously, community-building, such conclaves are among the indisputable ceremonial practices of academic participation. Anyhow, as we did every now and then, we undertook that strange mix of scholarly ritual and managerial intervention, talking shop on an unusually sunny late-winter afternoon. We read and approved the minutes from the previous term's meeting; we heard from our head of department; and we listened to faculty committees' reports concerning students, teaching, and research. Having ticked off all the items on our agenda, we had reached the apparent end of this organizational rite. Just then, in the twilight closing moment when one begins thinking ahead to the day's demands (office hours, a meeting here, an unattended inbox there) yet remains aware of the parting pleasantries, my mind snapped to attention.

"The school has requested us," began the head of department, "to come up with a list of journals that we consider prestigious in our fields of expertise—that define us as a department. They want to use this for our next evaluation, to have a better sense of our own standards of excellence." The chatter vanished, replaced by this infinitely more intriguing gambit. Silence followed, heavy with a combination of both incredulity and resignation. "This is an opportunity for us to decide how we are evaluated," the head of department nudged.

Several moments passed before an intrepid colleague ventured the first contribution: "the *British Journal of Sociology*, I guess." This sacrificial offer made sense: in addition to being one of UK sociology's flagship journals, the *BJS* was currently stewarded by our department. "*Sociology*," followed another, naturally forwarding the scholarly publication of our discipline's professional association. No argument there. "*City & Community*," said someone else, reflecting our department's investments and interests in urban sociology. "Certainly *Theory, Culture and Society*," said a fourth. "*Work, Employment and Society*," called out another, and I heard "*Antipode*" from a voice at the back of the room.

All these journals were (and remain) sensible suggestions. They were, after all, close to the topics, scholarly genres, and intellectual traditions followed by academics in our department. They contained the voices of our community, the traditions of our craft. But these suggestions were not, perhaps, as prestigious as they might have been, at least not in the eyes of the upper administration. They wanted to see "top journals," the kind that dominate rankings, rack up citations, and confer scholarly esteem to their contributors and affiliated institutions.

"Think big," urged the head of department. "The list has to be credible; it needs to convey we are ambitious and want to publish in the very top."

"Well then," someone in the room responded, "it's the *American Journal of Sociology* and the *American Sociological Review*, even if we rarely publish there." At the time, "rarely" was quite the understatement.

This seemingly banal exercise, at precisely this moment, became for me the sight that eclipsed the sun. There we were, a room full of sociologists anxiously fashioning chimeras, lists that combined tradition with aspiration, practice with expectations, and, in doing so, forging the very chains that would bind our knowledge, link by link, word by word.

• • •

Repeated across universities in the United Kingdom and often with far less participation from staff,[2] this exercise is a direct response to the cultures of assessment and evaluation that have proliferated throughout the British higher education sector in the past four decades.[3] Since 1986, when the British government first mandated that publicly funded universities submit regular, standardized assessments of research quality, scholars and managers have faced the vexing problem of evaluating the intellectual worth of articles, books, and other creative products of career academics, with the aim of rewarding "excellence."[4] With furrowed brows, we ask: When do we know that a paper *must all research be useful? or efficient?*

who decides?

who is funding?

is outstanding? How do we know if a book made a substantive contribution to knowledge? And we wonder whether the tallies we create answer the government's implicit questions: Is the public expenditure on science worth it? Is state funding being used efficiently, going to the best possible researchers in the most effective centers of knowledge production?

In this book, I am concerned with a pair of naturally extending questions: Do universities foster a form of scholarly excellence and selectivity that is, in fact, visible, measurable, accountable to the public? And how do the quantification and ranking of scholars and their work, through lists, assessment exercises, and other devices, affect the scholarship itself? The list my LSE colleagues were asked to produce was intended as an instrument that allowed managers and academic peers from other disciplines within our organization to make sense of our work, to assign us value. Being invited to craft this list certainly granted us a sense of buy-in, yet each scholar in the room understood it would be used as a measuring tape, of sorts—one more way we might be compared, quantified, and ranked, with consequences on the lives we lived, and on the knowledge we produced.

Knowledge is difficult to quantify; still, we try. In the following, I look at a particular instance of how trying to quantify the value and excellence of knowledge—specifically, the British evaluations known as the Research Assessment Exercises and, more recently, the Research Excellence Framework—changes the nature of scholarship and academic lives. In *The Quantified Scholar*, I argue that measuring value and excellence in science fosters specific forms of what sociologists Wendy Espeland and Michael Sauder call "reactivity"[5]: it introduces novel incentives for managers and shifts the goalposts for scholars, changing the way they think about and experience their careers and their craft. Quantification makes visible and organizationally durable specific and arbitrary hierarchies of worth that, when tied to the long-standing cultures of prestige in scholarly fields, change notions of who and what is valuable.

Studying the British case, this book shows how the adoption of standardized research evaluations changed the way social scientific knowledge about the world was produced. It did so in two ways. At one level, it perturbated local labor markets for academics, changing the structure of careers in a way that produced more homogeneous institutions within the fields of anthropology, economics, political science, and sociology. At another level, these evaluations changed the way academics made sense of their own worth, echoing in their everyday lives the hierarchies that were implicit in the practices of these formal assessments of research excellence. Slowly but surely, these vast and intrusive evaluation exercises made the conceptual schemas of scientists increasingly similar, ever more homogeneous, across the four disciplines that I study.

Although a book about the effects of the quantification on knowledge, however, the argument I make here is ultimately about academic vocations. If quantification holds a strong grip over the work of British academics—and those elsewhere exposed to the countless metrics of modern scholarly work—it is because of how scholars collectively come to accept and reproduce cultures of repute, overwork, and sacrifice connected to the ideals of research in science. Academics are often trained to hold research as the dearest of their obligations, striving to produce forms of knowledge that will be recognized by their peers and future generations. Even more, we are habituated to see ourselves in the research we produce. When we think of scholars celebrated for their contributions to the understanding of culture, politics, economy, and society—the types of names peppered throughout most introductory classes in high school and college—we casually equate their works with the lives of their authors. We talk of Max Weber as we do of his works; we conflate Hannah Arendt and her essays; we shorthand Adam Smith for his foundational books. They are one and the same: the carefully considered, curated, crafted, edited words on paper, and the messy, complicated, and contradictory lives of their authors, their bodies, and their careers. This is what we are trained to think, both as audience and as performers.

But in this training and vocation, scholars often reproduce a view of the world that dissolves bonds of solidarity in our workplace and profession. This is not a story of algorithmic or organizational inevitability but of choice—of recognizing our role in deciding how we value peers and their various forms of work. In the above vignette, what mattered was certainly how my LSE colleagues collectively populated the list; yet in accepting without dispute the role of the list as an instrument of value, we begrudgingly accepted the logic of standardized evaluations and what they expected about knowledge. Compiling a list of journals involved playing the game; but for a brief second, we had the upper hand to set the ground rules of our evaluation. The list we chose reflected our wants and aspirations rather than our community and strife. This is ultimately the challenge of the quantified scholar: choosing solidarity over the politics of prestige in a profession that sees repute as its prime currency.

COUNTING KNOWLEDGE

It is little wonder the measuring tapes would come for the sciences, given a vast and impressive literature that attests to measuring the world as an essential, centuries-old feature of scientific practices.[6] The social sciences especially count on counting to explain the intangibles that animate our ever-changing settings: economic growth, social class, political attitudes, religious conviction, unseen psychological dispositions, interpersonal trust, human suffering, commitment, taste, and so on. Quantifying these objects allows scientists to produce knowledge, making claims about various complex processes of the social world. But what happens on those occasions when science itself is quantified, particularly with a clear managerial intent?[7]

Metrics have long been used to organize, reward, and shape the course of science throughout the world. I still have vivid memories of my parents, both professors of biochemistry working at public institutions in Mexico, assiduously undertaking their annual rituals of verification. The national funding agency expected them to report the impact factors[8] of the journals in which they published their research as a way of guaranteeing the quality of their contributions. This onerous task meant securing print versions (often second- and thirdhand photocopies) of the Journal Citation Reports, in which these impact factors were organized alphabetically. When the internet made these measures more readily available, scholars began being asked to submit individual citation counts for their papers; these, too, were diligently gathered (regardless of expensive paywalls) and provided in order to demonstrate value and sustain state support. However often quantification is decried as "a cheap and ineffective method of assessing the productivity of individual scientists,"[9] metrics like these are routinely employed by universities, funding agencies, government bodies, and international organizations interested in learning what they get for their money, tallying their returns on investment.

Scientists are not uninterested in valuations of their work. Although largely an instrument of external management today, counting science arguably started within modern science itself, as a means of measuring quality and excellence in research. As Paul Wouters reminds us in his now-classic dissertation, for example, research librarians have "systematically applied citation analysis" since the early twentieth century, ostensibly to measure the usefulness of costly subscriptions.[10] The interest in counting was not limited to librarians but extended to the broader scholarly community. The notorious statistician Alfred Lotka, for example, sought to identify patterns in the distribution of publications as early as 1926 to "determine the part which men [*sic*] of different caliber contribute to the progress of science."[11] While motivated by intellectual concerns about the structure *of* scientific disciplines, the fields of bibliometrics and scientometrics are now established and frequently marshalled to determine the worth of scholars and their contributions *to* those disciplines.[12]

We might think of metrics, scales, and rulers as merely convenient devices for representing our world. In practice, however, most forms of measurement are tied to purposeful interventions. We measure to do things, whether to establish property lines with strings and trigonometry, understand the fundamental relations between subatomic particles, or cut a sheet of plywood into the components of a new drawer. But unlike tracing imaginary lines on the land beneath our feet, estimating the arc of a particle in a cloud chamber, or measuring bits of lumber, quantifying the productivity and quality of scholars is a particularly interventionist act. Measuring these "social kinds," to borrow from philosopher Ian Hacking,[13] alters the qualities of the objects under assessment—be they scholars, institutions, disciplines, or knowledge at large. When quantification is public and constantly visible, affording comparisons and competition, as Jelena Brancović and colleagues note, it triggers reactivity—that is, changes in the interests, practical strategies, and intellectual approaches of scholars in response to the incentives of rankings, numerical assessments, and metrics of work.[14]

How do quantification and its associated reactivity affect scholars and their scholarship? Does this process produce, over time, "better" knowledge? Or does its lead to "worse" accounts of the world? I'll be as straightforward and honest as possible: quality is relative. I cannot give you, reader, a definitive ruling on the future, long-term effects of quantification on scientific knowledge. (Being in the fortunate though entirely hypothetical position of knowing what is optimal for science would mean having cracked a quandary at the core of philosophic inquiry—what, precisely, separates science from other forms of knowledge—which I can't say I have.) Throughout this book, however, I will provide extensive evidence suggesting that efforts to quantify the value of science have affected knowledge production as well as the organization of scientific disciplines, fields, and academic units and the progression of individual careers. Whereas counting helps social scientists make sense of our world, being counted helps account for the questions we ask (and those we don't ask). By studying the mechanics of research evaluations in the United Kingdom, I show that knowledge produced by social scientists has become increasingly homogeneous within and across institutions. The actuarial demands of austerity, in which impact scores, journal rankings, and periodic evaluations dictate funding allotments and justify intellectual investments, circumscribe the types of topics explored by social scientists and the meanings associated with their concepts and theories of the world.

The consequences are stark: the uptake of quantification as a means for managing British science has resulted in ever more disciplinary logic and organization in academic fields. This occurs through a process I call "epistemic sorting": the cultures of evaluation fostered by quantification create incentives for scholars to sort themselves out across the institutional space of British higher education in ways that funnel their disciplines toward homogeneity. Epistemic sorting alters what scientists know—and seek to know—about the world in potentially fundamental ways. While I cannot say with absolute foresight that this is a negative outcome, my findings are shot through with an underlying value claim. For those who find worth in intellectual diversity and scientific serendipity, the effects of quantification that I document in this book are likely pernicious: scientists at the UK's leading institutions are, over time, conducting less risky, less innovative work.

• • •

Attentive readers will note my careful references to Britain and the UK. They are purposeful. The British case is particularly useful for examining the way quantification changes scientific work, given how it combines patterns of fiscal austerity, government-sponsored quantification, and the internationalization of academic work since the 1980s. While populated by institutions old and new, the British higher education sector is relatively standardized, providing a sort of natural experimental control. As explored in chapter 2, the various types of British universities—from the medieval institutions that served aristocratic elites to the newer ex-polytechnics designed to train the postwar professional masses—have converged through mimesis into a single institutional type.[15] Prestige and financial resources remain unequally distributed across the sector and teaching loads and research expectations vary, yet, by and large, most British universities operate under the same academic model: scholars are expected to publish, teach, and provide service to the institution and their profession, with the first of these taking symbolic prominence. Unlike the U.S. system, in which wealthy private institutions compete with flagship state colleges for both students and faculty, while also sharing space with a panoply of institutional types and forms, higher education in the UK is largely a public enterprise. It is regulated by the national governments of England, Scotland, and Wales and organized across a single workers' trade union, the University and College Union. This relative uniformity in organizational design allows for analyzing the effects of research evaluations with due care for teasing out extraneous factors that might otherwise create "noisy" data and inconclusive causality.

In addition to having a long-standing and established higher education system, Britain has periodically assessed academics employed in its public universities through vast peer-review-like exercises that are meant to determine the quality of research produced across institutions and their disciplinary units. These evaluations matter doubly: besides affording status and prestige (a form of currency that is central to science), they are tied to state financial resources. Pools of "quality-related" research funding are disbursed only to the best performing institutions in each field, as determined by the assessment exercises. Over time, these assessments have taken various forms and names—initially Research Selectivity, then Research Assessment Exercise, and since 2014 Research Excellence Framework—but in all cases they have involved evaluations of academic units performed by panels of disciplinary peers. These differ substantively from the more individualized forms of assessment that exist in other countries, which focus on each scholar's productivity or visibility as a measure of worth. This is not because individual scholars are not evaluated in the UK assessments, but simply because their individual results are never made public. So, in every iteration

·

since the first, in 1986, scholars of all British public institutions have been assessed, with their work read and scored by
peers across a scale of quality from "unclassified" outputs that
fall "below the standard of nationally recognized work" to four-
star research, "world-leading in terms of originality, significance
and rigor."[16] The scores of individual research products become
not a mark borne by each scientist (no one really knows how
their work was evaluated, with individual scores shrouded in
secrecy and destroyed shortly after the assessments) but, rather,
as cumulative calculations of their institutions' quality and disciplinary value.

In this, the forms of state-sponsored scholarly quantification observed in the United Kingdom are structurally closer
to the ways U.S. institutions are ranked (the emblematic case
being law school rankings, as revealed by the aforementioned
Espeland and Sauder[17]). Though the evaluations are ostensibly
high-level—department A produces more excellent research
than department B—the various ways administrators and peers
place value on, and react to, the outcomes of these evaluations
have consequences for individual careers and the disciplines that
scholars inhabit. The effects of these exercises are moderated
by distinct organizational cultures. In some institutional settings, the evaluations are hardly felt; in others, they are objects
of constant anxiety, directing hiring and promotion decisions,
resource allocations, and other consequential processes. Even
the administration of assessments can become a tacit game, with
institutions attempting to sway scoring (and risking mistakes
like submitting scholars' records to the wrong disciplinary peer
review panels, leading to poor results and negative consequences
for capable employees).

To study quantification, I have departed from some of the traditional approaches taken by scholars in the sociology, anthropology,

and philosophy of science. For decades, these colleagues have studied knowledge as constituted not through some universal method
of discovery but, rather, through piecewise processes of enrol-
ment, delegation, representation, intervention, looping, controversy, falsification, refutation, contestation, and closure. Scientific
knowledge is "socially constructed," insofar as it is created within
specific communities of experts who, on the basis of ongoing conversations and interventions, revise their claims about the world.[18]
These approaches clearly foreground the epistemic dimensions of
science, tackling the question of how practices, communities, and
institutions come together to assemble scientific knowledge. In
what follows, I am informed by these approaches, though I focus
not on the ways knowledge is made (how it encodes politics and
interests, how it depends on complex alliances between humans
and instruments, or how it produces or forestalls social action, for
instance) but on the conditions experienced by those who are in
the business of its production. That is, I consider the work world
of academic science. Laboratories are certainly sites for epistemic practices, but they are, too, invariably sites of work, of paid
employment, of managerial intervention.[19] By considering knowledge as a distinct product of labor, *The Quantified Scholar* finds that
quantification matters for how knowledge is produced because it
alters how the knowledge-makers experience their crafts and their
places of work.

TRAJECTORIES OF DEVOTION

The objects of this study are embedded workers whose intellectual labor is invariably shaped by the affordances, incentives,
biases, and barriers creating and curtailing the shop floors of the
modern university. I am inspired by a large sociological literature

on work and occupations, while emphasizing a particular facet of academic employment relations and the ways scholar-employees' experiences of evaluation shape the course of their labor over longer periods of time. The processes I trace in this book—the forms of epistemic sorting and linguistic change that are tied to the implementation of quantified research evaluations—are not punctual but processual, forming slow shifts in the register of scholarly conversations and the organization of disciplinary fields. These changes are connected to, yet overflow, the contractual relations between employers and managers, because academics are both workers, bound by contract to the universities that employ them, and professionals bound by the practices, traditions, and evaluation cultures of their individual intellectual fields.

Careers are fascinating meso-level phenomena to social scientists. Foundational scholar Erwin Goffman characterized the concept of the career as one that allows us to connect micro- and macro-level social processes by moving "back and forth between the personal and the public, between the self and its significant society."[20] In the present study, a scholarly career is what unites the individual, rational, isolated epistemic worker to the social agent who actively navigates institutional structures over the course of a field-based intellectual career.

Considering the tensions between the personal and the public provides a novel understanding of how knowledge and scientific fields change over time. Like others, barring exceptional luck or nepotism, scholars find establishing "successful" careers virtually impossible without expending some degree of individual effort—without putting in work and investments that translate into an intellectual contribution that helps maintain an institutional affiliation that provides a site for research. At the same time, careers are shaped by factors beyond the control of individuals: gender and racial biases saturate formal evaluations, peer networks amplify some work through frequent citation (and ignore similar work performed by out-group members), and life circumstances draw greater penalties to particular, often minoritized, groups.[21] Many of these well-documented biases—reflected in productivity gaps, promotion gaps, salary gaps, and citation gaps—surely reflect larger, economywide structures of discrimination and inequality (academia is not unique in this sense). Within academic science, however, these inequalities are additionally bound to the noncontractual expectations that shape our sense of commitment to academic disciplines.

Who we decide to include in our syllabi or cite in our works is rarely controlled by our employers—but is often policed by our disciplinary peers. Academia, in other words, is unexceptional as a form of employment in which the formal structures of our employing organizations impinge on our careers, yet exceptional in that our work is also associated with a form of vocation, evaluated and shaped by the invisible, weighty traditions to which we belong.

My strategy in *The Quantified Scholar* is to move back and forth between the individual scientist, with their personal experiences as managed workers, and the public, collective disciplinary settings in which their work is read, used, and assigned worth. These distinct but interrelated domains of the workplace (ruled by specific managerial expectations and contractual arrangements) and the discipline (where more tacit notions of value are produced and enacted through peer training and habits) are linked by the cooperation of research evaluations across both. Neither entirely "bureaucratic" interventions nor simply "intellectual" exercises, research evaluations establish expectations of productivity and scholarship that tie faculty work to institutional interests (with career consequences) and, by virtue of their connections to notions of scholarly quality, status, and prestige, reify disciplinary norms around relative value that, in turn, shape scholars' everyday intellectual decisions. More pointedly, because research evaluations are grounded in disciplinary peer review—with sociologists evaluating sociologists and so on—they lead to increasingly homogeneous scholarly fields. The diminishment of scope, which may be connected to less risky, recombinant, innovative forms of research,[22] is not then a direct product of scholars' individual choices and inclinations; it is a synthetic consequence of their conditions of work. Thus, to understand how research evaluations lead to the production of more homogeneous, paradigmatic forms of knowledge, I focus on their effects on scientific careers—the scaffolds on which we iteratively build our fields of academic practice.

These scaffolds are admittedly peculiar. A notable feature of scientific careers is the degree to which they are framed by the idea of a vocation, a "calling" to produce knowledge for its own sake, a devotion to the discipline, its logics, and its practices. This point was famously raised by Max Weber in his lecture on *Science as Vocation*, wherein he eloquently captured many scholars' personal enthrallment with and passionate dedication to scholarship in general as well as to their highly specialized objects of study.[23] This vocation is not practical—as sociologist Steven Shapin notes, the scientist's orientation does not encompass, in Weber's conception, "commercial goals and entrepreneurial means."[24] It is concerned solely with the production of facts and knowledge—finding truths that, however fickle and ultimately falsifiable, populate our shared fields of scholarship and pay the entry fee for a shared sense of academic, collegial, intellectual integrity. Although written almost a century ago, when performance management and scholarly evaluation were still incipient, Weber's account still resonates (decade upon decade, *Science as Vocation* warms the printing press). Despite the professionalization of scientists and the structural changes to higher education, the transformation of scholarship from a calling into a "mere" job is necessarily incomplete. Shapin reminds us that, to this day, the tension between employment and vocation, paycheck and devotion, alters the identity of scientists and how they value their own contributions to scientific advancement.[25] After decades of professional change, we remain vocational in a Weberian sense. Our work is a "mode of life" that encompasses our minds, our bodies, and the very fabric of our souls.

The survival of this vocational spirit in the sciences has concrete implications for peer evaluation. Yes, Weber was correct that scientists, carving out our niches, produce increasingly specialized knowledge claims on ever more particular fractions of our world. But even in today's hyperspecialized scholarship, where no single person can feasibly know their entire field, the larger structures of disciplines loom large. The tremendous rise in "interdisciplinary" research has not dislodged professional identities nor how organized performance evaluations hew to universities' departmental and divisional organization. Time marches on, and we continue to frame intellectual value and scholarly contributions in relation to the identifiable disciplines and subfields that anchor the objects of our vocation. Within these, loosely institutionalized forms of prestige become yardsticks, as the sociologist Richard Whitley argues: repute sits at the base of many of our organizational forms, a convenient means for assigning confidence to knowledge claims in an otherwise messy ecology.[26]

Our vocation is, in this way, bound to the numerous hierarchies—of institutions, of scholars, of traditions, of theories, of concepts—into which we are habituated. Quantification has surely ossified many. In *Grading the College*, for example, the historian of higher education Scott Gelber relates very early efforts to rank colleges in terms of how well they "prepared" their graduates for work in business and government (in 1912), as well as by increasingly intensive pushes to evaluate teaching quality starting in the 1920s.[27] That these rankings largely mirrored existing perceptions of institutional prestige should not come as a shock.[28] This finds echoes in the work of Jelena Branković and Stephan Wilbers, who identify both the long historical roots of academic rankings at the beginning of the twentieth century and the mechanisms through which they acquired postwar dominance. Moving away from their originally peripheral position to their place as primary managerial instruments required a shift in the logic of institutions of higher education toward framing excellence as a form of performance that could (perhaps had to) be constantly evaluated. Being an assiduous scholar was not enough: true devotion was only seen in ongoing, assessable, *measurable* actions and contributions.

We can return here to Espeland and Sauder's now canonical account of how such public evaluations transformed organizations and, in the process, our collective comfort with quantified hierarchies.[29] In their study, external rankings of law schools by *U.S. News & World Report* began as public instruments but soon became environments requiring organizational attention—the rising metrics came to change institutional strategies and priorities as well as the self-conceptions of their managers and workers (today, *U.S. News* ranks everything from high schools to mutual funds, ostensibly guiding consumers in a variety of crowded "marketplaces"). In part, we accept hierarchies like these because they are readily observable, patently material. They are "facts" that speak to the logic of our work and travel across organizational settings, making comparison of otherwise distinct objects possible and allowing for common conversations about worth.[30]

The use of metrics in the evaluation of scholarly work is certainly fascinating, yet what I find interesting about rankings, ratings, and scores is not that they exist and have performative effects (that, by design, they are self-fulfilling prophecies), but that we readily accept them and the forms of worth they imply. Our discussions of quantification seem to lack a link between the historical circumstances that made counting research possible and the way scientists continue to frame their work in vocational terms. What we have learned from the literature on self-tracking is that quantification is seductive, allowing individuals to evaluate their own worth and efforts, then aspire to selves prefigured by the devices and arrangements that measure them. The quantification of scholars is no different. While it depends on certain historical conditions of possibility, it is maintained by practices of status, prestige, and repute that hold affinities with our vocational ideals.[31] The quantified scholar is not merely a professional demand but a way to fulfill our desire to truly belong within our rationalized, modern, scholarly vocations. It is as if the numbers demonstrate that we have earned our place.

This explains, perhaps, why devices like the h-index, barely seventeen years old at the time of writing, so quickly became embedded in the global infrastructures of science metrics and research evaluation. The h-index measures the cumulative performance of a scholar's career by counting the number of publications for which they have been cited by others at least that same number of times. An author with ten publications only four of which have been cited four or more times would have, hence, an h-index of 4. The uncanny history of this metric shows that, rather than zealous administrators seeking to extract ever more from their scientist workers, the metric rose on the backs of scholars actively adopting it to better "judge the performance of researchers." "Most scholars," read an editorial in *Nature* in

2005, "prefer an explicit peer assessment of their work. Yet those same researchers know how time-consuming peer assessment can be."[32] In other words, if the gold-standard peer evaluations were too time-consuming, and measures like citations, journal factors, and institutional pedigree were regarded as less than adequate measures of quality, the h-index provided an appealing enough measure. It shorthanded a scholar's lifetime output against a discipline-specific proxy of impact. The h-index was soon adopted by scholars and refined as a frenzy of academic articles in physics, biology, sociology, computer science, and elsewhere tested its performance against previous metrics. Note that this was not about rejection, but calibration and acceptance. The success of the h-index did not stem solely from some powerful autonomous assemblage that, marketlike, sought to economize intellectual value, as the sociologist Roger Burrows suggests;[33] to the extent this form of quantification succeeded at all, it was at least as much because, deep within our modern vocation, within our training, habituation, and disposition, scholars have clear affinities for measuring their own prestige.

This is even more complicated because, as happens with artists and other creative workers, scholars have difficulty separating their personal and professional lives. Vocations are not 9-to-5 jobs, and they are not put on hold.[34] Academic careers are fuzzy cominglings of personal and professional selves (recalling Goffman, above), and this encourages us scientists to elide the personal and professional in our own careers. No lesser a sociologist than C. Wright Mills noted his early realization that most of the "thinkers and writers whom [he] admired never split their work from their lives."[35] We are what we do. Ours is a "strange intoxication," as Weber wrote, that renders the hierarchies of our fields and the criticisms and exultations of our work synonymous with our individual efforts or failures. Our identities and our careers, amplified, refracted, and modulated by quantification, alter what we see and think of as objects worthy of our individual passions or unjustifiably risky for our prestige.

REFLEXIVE KNOWLEDGE

Sitting around the new Formica tables of our departmental common room, the LSE faculty in the opening vignette were knowingly tracing the contours of our promised selves, committing to aspirational personas that would reflect back onto our work and our sense of scholarly vocation. This peculiarity is what erased my memory of the sunshine: my colleagues and I so quickly accepted—hell, *created*—a daily target of ten thousand epistemic steps though we knew little about the terrain ahead.[36] The looping effects of rankings, lists, and quantification were not alien to us: paper after paper, study after study in our very own discipline suggested that counting things matters in markets, organizations, and employment. We understood quantification as a fact of the social world, a matter of life and death. And yet there we were, trying to balance control and bureaucratic dictum, internal consistency and external legitimacy, forging our own chains of knowledge, creating our own boundaries, establishing our own measures of value. That they were required at all seemed beyond question.

Admittedly, this practice of setting goals and parameters of excellence is common to other academic disciplines, although it is put in practice in different ways. British sociologists have adamantly stressed the importance of evaluating books and papers by their contents rather than the status of their publishers or the affiliation of their authors, but this ethos is in no way shared across disciplinary lines. Fields like economics have readily accepted hierarchies of value, with clear tiers of journal quality (books are exceedingly rare as a research output in this field) mapping neatly onto broader evaluations of intellectual quality. In other domains, like political science (in Britain, more appropriately understood as politics and international relations), there are hierarchies, but these are noisy, defined by multidirectional tensions between European and American traditions of political thought as well as varying methodological approaches. In a smaller field like anthropology, the onus is traditionally placed on the peer-established quality of texts, though unofficial conversations and references regarding publisher rank and the discipline's institutional "golden triangle" (formed by elite departments in London, Cambridge, and Oxford) assert themselves throughout scholarly valuations. These different disciplinary cultures, as sociologist Michèle Lamont argues, vary in their definitions of excellence, as in how willingly they accept certain forms of self-quantification.[37]

These four disciplines share a sense of reflexivity—that is, a willingness to accept that the knowledge they produce about the world is inflected by the experiences and institutional situations of their scholars. Even economics, which seems to hold the most naturalized and individualistic view of the social, operates under the assumption that knowledge can be used to optimize or nudge the object of study in particular directions, including economists themselves. Part of this reflexivity involves a widespread recognition that quantification is a descriptor of research quality but that it can nevertheless be used with specific aims. What matters is not so much whether quantification is "actually accurate" as how it is made sense of by those it counts. Such self-awareness arguably leads to stronger forms of reactivity than in other fields like, say, high-energy physics or biotechnology. That is partly why I have chosen these four fields—anthropology, economics, politics, and sociology—for study in *The Quantified*

Scholar. In addition to lacking the fixed investments associated with disciplines in which laboratories and other forms of equipment make careers stickier (moving a lab is obviously a costly and fraught endeavor)[38] and displaying higher rates of single-authored works[39] (both of which explain my exclusion of fields like psychology), the vocation of the social scientist is modulated by a form of reflexivity that gives a different texture to discussions about excellence, quality, and performance evaluations.

The social sciences are also arguably more "flexible" toward their institutional settings, making them ostensibly better targets for studying how quantification changes their practices of knowledge-making. The sociologist Marion Fourcade's exceptional work on the development of economics, for example, shows that the variation in the organization and contents of this discipline—visible in its intellectual interests, theoretical approaches, and forms of institutionalization—observed in France, the United Kingdom, and the United States, is traceable to economists' position with respect to the state and industry in each country. A similar variation would be hard to find in the natural sciences—not because it cannot exist (national varieties of the "hard" sciences have been well documented by historians) but because these have experienced greater levels of global standardization than have the bulk of the social sciences.[40]

Within these four disciplines, I focus on academic careers—primarily, on movements of scholars between institutions (what the social scientific literature terms labor mobility)—to demonstrate how disciplines change over time in relation to the uptake of research evaluations. Knowledge is the product of communal efforts, yet it is ultimately tied to the bodies that make it possible. Academic social scientists' relative independence from physical research infrastructures like laboratories allows me to assess how quantification shapes their organizational strategies as they

Who & How far do we share credit | Institutes labs, Ones' resources / data set interrogated by 4 scholars @ different Unis? Who gets credit

attempt to govern and make sense of their immediate environments, while their employment contracts and disciplinary norms help them retain a degree of control over their labor. How they use this control is key: they can, in a sense, "play the game" of quantification or attempt to extract themselves from it, either through collective action or through changes to disciplinary norms. Though indirect, this control is practiced through internal organizational processes (for example, in scholars' approaches to assessing colleagues, serving on external panels, or reviewing peers' work). At the same time, the reliance of social scientists on shared knowledge infrastructures—things like data sets resulting from large-scale, high-quality surveys used by (and to train) large numbers of scholars—makes them subjects of distinct forms of disciplinary control. This tension between *organizational* and *disciplinary* control matters centrally for this book: even in settings with greater relative autonomy, quantification comes to matter in the way knowledge is made, cutting across the reflexive dispositions of scholars, the managerial logic of their institutions, and the prestige-based hierarchies of their fields.

The forms of reflexivity, autonomy, and institutional situatedness that attach to the social sciences point to opportunities to challenge some of the most pernicious effects of quantification. The central lesson of *The Quantified Scholar* is not that quantification is necessarily bad, but that when it becomes part of our way of making sense of the value of others and their knowledge, it leads to less hospitable, dynamic, and innovative disciplinary fields. The power contained in numbers, rankings, lists, and other measurement tapes hinges on their embedding organizations, with their sites of application and use potentially attenuating their effects. In looking at the spectrum of experiences under quantification in Britain, I will key in on cases in which scholars have actively resisted the disadvantages of quantification, fostering deeper consideration of the forms of solidarity that may serve as a balm against such corrosive outcomes. Reflexivity—of our shared condition, our common vocation, our collective knowledge—can be leveraged to produce more equitable, humane conditions of work and to tamp down the reactivity of our disciplines to bureaucratic demands.

STRUCTURE OF THE BOOK

To answer the question of how quantification changes scientific knowledge, I adopt a multipronged approach that combines various computational techniques of text analysis, quantitative models of career mobility, and interviews with British scholars active in anthropology, economics, politics, or sociology, as well as union representatives. Each tactic provides evidence that, jointly, suggests a process of increased homogeneity in the British social sciences driven by quantification's effects on careers. (A fuller description of my methods and data analysis, which echo the logic of the extended case method, are available in the appendix.)

I begin, in the next chapter, by exploring the origins of research assessments and quantification in the context of key transformations of the British higher education system. This story connects the drive to quantify scholarly excellence to the implementation of austerity measures and their attendant "audit cultures" (a term coined by anthropologist Marylin Strathern) across UK universities in the 1980s.[41] After additionally explaining how research evaluations quantify "excellence" in practice, I turn, in chapter 3, to the effects of quantification on academic careers, using evidence that links research evaluations with changes in the structure and organization of academic departments across time. Chapter 4 analyzes different fields' linguistic (and, ostensibly, knowledge) shifts in response to disciplinary pressures toward greater epistemic conformity. Together, chapters 3 and

4 present the concept and mechanism of epistemic sorting and its centrality to the effects of quantification on academic labor and scholarly careers.

In chapter 5, I take a different perspective, looking at how quantification has been experienced by academics in their workplaces. In particular, this chapter stresses the importance of local managerial implementation in understanding how scholars rethink their vocations under quantification regimes. One key observation is that quantification is moderated by hierarchies: individuals at the top of their field and their institution are less swayed by the pressures of quantification than are those in the "upward-oriented" middle of the hierarchy and peers at resource-strapped, teaching-intensive institutions that aspire to climb the league tables by expecting more "excellent" research from already overstretched staff. The interplay between quantification and prestige also offers an opportunity to discuss disconfirming cases, in which scholars were insulated from the negative effects of research evaluations by the support of their peers.

The Quantified Scholar closes, in chapter 6, by pitting quantification against the scholar's vocation. In this adjudication, I argue that the problem posed by quantification is fundamentally the way it triggers reactivity: it is not the quantification per se, but the way disciplines collectively deal with the individualization of scholars' professional worth. Having studied the practice and its implications for social science, I insist on the importance of rethinking our vocation, moving beyond devotion to scholarship as a calling toward devotion centered on academia as a lived, shared, multidimensional form of labor.

Hm can you not be an excellent scholar but still contribute your work only your hours?

2

MEASURES OF AUSTERITY

Necessity being the mother of invention, austerity has nudged higher education to reorganize around the distribution of ever-dwindling resources. In one way or another, the forms of quantification we observe in academia today are connected to a haphazardly constructed zero-sum game of financial resources and institutional prestige. The scarcity is evident—and everywhere. State support for universities decreases year after year, leaving researchers to squeeze the work of grant applications and funding requests into lives crowded with ever more courses, ever more students. Space is at a premium; though knowledge grows exponentially, classrooms, offices, and bookshelves seem only to shrink. And employment security is a waning dream for academics, with a previous generation's lifelong, single-institution careers obviated by precarity. Perhaps I use the example too frequently, but when the thirty-two-year-old Frederick von Hayek joined the London School of Economics in 1931, he could afford a well-appointed, five-bedroom house in Hampstead Garden Suburb. Tell that to an early-career academic today and, barring independent wealth, the rueful laughter may never stop.

In these meager times, we nevertheless enjoy an abundance of metrics. Numbers are the environments of our managed minds.

Our time is recorded in allocation models, rendering our busy-ness numerical. Our teaching is scored, weighed, plotted, and compared. Our employment is tied to ever changing perfor-mance metrics. Our publishing is measured and ranked through indices of prestige, visibility, and use, while our funding records function as monetary proxies for our intellectual value. As in other professional workplaces, metrics and their implied morals of accountability, thriftiness, efficiency, and control have grown as fast as the forms of austerity that gave them credence in the first place. They may not be new, but they have never been so important to the operations of the academic workplace.

The forms of quantification that I study in this book are part of the cultures of auditing and austerity that have charac-terized state logics in Britain (and elsewhere) since at least the early 1980s.[1] Among the miserly profusion, a very particular set of quantification practices is now all too familiar to British academics. Known under different names—Research Selectiv-ity (RS) initially, followed by the Research Assessment Exercise (RAE), and more recently, the Research Excellence Frame-work (REF)—these modes of quantification have sought to bring publicly funded research institutions to account for their intellectual and societal contributions. These interventions are hardly austere in themselves; quite the contrary, their execution has involved deploying vast and complicated bureaucracies that altered the organization of British universities and, as I demon-strate, the practices, careers, and knowledge of their academics. This chapter is not a comprehensive account of these measures but an explanation of how they work in the wild, how their prac-tice has become a polestar for academic knowledge production and has fundamentally changed the job. (For those less inter-ested in the history, a brief description of the mechanics of these assessments is found at the end of this chapter.)

A *VERY* SHORT HISTORY

Because the history of these systems of quantification echoes their effects on scholars' work, I will endeavor to outline, in the most humane way possible, how they came to be. To be sure, the history of research evaluations in the United Kingdom is decidedly complex, riddled by acronyms, committees, councils, ministries, parliamentary hearings, reports, government bodies, research institutions, sector-wide initiatives, techniques of management, and controversies about design. Let the twinge of overwhelmingness prompted by that list sit. It is a hint of the pressure scholars feel when those processes—RS, RAE, and REF—are deployed.

Britain has had universities for, one might say, quite some time (Oxford dates to 1096, Cambridge to 1209). Yet our collective images of cloistered old stone buildings, stained with the soot of industrialization and worn smooth by the feet of studious generations, are out of date. The dream of the modern public university as we know and experience it today is uncannily recent. Most universities currently involved in teaching and research in the United Kingdom are historically new creations—Victorian, perhaps, though more often post-World War II. Even those august institutions that we imagine stretch to times immemorial have been profoundly reconstituted over the past half-century around substantive changes in higher education and its relationship to the state.

In *What Are Universities For?*, Steffan Collini provides an exceptional account of the logic and pressures behind the twentieth-century transformation of British universities, a key period of modernization, expansion, and change for old institutions long the purview of elites. Oxford and Cambridge remained for most of their history residential, "character-forming" schools enclosed by steep barriers (walls, certainly, but more powerfully, class and privilege).[2] Newer, metropolitan institutions established around a professional, meritocratic orientation (in London, Glasgow, and Edinburgh, for example) provided some counterbalance to their older relatives, as did the new generation of civic, practical, aspirational "red brick" institutions that cropped up in late-nineteenth-century Manchester, Leeds, and Newcastle. Regardless, rates of participation in higher education remained exceedingly low: "on the eve of the Second World War," writes Collini, "fewer than 2 percent of the population passed through [universities]; they were not, for the most part, objects of media attention; and many of the recently founded civic institutions were very small and somewhat fragile."[3]

For most of this history, universities were financially disconnected from the state. Most of their income came from foundations, local initiatives of support, and student fees. It was only in 1919 that civil servants established the Universities Grants Committee (UGC) as a mechanism for disbursing state resources to institutions in need. The UGC was not a planning body, notes Michael Shattock, but merely an in-between, reactive mechanism for allocating government subsidies. Initially, it preserved institutional autonomy. This continued as the British state joined its peer countries in an expansionary pursuit of higher education after 1945.[4] Local colleges, such as the former University College Nottingham (founded 1881), were rechartered into universities, as, for example, the University of Nottingham (founded 1948). New institutions sprang up: the University of Sussex (1961), the Open University (1969), and a series of polytechnics that, like Manchester Polytechnic, would soon become universities in their own right. Throughout, the role of the UCG remained largely the same, relying on a rather mechanical model of resource allocation. As Shattock observes, well into the 1970s, the UGC favored decision making "irrespective of [universities']

attractiveness to research students or their research distinction."
Indeed, for most of this period, the funding disbursements provided by the UGC, ostensibly earmarked to cover the costs of
teaching and research expenses, were calculated largely based on
student enrollment. In these expansionary years, with resources
and demand flowing into higher education, new institutions
mushroomed. Absent pressures to make hard choices, "the hard
choices were not made."[5]

Despite the UGC's apparent indifference to the politics of
research prestige, its very existence had consequences for higher
education. It effectively created a single national system out of a
complex ecology of overlapping institutions with different logics
and interests. Establishing a common framework for these institutions, ranging from the elite universities bathed in tradition to
newer establishments oriented toward the growing professional
masses, invariably nudged organizations to converge onto similar models. Collini characterizes the pull as one toward "being a
national rather than a local institution; towards offering a full spectrum of subjects; towards offering postgraduate as well as undergraduate degrees; towards supporting research as well as teaching;
and towards having the autonomy and prestige traditionally
associated with . . . the older universities."[6] Effectively by the late
1970s, the universities meant to transform higher education after
World War II emulated each other, replicating the departmental
and disciplinary structures of the established elites. By 1992, when
the polytechnics were made into universities, whatever organizational diversity once existed within the sector was gone.

Convergence came at a cost. Mimicry made similar programs
and degrees available to students across socioeconomic divides.
That, however, required the growing expense of many large-cost
organizations performing essentially redundant work at ostensibly different levels of quality. With a physics department at
every university, students need not compete over a handful of

specific and venerable departments, but spreading expertise that broadly can leave it rather thin. Then came austerity. Did every university really need a physics department, or should these exist only when truly excellent?

Ken Mayhew and colleagues observe that, in the late 1970s and early 1980s, Britain's economic woes were compounding, bringing scrutiny to the historic levels of state support flowing to all these institutions of higher education. Spending per full-time-equivalent student peaked, beginning a sharp decline as public funding tightened significantly (see figure 2.1).[7] As early as 1981, the UGC was considering the "longer term balance of teaching and research in individual universities."[8] A move away from a slightly more egalitarian policy of funding to one that accounted for

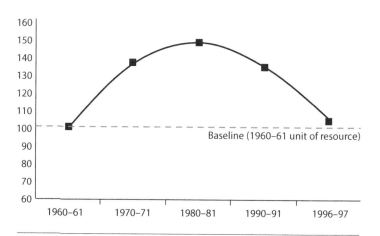

FIGURE 2.1 This graph, adapted from Mayhew et al., represents the spending in real terms per student for British higher education. The data, indexed to the values for 1960–61 (100), show an increase in expenditure per student throughout the 1960s and 1970s followed by a noticeable contraction in state support from the 1980s on. Overall, the 1980s marked a turn toward models of austerity that were characterized by dwindling levels of state support.

expenditure in more "efficient" and "responsible" ways was further bolstered by the fact that the UGC was itself facing extinction. This go-between for the government and universities was wound up in 1989 and eventually replaced by the higher education funding councils for England, Scotland, and Wales.

SELECTIVE AFFINITIES

There is a peculiar point of convergence between what Guy Neave called this emerging "evaluative state" and academics' unique vocational dispositions.[9] As early as the 1960s, UK funding agencies (outside of the UGC) were concerned about what seemed to be the thoughtless allocation of resources across institutions. The Science Research Council, in particular, was actively discussing the idea of "selectivity" as a means for concentrating funding in "particular areas and in particular laboratories."[10] Under a framework of selectivity, the funding councils would "select certain university departments on the basis of their leadership and their past and present achievements," supporting these as opposed to those where a "program had been completed or had lost impetus."[11] The selective allocation scheme would give centers of excellence the ability to maintain their research efforts and infrastructures despite the nation's intractable financial troubles.[12]

The UGC sidestepped this effort for some time, but after years of steep budgetary reductions, it adopted the selectivity paradigm in 1984. By then, a targeted approach to research funding was widespread in policy circles, with the Organization for Economic Co-operation and Development calling on governments to "concentrate their research resources in centers of excellence as a way to ensure that funds are not spread too thinly." How to know where to invest? How was the state to identify excellence? Positioned against the rising cultures of auditing and performance management (rather than extensions of them), public accountability measures emerged as the "best way" to resolve the problems of scarcity under austerity. As a 1985 green paper noted, the government already held "that there would be an advantage in the regular publication of a range of unit costs and other performance indicators by institution and by department [that will be] important for the internal management of institutions."[13] The stage was set for the first systematic research evaluation, UGC's 1986 attempt to identify and reward quality public research institutions.[14]

Within the higher education sector, particularly among research-prominent and historically prestigious institutions, the idea of distributing funds primarily on the basis of student enrollments had always been a poor fit. Academia prided itself on a shared, idealized culture of meritocracy, excellence, effort, and deserved rewards.[15] And since universities had been ranked by newspapers since the late 1970s, introducing a performance metric was not altogether unpalatable. Compared to the whims of journalists and editors, the UGC was offering a more objective, considered assessment of research quality based in expert opinion. Their Research Selectivity Exercise (RSE) was also politically astute, in that it erred on the side of incrementalism. The UGC forged a compromise, bridging the more egalitarian forms of funding from the past and the growing calls to fund excellence. Student numbers would still account for how 14.8 percent of the UGC's aggregate block grant was distributed to institutions, while another 14.2 percent, labeled "judgemental resources," would be "distributed between universities based on their research excellence as assessed by the UGC subject sub-committees."

The first RSE assessment went forward with simple principles. All universities were required to submit information, via their individual "cost centers," to subcommittees of

UGC-appointed experts representing key disciplines. The cost centers were accounting constructs that broadly mapped onto traditional subjects and departments (e.g., physics, medicine, sociology, biological sciences). What the exercise assessed, then, was not a particular department or unit, but rather the discipline as practiced in the institution, be it unified in a single entity or distributed across hallways, buildings, and organizational divisions. The cost-center reports included a several-page description of the university's principal achievements, five examples of the best publications produced in the previous five-year period, data about new hires, information on the cost center's success in obtaining competitive research funding, and peer reviews of the cost center's research performance.[16] Upon receipt and review of the files, the UGC's subcommittees graded institutions at one of four levels: "at international standard," "above average," "average," and "below average." Admittedly, it was not the most precise form of quantification. Nonetheless, the RSE, as a measurement, produced a ranking allowing institutions at the very top to gain priority of access to the UGC's selective judgmental resources.

Once the first RSE's results were published and the UGC stood back, the critiques rolled in. One big complaint was that the results happened to tidily replicate the hierarchies of status already at play in the British higher education system. The benchmarks, mechanics, weightings, and standards of this rather quaint assessment were unclear, in part because they were entirely out of view: whatever happened in the subcommittees went undisclosed and undocumented. Although scholars might appreciate quantification, tying funding to group-level rankings and clearly stating that some schools were better than others (at least at the cost-center level) seemed distasteful. Critic John Phillimore wrote that the selectivity assessment was "more divisive and pronounced than the more general funding cuts imposed since 1981. . . . Misery will no longer be shared equally."[17] As various scholars noted in the press, research selectivity threatened to amplify any number of inequalities. Writing in the *Independent*, for example, Ted Nield from the Universities Information Unit complained that "the slur cast by the UGC's dubious research gradings may mean that many small departments will not make it into the sunny uplands of the 1990s." Agreeing in the *Times Higher Education Supplement*, Liverpool Hope University professor Roger Brown noted that the exercise might "produce impressive marginal gains in efficiency," yet "the way in which judgements are translated into allocations, reinforces the reputational hierarchy that is the curse of the system, and which marketisation exacerbates."[18]

Despite numerous critiques of its cost, role in reproducing classed inequalities, and overall philosophy, the RSE was repeated in 1989—only with an individualist twist.[19] Instead of evaluating only five research outputs for each cost center, this second iteration of the exercise required institutions to submit two outputs per member of the research-active staff. A department with twenty-five scholars (largish but by no means monstruous) would now submit fifty rather than five research products, a tenfold increase in the number of submissions that had to be considered, prepared, submitted, read, graded, and included in the UGC committees' final tally. Critics had called for further transparency in the second RSE, but the metric exercise became, instead, more intense. Why?

The answer, I believe, is the affinity between scholars and the forms of prestige coded into the research evaluations. For instance, the Association of University Teachers (the AUT, predecessor to the existing Universities and College Union), regarded the selectivity exercise as a pernicious mechanism for creating a two-tiered system in British higher education. For them, selectivity would lead to an "inflexible hierarchy of universities where nearly all research activity will be focused in a favored few while others will be marginalized as *teaching-only* universities" (emphasis added).[20] Remember, by this point in the late 1980s, British higher education was already relatively homogeneous in its institutional form: universities differed by history, resources, and prestige but mostly shared the same operative logic, with research standing at the top of the hierarchy of desirability. That's why the AUT's statement lobs a reference to "teaching-only" institutions: a school that turns away from research is regarded as an affront to the vocation of scholars. Any shift from the research-intensive university model was understood as a form of marginalization.

So, too, was being overlooked in the high-stakes assessments. As one of my interviewees for this book suggested, being "left out" of the assessment, not having one's contributions included as part of the privileged package of five publications in the original RSE, was a signifier of irrelevance (a managerial purview that, as we will see, was wielded with precision). If "a majority of academics" abhorred the quantification exercise, they also tolerated it: inclusion, being *accounted for*, was tantamount to being valued and valuable.[21] How else to know one's worth, if not by participating in a market that gives us a price? The power of the state and its politics of austerity certainly played a role in the uptake of academic accounting, but so did the self-conceptions of academics who, seeking to establish their scholarly significance, actively accepted and participated in their quantification.

FIRST TIME AS TRAGEDY, SECOND AS FARCE

The structure and rationale of the original RSE were imprinted upon its future iterations: rather than assessing individual scholars, the evaluations focused on cost units[22] (individual academics' grades were quickly destroyed after deliberations were finalized); a four- or five-point scale scored research outputs, with "internationally excellent" research held as the shared standard of utmost intellectual quality (see table 2.1); funding was tied (more tightly over time) to the scoring exercise, with the secretary of state noting

TABLE 2.1 METRICS OF THE RAE 1992, 1996, 2001 (FOR UNITS) AND RAE 2008 AND REF 2014 (FOR OUTPUTS)

1992–2002 Rating scales of *units* and description	2008 Rating of *outputs* and description, distribution of outputs as outcome	2014 Rating of *outputs* and description, distribution of outputs as outcome
5* Research quality that equates to attainable levels of international excellence in more than half of the research activity submitted and attainable levels of national excellence in the remainders	4* Quality that is world-leading in terms of originality, significance, and rigor	4* Quality that is world-leading in terms of originality, significance, and rigor
5 Research quality that equates to attainable levels of international excellence in up to half of the research activity submitted and to attainable levels of national excellence in virtually all of the remainder	3* Quality that is internationally excellent in terms of originality, significance, and rigor but that falls short of the highest standards of excellence	3* Quality that is internationally excellent in terms of originality, significance, and rigor but that falls short of the highest standards of excellence
4 Research quality that equates to attainable levels of national excellence in virtually all of the research activity submitted, showing some evidence of international excellence	2* Quality that is recognized internationally in terms of originality, significance, and rigor	2* Quality that is recognized internationally in terms of originality, significance, and rigor

TABLE 2.1 (*CONTINUED*)

1992–2002 Rating scales of *units* and description	2008 Rating of *outputs* and description, distribution of outputs as outcome	2014 Rating of *outputs* and description, distribution of outputs as outcome
3a Research quality that equates to attainable levels of national excellence in over two-thirds of the research activity submitted, possibly showing evidence of international excellence	**1*** Quality that is recognized nationally in terms of originality, significance, and rigor	**1*** Quality that is recognized nationally in terms of originality, significance, and rigor
3b Research quality that equates to attainable levels of national excellence in more than half of the research activity submitted	**Unclassified** Work that falls below the standard of nationally recognized quality or work that does not meet the published definition of research for the purposes of this assessment	**Unclassified** Work that falls below the standard of nationally recognized quality or work that does not meet the published definition of research for the purposes of this assessment
2 Research quality that equates to attainable levels of national excellence in up to half of the research activity submitted		
1 Research quality that equates to attainable levels of national excellence in none, or virtually none, of the research activity submitted		

Data from http://www.ref.ac.uk and Bence and Oppenheimer, "The Evolution of the UK's Research Assessment Exercise."

in 1992 that "departments and institutions with poor research and publication records could not expect much funding in the future"; and evaluations were conducted by peer review by panels.[23] When the Universities Funding Council (UFC, the successor to the Universities Grants Committee) introduced its even more exacting Research Assessment Exercise (RAE), the template was largely set. "A panel of experts up to 10 strong," read a Glasgow *Herald* summary of the RAE process, "will assess submissions in each of the 72 units. Panel members have been advised to leave 20 working days free for rating research on a scale from one to five. Five denotes research of an international standing, four research which is largely at a national standing, three signifies research which is mostly to a national standing, two research which is up to 50 percent of the national standard, and one none of which is at the national standard. No funding would be allocated to the latter."[24]

The RAE was administered in 1992, 1996, 2001, and 2008, implementing three critical refinements of the original model of selectivity. First, the exercises cemented the emphasis on peer assessment as the most appropriate means for evaluating quality, even if it came with increasing costs in staff, institutional investments, and overall use of time when compared to the original selectivity exercise. An increase in the volume of submissions required more resources, both at the level of individual institutions (which had to consider and vet their submissions) and throughout the sector (where coordinating the work of peer reviewers became a more time-consuming form of labor). Some attempts were made to keep these rising costs under control by adopting more straightforward forms of quantification. The 1992 assessment, for example, asked institutions to submit a complete list of the publications for each scholar along with two pieces of research produced since the most recent evaluation as a way of using extended bibliographic information in the assessment. This was soon abandoned: consensus about merit and worth was seen as possible only through meticulous, interactional forms of deliberation like those observed in prize and award panels where experts discussed each submission.[25] From then on, every exercise involved gradings produced by elite panels of peers that, appointed by the funding councils, determined how various outputs stood with respect to their disciplinary landscapes (the language of "outputs" to refer to scholarly work, indexing an economized, investment-like mindset, was also coined at this time). Benchmarking exercises, in which external, non-UK members of the discipline were consulted for their opinions on highly graded outputs, gave further credence to peer auditing—though a clubby atmosphere was still said to be found among panel membership.[26] Unlike forms of scholarly quantification observed elsewhere (notably in Australia, where rankings were far more individualized by scholar, and in the United States, where the more informal journal rankings and prestige of publication outlets correlated with scholarly success), the emergent UK metrics more bluntly reflected the shared ideals of experts at the top of each profession.[27] As an instrument of disciplining, this form of peer quantification was more a mallet than a scalpel. It produced a ranking not of people but of institutions, marking their locations within disciplinary constellations of worth, merit, and prestige.[28]

Criticisms led to a second series of innovations to the RAE: the inclusion of "alternative" measures of research quality that sought to judge "research culture rather than just research activity." In addition to scoring recent research outputs—books, articles, exhibits, and so on—evaluators in 2008 were asked to consider other data points and indicators of "esteem" in reaching their gradings. With time, calls for expanded measures of quality would become a wedge in the evaluation system, leading to the inclusion of more formalized assessments of "impact" and research "environment" in future iterations.

The third major refinement from the RSE to the RAE involved how research outputs were selected for consideration. In particular, the 1996 Research Assessment Exercise introduced the designation "research active staff" to cover those who might be eligible to submit their works to the assessment. Managers and heads of department in each university had a considerable degree of flexibility in deciding on strategic grounds who was "research active" and should be submitted. This came at a cost for scholars: those not submitted were reclassified as "non research active" staff, leading to changes in their assigned responsibilities (for example, greater teaching loads) and a consequent loss of status in their institutions.[29] This was certainly a controversial and contested point: research assessments were not supposed to affect how staff was managed. This was purely aspirational. With research evaluations increasingly invoked as ways of identifying excellence, they became "the key instrument for performance management in institutions."[30] The fears of the Association of University Teachers had materialized: research assessments created new tiers not only *among* institutions (with evaluations largely tracking long-standing hierarchies of status in the system) but also *within* them, as a divide between highly productive scholars who benefited from economies of celebrity and their less visible peers who were redeployed to less prestigious and visible tasks like teaching.[31]

By the time the latest version of the countrywide evaluations arrived—the Research Excellence Framework (REF) administered in 2014 and 2021—all of these features were profoundly institutionalized. Except for a few changes—the number of outputs scored per research-active staff rose to four; research impact and environment were assessed independently; and special considerations were added to account for part-time staff, early-career scholars, and those who experienced interruptions in productivity—the logic of evaluation remained in place. Institutions sought to maximize their performance in the evaluations for both financial reasons and prestige, and scholars were incentivized to gauge their worth by the standards of the REF.

Of course, there was ongoing disapproval. Writing in the *Guardian* in 2014, Glen Wright jokingly advised academic readers to "cease all non-impactful activities, particularly teaching," avoid "writ[ing] a book or extended monograph: the REF makes no distinction between research outputs," and foster impact by becoming "ostensibly influential while actually contributing very little to society."[32] In addition to shifting the way academics thought (and complained) about their craft, research evaluations were tremendously costly for individual institutions, for higher education as a sector, and for the "austere" government. The original selectivity exercise in 1986 cost £4 million (about £11.5 million in 2020 prices) in combined costs across universities and government agencies. By 2014, the RAE had ballooned into a massive bureaucratic system costing anywhere between £250 million and £1 billion per cycle.[33] So much for austerity. In a 2011 *London Review of Books* lament, Keith Thomas pined for a "golden age" of scholarship, when academics "worked at their own pace and some of them would have fared badly in the RAE, for they conformed to no deadlines and released their work only when it was ready."[34] Not all the changes were for the worse: the more impersonal, quantified form of evaluation behind these assessments created opportunities for scholars ignored during the clubby and insular "golden age" of British scholarship. At the same time, however, it led to a more competitive, precarious, and pressurized system for scholars and their careers.

HYDRA

When I started this project, my experience as an academic in Britain and my professional interest in markets, quantification, and knowledge made me somewhat unsympathetic to the role of research evaluations in higher education. I shared, perhaps with

many colleagues, the view that the REF was a corrosive intervention, a means for marketizing a system that ought to be left
outside the realm of unfettered economic competition. I held a
somewhat romantic (and ultimately fragile) idea of academia.

As I spoke with academics for this book, my understanding
of research evaluations shifted. One interviewee in particular,
Susan, a sociologist working in London, radically changed my
perception. Sitting in her office late one afternoon, Susan and I
talked about how REF affected her practices. Susan agreed with
many of the preceding points—that the evaluations promote
certain forms of managerialism, incentivize productivity for its
own sake, skew the mission of universities and their professorial
crews, and discipline both knowledge and self. Yet, as our conversation wound to a close, Susan offered what seemed then a
peculiar plea in their defense: they documented and justified the
state's support for research under the now-endemic fiscal policy
of austerity. The REF, Susan noted, materializes a "national commitment to research. [It] is something that makes institutions
pay you at least a little bit for the research time you have. I know
it's complicated, but that was my experience."

Being counted was certainly a matter of status and prestige,
and that is part of what got us into this current mess: it served
as reasonable grounds for the expansion of assessments as toler-
able devices of valuation. Frankly, we academics often confuse
our vocations with a race for recognition. A. H. Halsey's account
of the massification of higher education and the decline of
established "donnish" professorship in Britain shows this well:
in surveys on preferred destinations of employment conducted
in 1964, 1974, and 1989, "the attractiveness of [a lectureship at
Cambridge] actually increased [from 33 percent to 40 percent
of respondents] despite the fact that it carries the lowest salary and formally the lowest rank" of the options presented.[35]

Survey respondents would trade money for association with the Cambridge brand. But, as Susan noted, being counted also mattered for the broader politics of the public university, for making sense of and justifying a higher education system that, however paltrily funded by the state, gave scholars the possibility to conduct their research.

Ambivalence is key for understanding research assessments. They are as much constraints as liberators, bureaucratic systems as marketlike mechanisms. Consider the work of Daniel Neyland and colleagues, who have argued convincingly that research assessments fostered forms of competitiveness that profoundly changed the dynamics of higher education. The RAE and REF not only measured departments in terms of their intellectual quality; they *valued* them in a marketlike way that initially created competition and fostered over time a distributed culture of competitiveness in the sector.[36] (Experimental data show that listing, ranking, and presenting objects of different sorts as comparable even when incommensurable lead to marketlike outcomes, whether the market is or not warranted.)[37] This same competition proved problematic in some ways. Research by Gianni de Fraja and colleagues shows, for example, how the REF 2014 was associated with a transfer market, in which the most productive and potentially better scored academics were rewarded with the opportunity to either move to better-paying institutions or negotiate higher salaries with their current employers. The valuations created by the REF thus became additional sources of inequality, not only increasing the funding and prestige gaps within and across institutions but also potentially damaging the sector by incentivizing highly rated researchers to concentrate in the best-funded institutions. This undoubtedly had an impact on the entire educational field.

That the competition was ambivalent suggests it introduced benefits alongside more questionable effects. At one level, it helped to erode the stability of the aforementioned donnish careers, sometimes opening spaces for scholars who were rare in the previous, more cloistered and insular system of the past. As a conversation with a senior scholar suggested, women academics as well as those from Black, Asian, and minority ethnic backgrounds found the evaluations useful in affirming their work and value, even opening paths to career advancement via transfer and negotiation. By no means were these sufficient advances, but they represented progress as the impersonal mechanisms instituted through the evaluations focused on where and what scholars published, not who they were or knew through personal connections. If one could demonstrate excellence outside the walls of established, elite institutions or show value as an underrepresented scholar, some careers paths became slightly more attainable, slightly more possible.

The premise of austerity, too, despite underpinning so much of the rationale of these interventions, is ultimately ambiguous. State budgets have contracted over time, and the higher education sector has been increasingly marketized and under stress. But as I remind students every year, our contemporary societies have never experienced such affluence. The austerity that we see is a choice (not *our* choice, perhaps, but one made by the governments we elect) rather than an unavoidable fate. These rituals of verification, these auditing devices, are both necessary and not, producing values legible to those who are assessed and those who control and replenish the monies that keep British researchers researching.

There is no moral to this brief story of research assessments other than that they exist and that they are not immutable. To understand their role, though, we must consider what they do in practice, how they operate in the wild. The assessments are not good or bad in any absolute, categorical way. By the same token, they are neither entirely bureaucratic rationalizations, nor pure effects of neoliberalism, nor administrative utopias, nor solely games of prestige. They are collective interventions that shape the conditions of our work and the experiences of our labor. Yet they far exceed their formal limits, never entirely self-contained within the work of government bureaucracies and subcommittees: the logic that animates these evaluations— peer assessment, selectivity, merit, quality, prestige—is not coded in the practices of the exercises themselves but shared as part of a pervasive, vernacular culture of self-auditing. This is where the problems reside. Selectivity skews notions of value toward research careers, simultaneously devaluing other types of work (including teaching and public scholarship). It demands both world-leading contributions *and* locally assessable research impacts. And it becomes an engine of inequality and anxiety. Selectivity changes the ways we collectively create environments, allowing research evaluations to shift our identities and the knowledge we produce.

It should encourage collectivity in that Collaboration - increases Citation rates

HOW THE (MOST RECENT) EVALUATION WORKED

The question of how quantification shaped knowledge requires knowing how the process actually worked. Thus, before moving to the next chapter, I will add a short account of how a recent UK research assessment was implemented in 2014. This will help provide a better idea of what interviewees discuss in later chapters and a sense of the meaning of the quantitative data in the accounts that follow.

The 2014 Research Excellence Framework, planned by the Higher Education Funding Councils of England, Wales, and Scotland, was intended to capture the quality of research produced over the previous evaluation period, between 2008 and 2013.[38] To this end, the research councils established thirty-six subpanels corresponding to different "units of assessment" (i.e., academic disciplines). Each subpanel was chaired by a scholar selected by the chief executives of the funding bodies and populated by an additional fifteen to twenty experts in the field, as nominated by 1,950 external organizations (such as professional associations). These thirty-six subpanels were nested within four larger main panels representing, roughly, the health sciences, the natural sciences and engineering, the social sciences, and the arts and humanities. These included international scholars (so-called assessors; for the social sciences, these included Trevor Barnes of the University of British Columbia and Jone Pearce from the University of California at Irvine) and user members representing nonacademic organizations with stakes in knowledge production. That the subpanels had their own assessors added a redundancy between the main and disciplinary panels (such as the nonprofit and industry representatives; for example, the assessors for sociology included Omar Kahn from Runnymede Trust and David Walker from Guardian Public).

As the research councils were establishing the expert scaffold for the evaluation, the funding bodies opened a period of consultation regarding the specific rules for the 2014 assessment. While changes seldom happen at this stage (this is more of a formal means for informing and preparing institutions about what is to come), the presentation and discussion of these rules with the community at large allowed for some minor adjustments. These included setting the census dates (the dates before and after which outputs counted for this REF), the weightings given to the different components of the evaluation, and the special circumstances that might affect certain scholars' output (such as being "early career," having experienced career interruptions, having part-time appointments, or describing themselves as "interdisciplinary" in one way or another).

With about eighteen months' notice, institutions were asked to prepare their files for submission. In 2014, these included four publications per full-time-equivalent research-active member of the academic staff; an environment statement in which the unit of assessment described its work, infrastructure, teaching, staffing, accolades, and contributions to research; and impact case studies that documented, with evidence, how scholars employed at that unit of assessment had contributed disciplinary knowledge with demonstrable effects on the public at large (say, developing a new vaccine or contributing to the drafting of legislation). The ultimate grade was determined by the subpanels' scores, weighted across outputs, environment, and impact. For 2014, outputs accounted for 65 percent of the final grade, impact statements for 20 percent, and research environment for 15 percent. The REF introduced impact as a distinct (and quite valuable) category: word on the street was that a four-star impact case study was equivalent to more than a million pounds in funding distributions.

After the lengthy process of preparation, the submissions were delivered to the funding bodies, which distributed the approximately 191,500 outputs (books, book chapters, articles, exhibits, and so forth) to the subpanels. The subpanels' chairs set the rules and expectations about the pace of grading but, in most circumstances, followed a standard sequence and procedure: the outputs were divided, with each allotted to at least two subpanel members, who then read and scored each output on a scale of one to four stars (with four stars indicating research of international excellence). The subpanels then compared and moderated the scores in an iterative process toward consensus. Notably, the amount of time put into scoring varied. Some readers spent a few minutes on each output (treating it like grading a pile of student papers), while others took far more time. The average (calculated by the number of outputs divided by the hours reported by panel members) was about two hours per output, less than what is normally dedicated by a scholar performing a peer review of another scholar's journal submission (and far less than required to peer-review a book). After subpanel members prepared their personal grades for discussion, they held one or two meetings to compare grades and conduct ever-so-important calibration exercises to define shared standards of excellence. Only then did they reach a final decision on scores.

The process of scoring is lengthy and expensive. In 2014, it took between six and nine months to complete. After determining all the grades for all the papers, books, chapters, exhibits, and so forth, the funding bodies report the proportion of work submitted at each level (one star, two stars, three stars, four stars, and unrated) along with the number of FTEs submitted by each institution. The evaluations provide no *official* ranking but several ways of evaluating the quality of units of assessment. In one, the grade point average is calculated without taking into account how many staff members were submitted (a department that only submits a few exceptional scholars performs particularly well in this case). The other (called research power) takes into account the number of scholars submitted, a method that privileges departments that submit many good scholars. Because funding bodies do not give institutions an official ranking, this managerial interpretation is left to the institutions.

It was only at this point, after all of the work had been submitted and graded, that funding allocations were made. There is always some uncertainty as to how quality-related funds will be distributed (at present, these amount to about £1.4 billion annually). The funding councils wait until the scores are in before deciding how best to reward selectivity: depending on the distribution of submissions, the different funding councils for the United Kingdom determine the weights for each category of research in the final calculations.[39] In the 2014 round, only research at or above three stars was considered for selective funding calculations, with a ratio of four to one between four-star and three-star publications. In practice, this meant that a scholar who contributed four "world-leading publications" to her department's submission would be responsible for sixteen times more funding than a colleague who produced just one "internationally excellent" article (regardless of how many they had scored at two stars or below). Less fortunate colleagues, those who did not publish any works considered "internationally excellent" by their disciplinary peers over the evaluation period, would not generate any quality-related funding for their institution. Weights are also assigned according to the type of discipline and the institution's location. High-cost, laboratory-based subjects, for example, had a weighting of 1.6 over lower-cost subjects in the 2014 exercise, and London institutions were given an additional weighting of either 1.12, for those in inner London, or 1.08, for those in outer London. The allocation per unit and institution was then determined by the number of FTEs who were submitted for evaluation and met the standards of excellence.

All of this translates into real money. At the London School of Economics, for example, our submission to the 2014 REF resulted in an allocation of £314,000 per year. Crunching the numbers, this implies that each four-star publication submitted by my colleagues was associated with about £8,000 of funding per year, three-star publications brought in £2,000, and otherwise classified research brought no monetary gain. As with any financial portfolio, diversification matters: a niche, thematically narrow department is unlikely to produce top research in adequate volume to garner a significant outlay, hence the scoring incentivizes generalist, rather than specialist, units. This may not be how academics understand their vocation, but at cash-strapped institutions living under austerity, administrators seeking to maximize revenues for their units and institutions readily perform the calculus of resource management. Indeed, given its anchors in the anonymous mechanics of disciplinary peer assessments organized around "world-leading excellence," this cash nexus links professional pressures, institutional responses, and individual behaviors in ways that significantly refashion knowledge and its production.

3

SORTED BY WORK

L ike farmers, blacksmiths, grocers, tailors, and marketing specialists, scholars are workers. The object of our toil—producing and disseminating knowledge—may be different, but an object of work it remains.[1] Making knowledge requires the skills of a dutiful, trained laborer as well as the persistency and care of the craftsperson. Knowledge may be pursued in the hermetic isolation of a lonely office or a midnight laboratory, but it ultimately requires a community of peers to sustain techniques, practices, and meanings. The extraction of knowledge from our world necessitates tools of myriad forms, from pristine clean rooms and particle accelerators spanning miles of Swiss land, to well-tended archives, digital recorders, coding languages maintained by communities, statistical processing applications, and the erratic yet unavoidable software that converts our clickety-clack into stories of theories, laws, formulas, and regularities.

The labor of scholars is often hidden within desktop folders and crowded shelves in offices, libraries, classrooms, and homes scattered across the world. Ours is a somewhat opaque line of work. The word *scholar* still conjures images of tweed-clad, slightly disheveled, often distracted professors surrounded

by aging papers, esoteric books, and the comparable comforts of
the ivory tower—think Indiana Jones, without the excitement,
looks, career stability, or generous funding. Yet the reality for
most scholars—from engineers and research scientists to critical
art theorists and musicologists—is that our work requires forms
of discipline, training, management, collaboration, material support, and professional development that make it quite comparable to other forms of labor.

A few fortunate souls may be able to smith words together
with astonishing ease and in the most precarious circumstances—
on crowded subways, in waiting rooms, at messy kitchen tables,
and in the company of raving toddlers. The rest of us require dis-
crete, dedicated parcels of time in which, like skilled workers, we
survey the state of the art, process and analyze data, and write up
results. These moments are rare. Scholarship is seldom a nine-to-
five occupation, and not just because the life of the mind fits
poorly with punch clocks. Our time is carved around teaching
and service, two additional, quite essential tasks for the modern
academic, with research, writing, and family and personal lives
vying for the same precious hours. As in any other job, planning
and support prove critical. And while certainly different from
the physical labor of the shop floor, construction site, emergency
room, or warehouse, scholars' work is but a varietal, managed and
surrounded by bureaucracy and its expectations of participation,
performance, and review.

The extent and degree of quantification imposed at universities includes the metrics of research excellence that I have begun
introducing, but it goes much further. Like other workers, scholars are currently beset by managerial accounting: all the elements
of our labor are given value in numbers, rankings, indices, and
scores. Contributions to service, or the ways we participate in the
life of our employing organizations and our scholarly disciplines,

are measured in terms such as hours spent in university committees, numbers of mentees supported, and counts of peer reviews performed for journals and academic publishing houses. Teaching is thoroughly measured and accounted for; whether as instruction, supervision, or office hours, the time spent with students feeds into the budgetary models of our institutions. And research is judged, in terms of both its content and the quantified traces it generates—the dollars received through grants, the citations gained for articles and books, the impact factors of our journals, and the various indices that precariously and haphazardly approximate our location within our field of expertise. As I drafted this paragraph, my email inbox pinged. It was an administrative request that the academics of my campus better report, in our preformatted curriculum vitae, just what share of our coauthored research we, personally, can claim. Did I contribute 50 percent of the thought, research, writing, and revising, or is it perhaps fairer to say 40 percent? A complex and multifaceted work life is forever reduced to a series of homogenous, comparable scales meant to capture each individual's relative worth.

This imperative to quantify knowledge is tied to a long trajectory of interventions by funders and academic institutions to administer the expanding armies of scholars and scientists they have supported over the past half century.[2] Its anchoring in the managerial logic of administration and the attendant economies of scarcity goes some distance toward explaining the pervasive, variegated, and contested practices of quantification across institutional, regional, and national contexts. Research on metrics documents their notable unreliability as markers of research quality, even in fields defined by clear theoretical and methodological paradigms (e.g., physics and biology), yet disciplinary positions on the quantification of research outputs are inconsistent. In my interviews with social scientists, for example, the economists were notably more tolerant of journal rankings and impact factors (considering them "good enough" proxies for intellectual quality) than their colleagues in anthropology and sociology, who insisted on the importance of "reading the paper" before making judgments about its value. Institutions, too, take different approaches. Some 40 percent of research-intensive universities in North America, for instance, use journal impact factors in review, promotion, and tenure decisions for scholars, but they do so with varying degrees of commitment. Handbooks may include explicit recommendations that faculty "publish in the highest ranked journals possible" as determined by metrics of citations, "impact," and visibility, though individual scholars are just as likely to espouse "various degrees of skepticism" about the value of the journal rankings and their utility as indicators of research quality.[3] This variation is even more pronounced across national borders, where the array of methods for measuring scholars and their productivity reflects how they and their work are valued by their colleagues, university administrators, and/or state bureaucracies. In some countries, academics are expected to publish in the upper tiers of internationally indexed, primarily English-language journals; in others, local publishers in native languages are seen as more than worthy homes for a scholar's craft. Some countries innovate; others imitate. All quantify.

These forms of quantification ultimately reflect the tensions between those who produce knowledge and those who manage the purses of higher education.[4] If quantification is so prevalent, it is generally because it has become a relatively uncontested, apparently objective mechanism for managing scholars and allocating resources in large and complex organizational settings. Administrators understandably appreciate, when deciding how to divide up scarce funding pools, metrics that allow them to compare an art theorist to a neuroscientist or a demographer to

Nope.

Not Comparable

a sociologist, their trades made commensurable with the spread-
sheet and the institutional form. As a universalizing exercise,
befit for institutions with universal aspirations and insular lega-
cies, quantification is embraced as a less biased, more modern
way of managing scholars by rewarding productivity rather than
friendships or acquaintances. In addition, quantification allows
for planning into the future by creating points of comparison
that become goalposts for institutional action.

All this is to say that quantification is not just a convenient
means for comparison but also an instrument of labor control.
Because it is practiced and assumed by both administrators and
scholars, each invested in distinguishing the alpha from the beta,
the grain from the chaff, and the gold from the pyrite, this measurement spans institutions, academic disciplines, and national
settings. Quantification, proliferated across levels and fields,
has created an "evaluation culture," to use the term proposed by
sociologists Donald MacKenzie and Taylor Spears, a convention that guides practices and professions, linking institutional
domains and shaping their priorities and resources around specific notions of value.[5]

How do these evaluation cultures shape the production of
academic knowledge? Metrics and other forms of quantification
do not transform knowledge directly. They influence the ways
scholars plan and execute their work and establish communities of peers that persist over time, indirectly shifting scholarly
products and disciplinary consensus. For several decades, authors
in the field of science policy have analyzed how certain metrics
associated with the production of knowledge, such as citations
and impact factors, become instruments for management. Many
of these studies were both inspired and facilitated by the uptake
of new forms of counting, evaluating, and rewarding scholars. As
organizations and governments throughout the world introduce

new techniques of counting, scholars of science policy are able to study how these alter the organization of scientific communities and the strategies that scientists adopt as researchers.[6] One key insight from this literature is that metrics' distinct effects on the behavior of individual scholars trace to how they are bound up with career advancement, financial incentives, and collective notions of prestige. When national research systems indicate preferences for journals included in some citation index or another, scholars change the publication venues to which they submit, regardless of whether that means publishing in less relevant outlets than they otherwise might. When researchers are rewarded for publishing in top-ranked journals, they design their studies and write their papers so as to make them more attractive to the editors and reviewers of those few publications. And when scholars are assessed for volume and productivity, they will splinter their work, breaking their research findings into as many parts as possible, even if it means that the separate papers are far flimsier and less informative than a single study might have been.[7]

Science policy scholars' findings sketch the contours of quantification's effect on academics' experiences and labor strategies. Still, most of this research has focused on the behaviors and decisions of *individual* scientists when evaluation systems change. These shifts are certainly important, but they fail to account for how larger, discipline-level changes are connected to quantification. This is particularly relevant because some of the patterns associated with the adoption of metrics already reflect long-standing cultures of evaluation among scholars, as I discussed in chapter 1. Distinguishing the effect of metrics from the effect of an internalized quest for excellence is challenging. Most academics would like to publish in the most visible and best-cited venues, and while few would put the cart before the horse, many of us plan our studies and write up our findings with the aim of hitting journals and publishers in the highest possible tiers. Disentangling the dynamics of prestige from scholarly logic is a nontrivial task, and if it were accomplished, we still would not understand a great deal about quantification-related changes to intellectual communities and institutional contexts. Science does not exist in the absence of other scholars, and while the actions of individuals matter to how scientific disciplines evolve, changes in shared knowledge require collective forms of realignment, agreement, and convention making that cut across idiosyncratic practices and worldviews.

Taking a labor perspective helps transcend individuals and their behavioral accommodations to learn about how *collectives* agree (however tacitly) to produce knowledge in the face of distinct possibilities and constraints. Indeed, if scholars choose to react to metrics, rankings, and other quantified devices, it is not only because their individual responses are tied to prestige and visibility but also, as importantly, because their actions are oriented by and coordinated through the relations they establish with colleagues and managers, the resources they obtain from their employers and funders, and the peer-moderated mobilities they experience throughout their careers.[8] The quantification of knowledge is not just a managerial technique or an external shock but also a control regime of labor, the outcome of how struggles among scholars, managers, and employers/funders are resolved in the context of a competitive marketplace for cognitive workers and the knowledge they produce.

TRACING INSTITUTIONAL MARKS

Studying scientific careers offers a means for understanding how labor configures academic fields in terms of both their stocks of knowledge and their overall institutional organization. More generally, careers, which I noted earlier are meso-level phenomena (see chapter 1), sit between, and are influenced by, individual, voluntarist actions as well as larger institutional structures.[9] For example, careers involve a commitment from individual workers without which some of the most desirable outcomes—prestige, visibility, resources, and higher wages—are practically unattainable. A scientist may well wish to produce pathbreaking research, to transform knowledge in a fundamental way, but without putting in a considerable amount of effort—from gaining access to prestigious and highly selective graduate programs and then commanding the state of the art in their field to fostering specific intellectual networks and laboriously applying for grants and drafting and redrafting manuscripts—it is unlikely they will find success and recognition in their field. Careers are necessarily shaped by individuals and their concrete investments in care, vocation, and devotion, as well as a certain abject commitment to the ideals of scholarly work as a skeptical, universalistic, meritocratic endeavor. To build an academic's scholarly career, in other words, takes work.

These efforts do not guarantee scholarly success. Most people might think that they have their careers "under control," that their position in professional life is the product of individual strengths, and that the rewards they have reaped are a product of sweat, strategy, and forethought—they buy into the meritocratic ideal. To the extent that equality of choices, opportunities, and evaluations is fostered by institutional contexts and historical moments, this may be true. More often, however, careers are heavily mediated by how institutional settings make some paths and professional moves more probable (and more probable for some people) than others.

Consider gender. Men's and women's vastly different professional lives are a mainstay of the literature on labor and employment. A widely confirmed finding across economic and sociological research, for example, is that women earn less and are less likely to be promoted than men with comparable professional credentials, education levels, and socioeconomic backgrounds. This is true even within the purportedly meritocratic field of science: as recently as 2019, *Nature* reported U.S. National Science Foundation studies showed an $18,000 salary gap between newly minted male and female PhDs.[10] More generally, economists have shown that women are more exposed than men to "penalties" associated with important life events and transitions. Globally, looking at earnings and parenthood shows a permanent contraction in women's salaries, but not men's, following a first child—a reflection of compounding historical inequities (e.g., in the distribution of housework responsibilities, levels of institutional support, and employer- and state-provided infrastructures of care) that structure careers and their professional and economic outcomes.[11] Constituted by the micro processes and interactions of everyday life, careers are also shaped through a series of macro constraints beyond our individual control: the legal arrangements that define employment relations, institutionalized stereotypes about fit and adequacy, the availability (and entrance into) networks, "career scripts" that prescribe evaluations about the worth of different types of activities, and on and on.

In the case of science (and academia more generally), these micro and macro processes interact with evaluation cultures primed on ideas of prestige and recognition. The resulting career patterns are directly associated with how knowledge is produced. Among the best known is the "Matthew effect," studied by sociologist Robert K. Merton in his now classic 1968 contribution to the sociology of science, which highlights visibility as a concentrating, self-perpetuating force in academic fields.[12] Because of their position, eminent and well-regarded scholars attract greater attention to their contributions than their lesser-known peers, independent of the "actual" worth of those contributions. The heightened status translates into higher personal confidence, leading prominent scholars to take on riskier research projects with potentially greater payoffs. With more stable, more visible careers, these scholars exert greater control over their areas of expertise. This finding holds at the level of methodological innovations, with Sharon Koppman and Erin Leahey confirming that scientists in greater positions of prestige and authority—in particular, male researchers at elite institutions—pursue more unconventional methodologies that can result in pathbreaking work that bridges knowledge in new, atypical, innovative ways.[13] They are granted a sort of fast pass to "genius" that others are not.

Arguably, Merton's work smuggled in the assumption that the effects of prestige and visibility merely reflected the self-selecting, meritocratic institutions of science, but growing evidence suggests that luck plays an oversize role in how status shapes scholars' careers and knowledge production. Studying the effects of early funding on scientific careers, Thijs Bol, Mathijs de Vaan, and Arnout van de Rijt recently showed that otherwise identical scientists—sharing similar skills, research quality, and intellectual capacities—distinguished only by having or not received a prestigious grant, had notably different long-term career outcomes.[14] Young scholars chosen by selection panels as being marginally better than their peers (really, a matter of chance) were associated with winning additional competitive grants and experiencing faster promotions than their peers. This effect produced tremendous gaps in incomes and research funding (estimated at €180,000 in the eight years after the first award) that heavily advantaged the ability of one group of scholars to shape their areas of research (how scholars are categorized across the spectrum of perceived value clearly has material consequences). This difference in authority and resources is not a reflection of fundamental, underlying differences in capacities. On the contrary, the "surprise" is that radically different career paths can result from somewhat random decisions over the distribution of prestige and their compounding effects over time.[15]

We also know that knowledge changes as a result of the organization of research. In their impressive study of scientific change, Pierre Azoulay and his colleagues investigate what happens to a field of research when one of its "superstars" dies.[16] The team identified 12,935 elite scientists who commanded their fields in terms of funding, citations, and awards—an estimated 5 percent of the relevant labor market. Of these, 452 individuals died prematurely (at an average age of just above sixty years). By comparing the productivity of subfields with and without one of these premature deaths, Azoulay and his coauthors revealed a clear pattern: when superstars die, their less-renowned peers' ideas gain more visibility and support, leading to noticeable advances in the state of the art. Azoulay's research underscores the strong connection between the type of reputational positions that animate the Matthew effect, associated with a concentration of intellectual and institutional resources, and the direction and speed of scientific change. Combined with Bol's findings, Azoulay's results are doubly suggestive: our knowledge about the world—from biochemical compounds and astrophysical laws to sociological theories and economic prescriptions—is inevitably shaped by the way scholarly careers are constructed (through both individual merit and collective efforts) but ultimately fated by chance.[17]

COUNTING CAREERS

Quantification not only acts upon the careers of individual scientists in the context of their organizations (as through hiring, productivity assessments, and decisions on promotions) but also informs shared cultures of evaluation that shape the context of publication patterns, the dynamics of academic units, and the mobility of scholars across their fields. Each of these—in both their individual and collective manifestations—affects the connections between careers and knowledge, between the experiences of scientists as epistemic workers and the products of their bodies, hands, and minds. That is why quantification is an evaluation culture: it percolates through academic and institutional lives.

Amid all this complexity, it is rather a tangled endeavor to observe how quantification impinges on scientific knowledge through scholars' careers. We need a case that, in the lingo of quantitative social sciences, controls for as many situations as possible—a quasi-experimental setting in which the randomness and chaos of the social world are attenuated to facilitate analysis. In the introduction, I outlined why the American system of higher education is a poor case. Its public universities compete in the same space with elite private universities, liberal arts colleges, research-intensive institutions, and other peculiar organizational forms. There are too many moving parts in this, likely the world's largest research and innovation complex (as of 2020, the U.S. Department of Education counted as many as 4,800 degree-granting institutions). Further, U.S. scholars' work is funded not primarily by the state but by a constellation of organizations, government bodies, corporations, and so on. The quantification to which they are subject takes just as many forms, fragmented across institutional landscapes, priorities, and subcultures of evaluation. Local, state, and federal imperatives operate alongside public and private evaluations, creating a cacophony of metrics and interpretations.

The data, happily, are far less noisy in the British context, where roughly one hundred public institutions of higher education are subject to a uniform research-quality exercise (see chapter 2 for more on the structure of the iterations of this periodic survey). Here, we have a neat empirical case in which to observe how numbers, rankings, and evaluations of different sorts alter the careers of scientists and the knowledge that they collectively produce. The size and structure of the British higher education system helps, too, in that every type, from hallowed institutions such as Oxford and Cambridge to freshly founded postwar polytechnics, operates under the same model of government sponsorship and funding. This condition removes many potentially distorting effects. Finally, the British case suits our needs here in that it has been the subject of numerous *official* state interventions seeking to "objectively" evaluate teaching and research quality. League tables, student surveys, and other unofficial metrics certainly matter for these schools, but it is the government-sanctioned evaluations that help justify public expenditures on what is considered a privileged, protected domain. This smaller, more contained, and more homogeneous world of higher education provides an exceptional instance—a sort of natural experiment in which we can study how quantification affects knowledge.

The veritable panoply of evaluations and assessments that comprise the "audit culture" of the UK's higher education sector seek to verify the "performance," "effectiveness," "value for money," and "efficiency" of institutions that receive some support from the coffers of an abstract public.[18] What is particularly interesting about the British case is that, as Marilyn Strathern and other students of evaluations have observed, its "audit cultures" are not merely managerialism dictated from the top down. Though calls for quality assurance, efficiency, and fiscal prudence may start their lives within the logic of government austerity, they soon find echoes and affinities in the ideas of responsibility, worth, prestige, and value held by many academics. Auditing, and more generally the politics of visibility and status on which evaluations hinge, has urged the active participation of scholars, who have a number of interests in crafting the administrative instruments and higher education policies that have become part of their fields. Evaluations are imposed rituals, yet they are also manifestations of a begrudgingly accepted "culture of counting," as James Wildson calls it, shared by administrators, academics, and state bureaucracies.[19]

To explore how these evaluation cultures have transformed knowledge in Britain, we can study how they have interacted with and altered the structure of academic careers. At the most fundamental level, research evaluations are perennial features in the lives of British academics; they operate as almost taken-for-granted elements of their employment, naturalized ways of counting, measuring, and rewarding that matter for how labor is ultimately organized. Evaluations and their distinct modes and languages of quantification permeate the careers of scholars, from their earliest and most tentative moments entering paid full-time academic work all the way to their institutionalized exits. When I finished my PhD at the University of Edinburgh in 2010, for example, the Research Assessment Exercise (RAE) of 2008 had just passed. I was spared its gaze as a PhD student, but I absorbed its import: an aspiring academic must assume these government criteria as personal targets. As an early-career scholar, I saw I would need legible, assessable "outputs" to get a job and advance in my field. I needed, to borrow a term with rising popularity, to become "REF-able" before the looming Research Excellence Framework of 2014 got under way.

I am not alone in this experience. The imaginations and anxieties of early-career British scholars are rife with similar encounters with the evaluative apparatus.[20] This came across in several of my conversations with established social scientists. Peter, a political scientist at a large Scottish institution, recalled his changing relationship to the REF. As a PhD student, he mused over coffee, "I was aware it happened, and I think I heard people talking about it. You would hear people talking about how it affects their job prospects. I didn't pay that much attention." Then, "The following one, I did pay attention to it 'cause that's how I got a job."

Making oneself REF-able—producing sufficient and sufficiently visible publications in each evaluation period—allows an academic an illusion of career security, the sense of having savings in the bank. And so, knowing the rules of the game became part and parcel of how I thought about my work and position in the British academic landscape. Though my interests and projects were never directly driven by research evaluations, I was never unaware of their existence or power. The collective, shared stories of my profession and my discipline were full of quantification and its effects—remembrances of reviews, promotions, and institutional worth obliquely attenuated not *what* I studied but *how* I conducted my research and *where* I presented my findings. My career tilted toward the metrics.

This experience is echoed in Sharon McCulloch's study of the writing practices of British academics.[21] McCulloch followed sixteen scholars across mathematics, history, and marketing through repeated interviews, trying to tease out how research evaluations bear upon a critical part of their work: writing. Her argument is certainly an epistemic one—about the effects of evaluations on how knowledge gets produced. But it is also profoundly about labor practices: writing is a critical task that scholars must perform, for it is the only way their products can travel and endure across time.

McCulloch's respondents sometimes spoke indirectly of research evaluations, referring to them as "quality" objectives rather than intellectual constraints. One respondent, for example, noted her efforts to produce "internationally excellent" work. As you will recall, this term is native to the research assessment's language of value commensuration, in which only work ranked at the top of the international hierarchy generates additional income for institutions. Publications, noted another respondent, had to be "good" to count, which this scholar stipulated meant carefully optimizing the number of authors (the fewer, the better) and the ranking of the journals they targeted for their publication submissions.

Other respondents experienced the tiers of quality associated with the exercises—one, two, three, and four stars—as explicit, manager-set expectations of performance. As one of McCulloch's interviewees noted, his employer expected he'd have "a four-star journal" in each evaluation. That meant he was to publish world-leading, groundbreaking research at least every five years. For some, particularly those at less resourced, teaching-intensive institutions, these expectations of productivity are quickly interpreted as barriers to professional mobility. Scholars anxious to meet these higher teaching and service loads understand that they are disadvantaged when it comes to the rankings: "I don't get any hours for research whatsoever," noted an interviewee. The structure of their workplaces seriously curtails their ability to ever move to more privileged, more prestigious, research-extensive universities, contributing to anxieties about not being "proper" academics, more so when it is inflected by high-stakes quantification.

THE LIVES OF OTHERS

We can see from these observations how evaluations might shape the choices available to individual scholars, but individual stories lack the bird's-eye view needed to see how they might affect academic disciplines over time—unless we attend to the way these individual anecdotes suggest a connection between research evaluations and the paths that make up a scholar's career. Looking to the meso level lets us ask and answer, with some clarity, whether evaluations shape careers and, if so, whether it matters for knowledge.

With the help of an exceptional team of research assistants, I undertook my own quantification exercise.[22] I compiled a partial census of the British social sciences that provides a reasonable account of the movement of academics across institutions between the late 1980s and 2018. The data already existed, contained in a widely used source of information on scholarly publications known as the Social Science Citation Index. As one of the most recognizable infrastructures of bibliographic data, the Social Sciences Citation Index and its embedding Web of Science contain detailed information about the articles, comments, book reviews, and announcements published in more than three thousand academic, peer-reviewed journals across more than fifty disciplines since 1988.

Each entry contains standard bibliographic information: the publication's classification (is it a research article or a book review?), its title, the journal where it was published, the year of publication, the names of its authors, the page numbers and volume information, and the list of references used in the main text (see figure 3.1 for an example of the source data). In about the mid-1990s, entries begin to include the complete abstracts for research articles, providing precious textual data. More importantly, however, each entry contains a specific field whose existence seems anachronistic in the age of emails, the internet, and electronic publications: the corresponding address for at least one of its authors. This vestigial data point allows the attentive researcher to identify the institutional affiliations

```
PY 2018
VL 22
IS 7
SI SI
BP 1808
EP 1824
DI 10.1017/S1365100516000882
PG 17
WC Economics
SC Business & Economics
GA GS7SD
UT WOS:000443902600006
DA 2018-10-10
ER

PT J
AU Pavlidis, EG
   Paya, I
   Peel, DA
AF Pavlidis, Efthymios G.
   Paya, Ivan
   Peel, David A.
TI A NONLINEAR ANALYSIS OF THE REAL EXCHANGE RATE-CONSUMPTION RELATIONSHIP
SO MACROECONOMIC DYNAMICS
LA English
DT Article
DE Exponential Smooth Transition Regression Model; Volatility Shifts;
   Conditional Heteroskedasticity; Impulse Response Analysis
ID AUTOREGRESSIVE MODELS; INCOMPLETE MARKETS; NONTRADED GOODS; PUZZLES;
   COSTS
AB A variety of international macroeconomic models predict a relationship between the real exchange rate and consumption. The empirical evidence in
   favor of such a relationship is limited, the so-called Backus and Smith puzzle. In this paper, we extend the analysis to allow for nonlinear dynamics
   and volatility changes across exchange rate regimes. Our findings suggest that long-run relationships in line with standard international business
   cycle models do exist for many Organization for Economic Co-operation and Development (OECD) countries. Further, Monte Carlo experiments illustrate
   that the nonlinear models can generate the Backus and Smith and the exchange rate disconnect puzzles. In this paper, we also contribute to the
   nonlinear real exchange rate literature by establishing a theoretical relationship between volatility and persistence. In accordance with the
   theoretical results, our empirical findings suggest that the increase in volatility in the post-Bretton Woods era is associated with relatively fast
   mean reversion of the real rate toward its equilibrium value.
CI [Pavlidis, Efthymios G.; Paya, Ivan; Peel, David A.] Univ Lancaster, Management Sch, Lancaster, England.
RP Paya, I (reprint author), Univ Lancaster, Management Sch, Dept Econ, Lancaster LA1 4YX, England.
EM i.paya@lancaster.ac.uk
OI Paya, Ivan/0000-0002-2857-057X; Pavlidis, Efthymios/0000-0002-4892-1955;
   Peel, David/0000-0001-5281-2041
CR BACKUS DK, 1993, J INT ECON, V35, P297, DOI 10.1016/0022-1996(93)90021-O
   BALASSA B, 1964, J POLIT ECON, V72, P584, DOI 10.1086/258965
   Benigno G, 2008, J INT MONEY FINANC, V27, P926, DOI 10.1016/j.jimonfin.2008.04.008
   Bombardini M, 2012, J EUR ECON ASSOC, V10, P1348, DOI 10.1111/j.1542-4774.2012.01086.x
   Chari VV, 2002, REV ECON STUD, V69, P533, DOI 10.1111/1467-937X.00216
   Chetty R, 2006, AM ECON REV, V96, P1821, DOI 10.1257/aer.96.5.1821
   Dmitriev A, 2012, MACROECON DYN, V16, P312, DOI 10.1017/S1365100510000957
   DUMAS B, 1992, REV FINANC STUD, V5, P153, DOI 10.1093/rfs/5.2.153
   Granger C. W., 1993, MODELLING NONLINEAR
   Head AC, 2004, CAN J ECON, V37, P782, DOI 10.1111/j.0008-4085.2004.00248.x
```

FIGURE 3.1 What the data look like.

of scientists over time. Using this field, our team could match authors, addresses, and institutions, building a relatively comprehensive data set that told us where scholars were employed across evaluations.

With this affiliation data, we could reconstruct the careers of academics across four key social science disciplines (anthropology, economics, political science, and sociology) over nearly four decades. The variable of interest to be explored with this synthetic data set is labor mobility, that is, the rate at which members of these four disciplines changed institutions throughout their careers. The data at hand are admittedly imperfect, lacking specific demographic and organizational details; we cannot tell, for example, if a scholar's move was due to a promotion or implied a change in job descriptions. What we have is closer to the type of "geographic mobility" data used by economists, although our interest is not in space but in institutions.

The forms of academic mobility that we capture are, nevertheless, exceedingly useful because they reflect the indirect role of the academic market as a partial coordinator of intellectual resources. What directs this market is not only the myriad individual efforts of those scholars who participate in it but also, as importantly, the efforts of higher education institutions to compete for talent, students, funding, and visibility. Indeed, as the sociologist Burton Clark wrote more than two decades ago, "if there is an institutional market in higher education, its apparent coin is prestige." Interventions like the research evaluations explored in this book are ways of "governing the relations among institutions" by disbursing funding and repute across the sector, thereby shifting the incentives for people to move.[23] The importance of prestige as an underlying feature of mobility remains valid: while definitively shaped by familial and financial considerations as in other forms of work, "in the academic labor market, research and 'reputational' factors could be as, or even more, important than salary in the decision to accept or reject an offer," write economist Fernández-Zubieta and colleagues.[24] Focusing on mobility thus allows us to analyze the forms of sorting between scholars and institutions that, tied to structures of prestige, shaped universities and academic disciplines as research evaluations became endemic to British higher education.[25]

There are important limits to our data, however. Like any data set, the Social Science Citation Index is immensely idiosyncratic. Over the years, the depth and quality of its contents have changed dramatically, making some connections between people and affiliations difficult to trace.[26] For example, the earlier standards of record keeping for the index registered authors only by last name and initials. This made disambiguating individuals tricky. Our team had to manually check hundreds of examples, dropping those whose names overlapped and were difficult to distinguish through additional data and cleaning those for whom ambiguity could be reduced. Identifying individual addresses and institutional affiliations required some similar manual tinkering. The way affiliations are reported in the data set changed over time, and what appeared at first glance to be movements of scholars were soon demonstrable as artifacts in the data. Identifying mobility required multiple rounds of analysis, recoding, and testing. The most important limitation, though, is that the SSCI data set reflects specific assumptions about disciplines. Like data sets used in the realm of computational social science, particularly those that involve administrative records or other forms of digital, organizational traces, the SSCI incorporates fields and classifications that are meant to be useful to particular groups of users. Thus, the discipline ascribed to articles and journals maps only partially onto the practices and expectations of actual scholars. Some journals classified by SSCI as belonging to economics, for example, were better aligned with sociology and anthropology, and several publications in the area of politics identified with sociology or economics. We inserted an additional step to disentangle some of these overlaps and misattributions, recognizing that the disciplines our team added to our final data set remained only imperfect encodings of "actual" disciplines and units on the ground.

CHECKING OUR DATA SET

Despite practical challenges, we were able to produce a remarkably compelling account of the trajectories followed by scholars across anthropology, economics, sociology, and political studies over the period during which research evaluations took hold of the British academic landscape. How good is our data set? A straightforward way of evaluating its quality is checking for how well it approximates well-documented patterns of change in the British social sciences and the systemic inequalities that shape the productivity of their scholars. Do our data, for example, capture differences in productivity across disciplines and scholars? Do they replicate widely documented publication patterns? Do they stand as a reasonable mirror of the British academic world?

Our data might be quirky, but they are definitively illuminating. From nearly 150,000 articles extracted from the Social Science Citation Index (SSCI), we identified slightly more than 16,500 individual scholars in our four focal fields (2,208 anthropologists, 6,384 economists, 4,271 political scientists, and 3,668 sociologists). Compared to the size of the membership of some key professional associations, these numbers are decidedly reassuring because they suggest that our findings mirror those of purpose-built surveys, at least in terms of the size of disciplines (the British Sociological Association has about 3,000 members, while the British International Studies Association and the Political Studies Association have a joint membership of around 3,200). Further, because we had the first names for about 80 percent of the individual authors, we were able to computationally infer their gender using patterns from the 1991 United Kingdom Census. Caveats apply, of course, but this variable provided a critical additional dimension for tracing the ways mobility, productivity, and assessments were experienced by academics and their distinct disciplinary cultures and constraints.

Confidence in our data is further strengthened by looking at its predictions on gender and productivity in comparison to established observations reported in the literature. Overall, the

data suggest that the British social sciences have reduced the
gender gap over the previous thirty-five years, with anthropology and sociology nearing parity and economics and political
science lagging but with some relative improvements. Because
our numbers are derived from the SSCI's data, the demographic
profile of each discipline aggregates both permanent and temporary scholars leading to some slight over- and underestimates,
depending on the structure of each field. The 2016 report on
gender balance from the Royal Economic Society, for example,
noted that only about 28 percent of all academic staff in UK economics departments were women—a rate lower than the 30–33
percent estimate obtained from our citation data. In part, this
is due to our data including economists working in other units
across universities and those who have only part-time contracts.
The figure for sociology is, conversely, a likely underestimate: a
2009 report by the UK's Higher Education Standards Authority
mentioned that women accounted for 46 percent of the discipline's academic staff, whereas we estimated 42 percent estimate
from the SSCI data (see figure 3.2). Overall, our data set passes
these demographic tests with a close, if imperfect fit, allowing us
to trust that it provides an adequate foundation for more complex analyses.[27]

This relatively simple data set provides additional insights
about large-scale transformations in academic practices. The
most important, perhaps, refers to a notable change in the productivity of British social scientists (or at least in the rate of publication of articles contained in the SSCI): from an average of
fewer than two peer-reviewed articles published by each scholar
in the earliest evaluation period, productivity rose to about five
peer-reviewed publications per scholar in the most recent period
of assessment. This growth was gendered (women publish an
average of 4.6 peer-reviewed articles, in comparison to men who

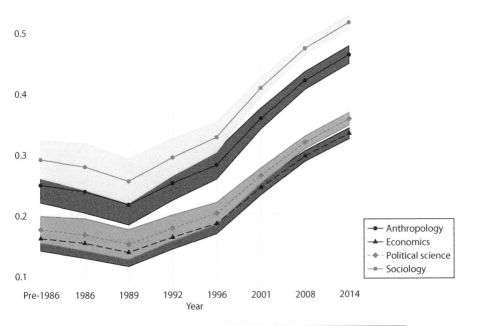

FIGURE 3.2 Gendered composition of the British social sciences as estimated through publication patterns. The graph shows the inferred proportion of women in each field at the time of each successive research evaluation.

publish an estimated 5.8), and it is associated with an increase in the number of multiauthored articles (from less than 30 percent in the early 1980s to just shy of 50 percent in 2013).[28] Publications are patterned across disciplines: economics and political studies have the highest publication rates, followed closely by sociology, but there is a steep drop-off when it comes to anthropology (figure 3.3). These findings are necessarily partial. Lacking a complete census of publications—from indexed and nonindexed journals, book chapters, and complete monographs—our data can only refer to a specific type of output (peer-reviewed articles

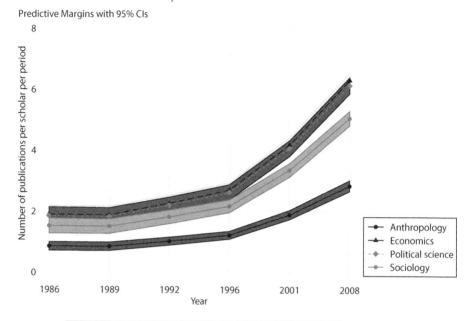

Predictive Margins with 95% CIs

FIGURE 3.3 Changes in publication patterns over time. The graph represents the number of peer-reviewed articles published per evaluation period. Our data set suggests that the number of peer-reviewed articles published by social science scholars across the UK increased by a factor of about 3.

published in journals indexed by the Social Science Citation Index). The evidence from this data set, however, is strongly suggestive of transformations in the incentive structures and practices of British social scientists.[29]

Before performing any complicated statistical analyses, it is striking that the data confirm several unequal structural features of scholarly work. For one, it supports long-standing evidence of gender gaps within and between academic fields. Not only are there publication gaps between genders, but the data also reveal (controlling for both number of publications and journal prestige), that women are cited 20 percent less often than are their male counterparts. If women are, on average, published less often than men and cited with lower frequencies, they are doubly disadvantaged in seeking jobs, promotions, and higher pay.

Now, given that scholarly fields have different disciplinary cultures that mediate how prestige, rewards, and mobility intersect at the individual level, it is interesting to see other patterns in the data. For instance, some academic fields are more invested than others in the production of peer-reviewed articles—the object of the SSCI. Economists would find building their careers around monographs difficult, if not impossible, so it makes sense that they have higher numbers of publications included in the data set than do anthropologists, for whose careers journal articles are arguably less critical. These, again, are simple though telling results that already suggest important patterns in the organization of academic labor in the British social sciences. The next step involves building on this data set by adding complexity to explore how careers are structured and how they structure knowledge.

WHAT WE EVALUATED: MOBILITY

Having gained some confidence in the data as a snapshot of the British social sciences, we moved on to scholars' mobility, our dependent variable. Aggregate mobility—defined as the rate or likelihood at which academics change institutions—is an admittedly peculiar measure.[30] All we can know from this data set is where people worked across time. We lack information about their salaries and ranks and about the nature of their positions, all of which would be exceedingly valuable for disentangling upward, downward, and lateral mobilities (a scholar can move institutions for many reasons, and not every move will bring higher salary or rank). Still, this imperfect aggregate measure of mobility captures the movement of people and the knowledge they carry. A manual analysis of a random sample of four hundred cases from our data set shows that, as with the trends noted previously, the dependent variable of mobility is consistent with patterns described in the literature: when scholars change jobs, they disproportionately experience stable or upwardly mobility in rank and in the status of their institutions.[31]

Our mobility measure is also revealing because it reflects what sociologist Rachel Rosenfeld called the "opportunity structures" facing individuals in their economic and professional lives.[32] These tend to be made apparent in patterned labor market shifts. Looking at aggregate mobility may reveal, for example, the existence of shared norms about value and prestige that make some career paths more available and desirable than others. It may also show the differential effects on careers of gender, race, and class. Indeed, studies of academic mobility have underscored both differences from and similarities to some of the patterns observed in other labor markets. Like mobility in most other markets, academic mobility is distinctly stratified by age, gender, and status.[33] For instance, more established scholars tend to change jobs less often than early-career scholars; women change jobs more but gain less from each transition in terms of earnings and rank (in fact, women's employment changes are more frequently associated with exits from academic employment); and scholars in well-resourced, elite institutions—the most prestigious ones—experience better mobility outcomes than their peers working at lower-prestige universities.[34]

Contrasting, perhaps, with other occupations, in which economic incentives have a strong bearing on the shape of careers, the opportunity structures surrounding academic mobility are tied to specific vocational identities and disciplinary norms. Changing jobs is not only an economic calculation; in cases where mobility is voluntary, as it often is in academia, job changes seem to respond to a search for intellectual correspondence between the scholar and the organization. In their study of the National Survey of Postsecondary Faculty, for example, Debra Barbezat and James W. Hughes found that a key impetus for changing jobs among academics is not higher salaries but, rather, what they will do (or be able to do) in the new job.[35] Sociologists Paul Allison and Scott Long observed the same dynamics, writing that scientists' moves are more often than not voluntary, with scholars choosing jobs (both the ones to which they apply and those that they eventually take) on the basis of complex, individual criteria, including "academic environment."[36] This apparent break from a simplistic model of wage maximization is a crucial reason that academic mobility matters for transformations in scholarly institutions and disciplines.

None of this is to say that finding and changing jobs is any easier in academia than in other labor markets. Quite the contrary, academic markets are often highly constrained. With more and more PhDs being granted each year, there is a distinct oversupply of academic job seekers, and when positions open, they are frequently narrowly defined as searches for scholars in particular subfields and specialties. The hiring process requires enormous investments, especially in terms of that precious resource, time. So, academics' mobility is a matter of both strategic pursuit and luck. But when changes are possible, when academics invest in finding a new position and happen to get hired, their jumps across institutions are about renumeration, prestige, *and* their pursuit of individualized intellectual projects.

Although imperfect, our focus on aggregate mobility works: in addition to reflecting the physical displacement of knowledge workers across space and organizational work sites, it is also shaped by the institutional and intellectual affinities of scholars. At the end of the day, scholars who change their institutions alter, consequentially if only slightly, the distribution of knowledge in their fields. As new departmental colleagues interact, mobility can facilitate transformations in how the scholars individually and collectively understand their discipline, its structure, and its future. Movement can result in novel collaborations and communities of scholarship as scientists come into contact with their proximal peers. As mobile scholars come to train different cohorts of students, mobility can reshape the ways new generations of scholars are inducted into the traditions, practices, and commitments of their disciplines. And by redirecting funding, resources, and citations, mobility can reshape a field's prestige structures. The question then is: how have these subtle changes contributed to producing the transformations we observe within British social sciences?

HOW WE MEASURED
CHANGES IN KNOWLEDGE

Our data set continues to fit with extant scholarship in terms of knowledge about academic job markets and mobility. Both suggest a steep decline in British social scientists' annual rates of job changes, from close to 13 percent in the early 1990s to 4 percent in recent years. This may indicate slowing growth in the educational system as well as longer-term occupancy of current positions. Gender differences in mobility rates are conclusive in our data, too: women scholars are about 1.28 times more likely to change jobs than are men, a trend that is patterned by discipline so that, at the extremes, women sociologists are 41 percent more likely to change jobs than are men in politics and international relations. Again, our analysis shows that shifts in labor markets are gendered: women tend to move within the same rank (that is, their mobility is less likely to be associated with promotions), and men tend to move and experience promotions.

What matters in these data are not only rates of change but also the predictors of mobility associated with transformations in the structure of disciplines and the distribution of knowledge across fields. This is really the crux of this book's argument, and it is the most important reason that our data set is suited to the task. Yes, the SSCI data allow us to associate each scholar with their individual publications. But key is that, in more than 50 percent of the cases, they provide a snippet of each work's text in the form of a full abstract, or short summary of the paper. These abstracts allow us to construct a detailed image of the textual characteristics of the British social sciences from the mid-1990s onward—what authors in individual institutions and disciplines were writing about, what they were mentioning, and how these patterns changed over time.

Thus, leveraging techniques from computational text classification, we produced two measures to account for both a scholar's work and its position in their field. Both rely on the use of so-called topic models, a family of algorithms that classify texts into a finite set of bins on the basis of their unique distributions of words. Topic models were originally developed to automate the classification of large collections of texts where the distribution of words allowed for quick inferences about their content (as you may imagine, this is extremely helpful for internet search engines).[37] Scientific texts are often identified by very distinctive terms—such as *mitochondria*, *punctuated evolution*, *tensile strength*, *ensemble*, or *structuration*—that are strongly associated with their core topics. By using the distribution of words

TABLE 3.1 EXAMPLES OF TOPIC MODELS FOR THE FOUR SOCIAL SCIENCES IN BRITAIN

Anthropology

Topic 29	archaeologi; data; develop; record; past; review; interpret; issu; discuss
Topic 30	network; structure; social_network; commun; reserve; ti; central; social; measur; time
Topic 31	anim; dog; owner; behavior; attitud; human; emot; pet; hors; cat

Economics

Topic 29	optim; process; option; time; function; price; stochast; method; deriv; dynam
Topic 30	inform; contract; agent; incent; effici; optim; auction; mechan; effort; cost
Topic 31	polici; reform; market; govern; regul; privat; service; competit; sector; uk

Politics and International Relations

Topic 29	parti; issu; left; elector; posit; polit; polit_parti; support; polici; ideolog
Topic 30	public; tax; cost; spend; budget; govern; effect; polici; expenditure; fund
Topic 31	labour; conserve; polit; british; parti; leader; leadership; govern; british_polit; britain

Sociology

Topic 29	class; culture; music; bourdieu; field; habitu; middl_class; social; capit; distinct
Topic 30	knowledge; scienc; technologi; genet; practice; scientif; human; power; form; natur
Topic 31	manag; worker; labour; profession; employ; service; industry; organis; organ; employe

Note: The classification is described by the key terms most strongly associated to each topic.

across an entire collection of documents and comparing this in an iterative way with the specific distributions of words for each document, topic models provide an estimate of the clusters of terms that identify units of text. These clusters, which reflect the probabilistic co-occurrence of words and concepts, can be interpreted to obtain a sense of how frames, meanings, and ideas are distributed across the text.

Digital humanities scholars and social scientists have used topical models to classify texts and to study the properties of large collections of documents. Using topic models, for example, we can observe the emergence and decline of certain types of discussions in newspapers, the rise of new fields of scholarly work, or changes in the priorities of regulatory agencies. In a way, by combining iterative, expert review with the affordances of machine learning, topic models allow us to scale up the manual process of coding texts used by sociologists and other social scientists to make sense of the world for untold decades. They cannot displace the qualitative sensibilities that matter for the study of culture, knowledge, and meaning, yet these techniques are invaluable for assessing vast collections of texts for thematic structures and thematic change over time.

Using topic models as rulers allowed us to define two variables that describe the organization of knowledge in the UK's social sciences. The first is *similarity*, which captures the proximity of a given scholar's work to that of their immediate institutional colleagues. To calculate this similarity of scholars, we represented their articles in each evaluation period as distributions across forty fixed topics (see the methodological appendix for further details). Then we compared each individual distribution to the overall topical distribution of their colleagues' published articles in the same period (formally, we used the cosine similarity between the focal scholar's topical distribution and the distribution of their departmental colleagues' work). This comparison provides a scale of thematic affinities between academics and their institutional colleagues, with a value of 1 representing maximum similarity (or total overlap) and a value of 0 representing no thematic overlap. Imagine a specialist department in which everyone studies the same type of topics and writes closely related research with the same audiences in mind. The computational topic models would produce very similar profiles for scholars within this imagined department, and each scholar would have a high value in their measure of similarity. Contrast this to a situation in which every member of a generalist department studies something completely different, without any topical overlap. In this "orthogonal" situation, we would observe minimal similarity. Of course, the typical case lies somewhere in between these extremes: scholars tend to partially overlap with their colleagues, though with some level of distinctiveness (figure 3.4).

The measure of similarity is a local measure; it only makes sense in relation to a given scholar's institutional colleagues during an evaluation period. To represent the global, structural position of units within academic disciplines—to see how the departments compare with one another—we used the results of the topic models to calculate a second variable. This is the *typicality* of institutions in the UK's higher education system. The construction of this measure was slightly more complicated but recurred to the same logic of topics-models-as-rulers used before: for every period, we estimated the distribution of forty possible topics associated with each institution across each discipline. These distributions were then compared by measuring the "distance" between units: after normalizing the topical distributions for each institution, we calculated their Pythagorean distance to get a sense of their thematic proximity. With this procedure, two institutions with the same topical profiles have zero distance,

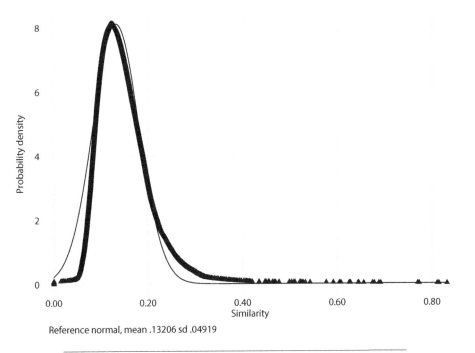

FIGURE 3.4 Calculating the similarity of scholars.

while two institutions with diametrically opposed investments in research areas have the greatest possible distance. This procedure was performed on every pair of institutions across all periods, resulting in a precise description of thematic affinities.

Next, the thematic affinity pairs were used to create network maps of the four disciplines we studied, in which disciplines appear as graphs of connected institutions. Institutions with the same thematic profiles overlap in the network, while those with maximal distance in topics are far apart (figure 3.5). Our measure of typicality derives from this structural representation: instead of using the pairwise distances of institutions, we use

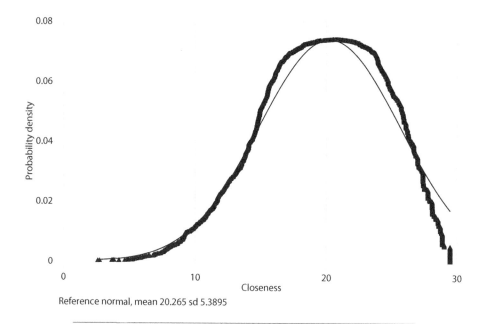

Reference normal, mean 20.265 sd 5.3895

FIGURE 3.5 Measuring typicality. Using topic models as a ruler, we can determine the similarity between departments as positions in a network. The centrality of institutions in the network is taken as the measure of typicality. The graph shows the distribution of the values of typicality for all our data set.

their position in the graph as a proxy for their overall place in the discipline. Institutions at the center of the graph will be more similar to each other, and those at the edges will share fewer characteristics with their peers. The typicality measure, then, results from calculating the centrality of each institution to its disciplinary network (more formally, we use the eigenvector centrality given its association with concepts of status and repute).[38]

Similarity and typicality are linked through data (the abstracts we collected from the SSCI) and methods (computationally estimated topic models), but these metrics are built to describe

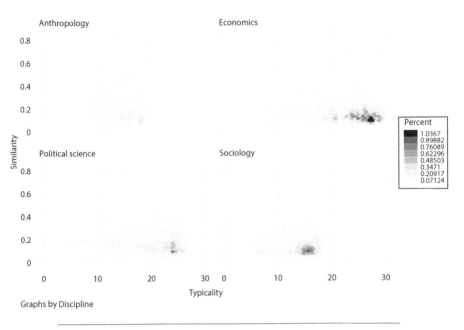

FIGURE 3.6 Distribution of typicality and similarity across disciplines. Observe that disciplines vary not only in the organization of centrality of units but also in the relative diversity of scholars in context. In some disciplines (such as economics), high values of typicality are more common than in others (such as anthropology).

entirely different situations. The first operates at the level of the individual, providing information about the immediate context of a scholar's intellectual work. The second operates at the level of the academic discipline, a representation of an institution's relative position in the field. For all practical purposes, these variables are entirely uncorrelated (the correlation is a meager 0.06); it is at least partly for this reason that they jointly provide a sense of the variety of organizational forms and experiences in the British social sciences (figure 3.6). Some scholars work in more typical departments and conduct work that is close to that of their colleagues (they are doubly typical, so to speak); others work in very atypical units yet are themselves rarities in those settings (think, for example, of an orthodox economist in a heterodox department). If mobility is unstructured and independent of scholars' "fit" with their disciplines and their sites of employment, we would expect neither variable to have much consequence in predicting career patterns. If, on the contrary, they matter, we would expect them to predict mobility across time. This is the hypothesis we put to the test in our expanded model.

A third variable is useful to further tease out the "fit" of individuals, particularly in relation to how it is tied to the quantification of their work. Essentially, this variable—which I call *categorical dissonance*—approximates the question of who is counted and who is not. In addition to the computational representations of the four social science disciplines, we cross-referenced the affiliation of individual academics to the outcomes of wave after wave of research evaluations. We know, for example, what grade point average was awarded to each department across the different cycles of the Research Assessment Exercise and the Research Excellence Framework, and we can tie these scores to each scholar's mobility (or stability). We can also determine whether a given academic was considered at all in the evaluation—or whether they were left in an awkward, potentially marginal position in their institution.

Being left out or counted in the wrong category is not ideal. Recall that each paper, book, and chapter submitted to the peer panels can, if deemed of sufficient quality, contribute to a university's bottom line. There is value in being counted. Yet what, how, and to which assessment panel research is submitted is not the scholar's choice; it is up to institutional strategy. An institution might want to strengthen a particular element of its submission by excluding some scholars or submitting them elsewhere (submitting heterodox practitioners that do not fully match the discipline's canon to a different subpanel, for instance). Or it may simply decide not to submit to a particular panel because the discipline lacks a critical mass at the institution (for example, an anthropologist working in a school heavily driven by research in health and medicine might have their work submitted to the medical panel rather than to the more epistemically proximal anthropology panel.) Indeed, universities may choose not to submit scholars to their predominant fields of practice or might not even submit them at all.

This is only possible because the panels formally evaluate "units of assessment," those artificial constructs loosely defined by institutions to group scholars within distinct academic fields (see chapter 2). Institutions play the game of the research evaluation, seeking to maximize their grade point average and the resulting financial rewards. In assigning scholars' work to units of assessment, institutions can create the sort of dissonance in which the aforementioned anthropologist has their work delivered to the critical examination of medical scholars or a sociologist's research is ranked by a panel of business and management experts. If research evaluations are unrelated to career structures, these forms of dissonance should have no association with mobility: workplace climate and incentives structures would be independent of these and, as such, a scholar should not feel compelled to change institutions if "improperly" assessed. Including this variable in our model, in other words, lets us determine whether being counted counts at all.

PATTERNS OF MOBILITY

Together with the demographic and productivity data for each scholar, these three variables—similarity, typicality, and categorical dissonance—give us further information on what shapes mobility in the British social sciences. In addition to these, the statistical model contains most of the variables that are commonly used in other studies of academic careers. These include the length of a scholar's career; their productivity (measured cumulatively and by publications per evaluation period) and visibility (proxied by cumulative and periodic citations); the prestige of their publication venues (approximated by journal impact factors); their success at receiving extramural research funding (gathered from grant data reported in papers on support provided by national organizations, such as the Economic and Social Research Council, and large international bodies, like the European Research Council); and their institutional status, inferred gender, and discipline of practice (see the methodological appendix for a fuller description of the models). Our resulting findings control for a variety of individual situations—productivity, visibility, resources, and institutional status—better clarifying the local and global dynamics of disciplines, institutions, and individual mobility associated with research evaluations.

Testing between-variable associations yields some results consistent with previous work on academic labor markets. Gender, prestige, and age all affect the odds of changing jobs. For example, we see, when controlling for productivity, that women are about 35 percent more likely than men to change jobs between evaluation periods (remember that mobility per se is not positive or negative but that our manual analysis of a small sample suggested that men were 1.3 times more likely than women to use mobility as a means for promotion rather than lateral moves or exits from academia). Consistent with well-established findings regarding the importance of prestige in science, our data show that recent citations and productivity increase rates of mobility. And age, in our data, was a strong predictor of mobility—or rather, stability. Lacking each scholar's precise age, we counted their years of activity in the field (the time elapsed since the first recorded publication in our data set) to approximate a "professional age" and found that every additional year of activity reduced the chance of mobility by about 4 percent. Over the typical career, this means that about 24 percent of scholars will remain with the same institution where they began their professional lives. This drop in the rate of movement makes intuitive sense: over time, most people establish relations, create roots, and reap the rewards of investing in their communities, increasing the "friction" involved with moving jobs and possibly cities or countries, disrupting families, and breaking networks. Within the rarified field of established scholars with more than twenty-five years of activity who happen to change institutions, the only statistically significant predictor of mobility is recent publications (an indicator, perhaps, of sustained intellectual contribution). Even that is a very modest effect, an increase in the likelihood of changing jobs of just 3 percent per published article (which, given the precipitous decline of mobility rates against a scholar's productive age, is a modest increase indeed).

Arguably more relevant for grasping the bigger picture of scholarly mobility are the results when we turn to the textual variables created by our computational analysis. These lend strong support to the idea that research evaluations are tied to an assortative process of academics throughout institutional space—that scholars move, in part, on account of their fit within their institutions and disciplines. A scholar's similarity with respect to their department, for example, was dramatically associated to mobility. A hypothetical scholar who closely mirrored all of their colleagues' topics, for example, would be 8.42 times more likely than a completely dissimilar colleague to change institutions between evaluation periods. Such a scholar does not exist, of course; the most extreme case of similarity in our data was a score of 0.17, well above the baseline on this 0–1 scale. Still, small deviations from the mean affect mobility: scholars who are just one standard deviation "more similar" to their local colleagues are between 12 and 40 percent more likely to change jobs than their average peers. To the extent that similarity is about topics, themes, concepts, and domains of knowledge, this increased likelihood of mobility has structural consequences for the organization of disciplines. Specifically, the positive association with mobility suggests that scholars with similar interests will not tend to cluster in specialist departments over extended periods but will sort themselves, through labor markets, more evenly across the institutional field. As a result, institutions will tend to converge on a "diversified portfolio," to borrow a financial term, or generalist departments containing specialist elements from across the academic market.

This is a rather unexpected finding. Research evaluations do not explicitly require departments to pursue strategies of disciplinary breadth, yet this seems to be how scholars are sorted across the institutional space. We will see in chapters 4 and 5 that some of this is tied to how organizations institutionalize their response to research evaluations. But the more direct cause is how the incentives of these exercises push departments to pursue research excellence of international acclaim. Only research considered to be of the highest quality in the discipline gets funded by the government. A specialization strategy would be counterproductive, if not risky. Populating a department with many exceptional scholars working on similar topics might be difficult, particularly in relatively small subfields, and likely counterproductive as colleagues would compete for similar publication venues, awards, and other sources of prestige. It is also risky in the long term: subfields fall out of fashion, but employment contracts are long-lasting arrangements. Putting all the epistemic eggs in one basket could lead institutions to make costly overinvestments and fall behind in disciplinary excellence should that subfield go dormant.

So, the relatively low similarities we see among institutional colleagues suggests that there is a certain pressure on the British social sciences to conform to a diversified or broad department type. This pressure is also evidenced by the association between institutional typicality and academic mobility. Typicality, remember, captures the structural position of a department within its discipline. Highly typical organizations are more like each other, and less typical ones are distinct from the pack. Because of how it is calculated, typicality changes over time as academics join and leave institutions, establish external collaborations, or take on new research interests. These actions alter departments' positions in the field by changing the underlying collection of texts that the departments contribute to the field. In our model, typicality is clearly associated with mobility rates. For every unit increase in this measure, a scholar in a given department is, on average, 2.3 percent less likely to change institutions. At the extremes, this apparently small effect has tangible consequences: after controls, scholars in the most typical departments, closest to the core of the field, are about 50 percent less likely to change jobs over each period than their peers.

Jointly, similarity and typicality indicate a pattern of slow institutional change in the British social sciences, a pressure to conform to both an organizational and a disciplinary canon that is reinforced by how scholars move across their fields. Figure 3.7 represents this process in just one discipline, economics. Each hexagon represents the odds of mobility for individuals across their endowments of similarity and typicality in the field. Scholars associated with the lighter positions on the graph are less likely to change jobs than those in darker hexagons. The mobility

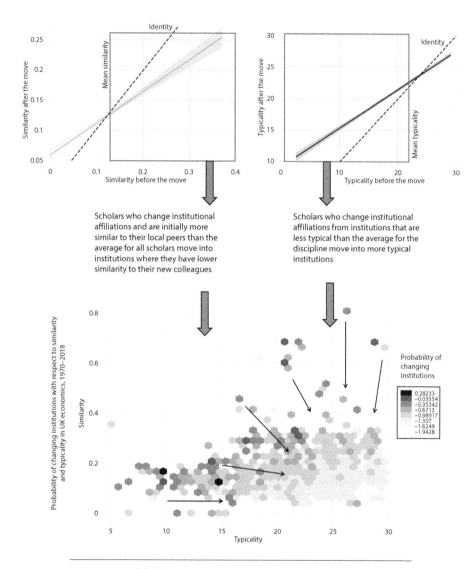

FIGURE 3.7 Mobility in economics, an overview. Observe that the most mobile situations are for scholars in very atypical institutions or those with high degrees of similarity with respect to their colleagues.

pattern is not a random cloud of unstructured lives, with position disconnected from careers; it is concentric and organized. Those at the fringes—in both similarity and typicality—move more and do so in specific directions that reflect the field's intellectual and organizational paradigms.

We have added confidence that this pattern is not spurious by restricting our analysis to only those individuals who have moved institutions in the past two decades. Comparing the degrees of similarity and typicality both before and after changing institutions, we find convincing evidence that the scholars who were more likely to change institutions moved from situations of higher similarity to situations of lower similarity and from situations of lower typicality to those of higher typicality. Slowly but surely, invisible opportunity structures built into the quantified labor markets of British academics have sorted scholars, restructuring the way knowledge is distributed across the institutional space.

I have not yet presented any evidence connecting mobility patterns to research evaluations. To find this link, let us return to the variable of categorical dissonance. The statistical model estimates that scholars whose work is not submitted to their disciplines of practice are 39 percent more likely than their peers to change jobs between evaluation periods. Categorical dissonance, in other words, is similar to gender in terms of its effect on mobility. If we take the accepted reading of academic mobility as a strongly voluntaristic process, this result can be considered further evidence of the importance of quantifiable "fit" in scholars' work environments. Scholars who are not taken into account within their fields of practice and specialization—those who are somehow left out of their peers' evaluations and are measured, instead, through the gaze of a different intellectual community—are ostensibly less commensurable to their

local managers and colleagues, which could mean less rewarding, satisfying workplace experiences. I delve into this issue in
the following chapters, but for now it is sufficient to say that
the strong signal associated with this variable confirms the role
of dissonance in shaping careers (a difference-in-differences
analysis using this variable shows it to be a significant treat-
ment, which suggests a causal association between mobility and
assessments). Indeed, categorical dissonance matters to outcomes because of what it says about the importance to the work
of scholars of feeling part of a disciplinary, intellectual community. When this sense is lacking, scholars will seek to move to
situations where they are closer to their scholarly communities
and their comparable peers.

EPISTEMIC SORTING: FROM CAREERS TO DISCIPLINES

The mobility patterns identified by our statistical model highlight the couplings among a scholar's research (measured through
citations, impact factors, and productivity), position in the field
(seen in the form of institutional prestige and departmental
typicality), and organizational context (measured through both
similarity and categorical dissonance). All things considered,
scholars who are at the fringes of their disciplines or are slightly
redundant within their departments are more likely to change
institutional affiliations over time, leading to what I call *epistemic
sorting*. Epistemic sorting matters not only because of how it
shapes individual careers—how it modulates the experience and
texture of mobility—but because of what it implies for academic
fields. As scholars move from less to more similarity and from
more to less typicality, they change the organizational diversity

of their disciplinary fields.[39] Departments become more similar to each other, organizationally and thematically.

So, how does this process of epistemic sorting change not only organizations but knowledge itself? Above all, our findings here point to the importance of the institutional environments that scholars are presented with, co-construct, and inhabit. Complementing existing studies on academic labor markets, our data show, for example, that gender, age, and prestige influence academic career structures. Women experience higher rates of mobility with comparably worse outcomes. Highly visible scholars (who tend to be men) are more able to transform their visibility into upward mobility. Yet our data also show something decidedly new: by including variables that speak to the textual organization of each field, our models suggest that the logic of disciplining that lies behind research evaluations—the exercises in quantifying, valuing, and rewarding scholars' publications—has distinct effects on how academics move across spaces of employment. Quantification and its disciplining logic join gender, age, and prestige as constituent parts in the opportunity structures that constrain some movements and make others possible.

In particular, the opportunity structures augmented by research evaluations and their disciplinary pressures mean that scholars who happen to change jobs now do so in particularly patterned ways: they more often move from atypical to typical departments and from settings of higher similarity to ones in which their expertise is less redundant. All of these jumps, changes, and transitions are, of course, noisy. Scholars faced with the possibility of moving institutions do so voluntarily, with complex and often personal motivations, and not always to gain a promotion in pay or prestige. Few academics would uproot just because someone else in their institution is doing similar work.[40] But as slight nudges and modest pressures that haphazardly

shape the course of our institutional lives, the opportunity structures created by research evaluations—the ways these standard-
izing exercises count and discount, include and exclude, compare
and contrast—shape the distribution of knowledge in the long
run, slowly contributing to the sorting of the bodies and minds
that labor in scholarly work.

Like demographic change, operating over generations, these
peculiar evaluation cultures do not change disciplines and
knowledge immediately but do so over longer spans of time. At
the end of the day, the quantification of a scholar's work does
not directly affect the skills or tools of their trade; it affects the
dynamics of their workplace, the setting where knowledge is
weighed, crafted, and molded into form. Mobility captures this:
changes to the workplace through the movement and displacement of workers. Quantification may not directly change the
widgets on the production line of academic work, but it certainly
contours the experiences of its workers who tend to their making. And insofar as the knowledge we make is tied to the experience of our lives, quantification will have an effect on both. This
is the next step: discerning how knowledge has changed in this
quantified environment.

4

SHIFTING WORDS

The knowledge about the world that we produce as social scientists is fashioned, molded, perfused, trampled, wrecked, and nurtured by the experiences of our lives. We are never truly disentangled from our objects of study or matters of concern, whether because of methodological constraints (we sometimes live and break bread with our informants), the affinities of our own meanderings (we bump into research by transforming the "debris of the old" into knowledge of the new), or the sheer importance of care and maintenance work involved in making science possible. That this is the case, that our personal trajectories come to bear so centrally upon what we know and how we know it, is almost a commonplace.

Our shared scholarly historiography teems with examples. For the eminent cultural scholar Stuart Hall, the experience of living and studying in England, which he found "simultaneously familiar and strange, homely and unhomely, domesticated but at the same time a thoroughly dangerous place," was utterly inextricable from the development of what became the influential field of cultural studies. The textual turns and linguistic whirlwinds in the sociologist Pierre Bourdieu's work reflect not only the intricacies of his theories but also his position and movement through the densely classed and cultured structures of mid-twentieth-century French academia. The economist Eugene Fama's information-theoretic account of stock markets is arguably anchored in his direct and unique acquaintance with the cleaning, processing, and storing of price data on digital computers; the feminist philosopher of science Donna Haraway's *Companion Species Manifesto* necessarily depended on the existence of her everyday canines; and Max Weber's Protestant ethic is nigh impossible to extract from his familial background and vocational devotion. The claims of our papers, the accounts in our books, the lessons spoken in our classes, and the webs of words we cast are always, in part, reflections of the events, paths, affordances, and constraints of our own lives.[1]

This book is no exception. Its framing, methods, and claims encode the movements and encounters of my career. As I write, I live thousands of miles from their realm of influence, but the evaluations that I study in these pages became my focus, in part, because I experienced them as a staff member in British higher education. The computational techniques that I have used to explore how quantification might shape the social sciences cannot be separated from my changing disciplinary affiliations: I started my intellectual life in physics, where I became fascinated with the measurement, simulation, and analysis of economic processes using the tools of numerical statistical mechanics, then soon discovered science and technology studies and its concern for the situatedness of knowledge and its epistemic institutions. The lessons and conclusions that I draw from these observations, about solidarity, epistemic diversity, and the troubles of disciplining, speak as much to straightforward sociological puzzles—the gaps and lacunae prefigured in and by the literature produced by my forebears—as to my affective commitments toward my past and present colleagues, friends, peers, and the institutions we collectively inhabit. Like all of my work, this book crystallizes both apparently calculated labor and the vicissitudes of a quantified yet unpredictable life.

If knowledge is ultimately a biographical product, encapsulating the myriad, concatenated events and contexts that shape scholars' theoretical, practical, and political schemas, then the structure and lived experiences of academic careers necessarily matter for understanding the emergence of and change within larger configurations such as disciplines. Shifts in careers imply bodies moved, relations and communities transformed, and conversations and knowledge redistributed. When we move institutions, we transform our everyday networks of acquaintances, the texture and tessitura of our exchanges, the terms of our discussions. We encounter and contend with new students, interlocutors, managerial pressures, and collective points of concern. We change the lifeworld that defines our vocation, attending to "multiple groups, either simultaneously or in succession" that shape our register of attention and import, our concerns and puzzles, our values and conceptions of intellectual worth.[2]

With each jump, each transition, each event, career shifts map onto slippages in our understanding of the world. Concepts once peripheral to our theoretical repertoires acquire lived and scholarly significance. We change lexicons, meanings, and ways of framing our environments. These are not always so obvious or dramatic as exchanging knowledge for organizations, epistemic for cognitive, structural class analysis for approaches attentive to the intersections of gender and race, or oral histories for robust estimators, but they are material to the way our disciplines are organized. Scholars' career moves can be productive—recombining and allowing schemas to travel (however slowly) across institutional divides—and disruptive, upending established ecologies of texts and dislocating established orders of epistemic worth, the sorts of shocks that require recovery and assimilation.[3] The movements of scholars across institutions can be almost geological: explosive on occasion, like volcanoes that rapidly transform fields and their horizons, but also slowly cumulative, changing the landscape through piecewise bursts, adjustments, erosions, and sedimentary deposits.

The research evaluations that I study in this book, in that they shape the careers and intellectual ecosystems of British scientists and scholars, are also metaphorically "geological" forces altering landscapes of shared knowledge. By creating incentives for scholars to move across institutional spaces, the evaluations spur possibilities for recombinant knowledge and bursts of innovative literature that might alter disciplinary understandings and relations. Such momentous transformations, however, are rarities, frequently disconnected from the act of quantification. More often, quantification effects change through slower processes. They rechannel the scholarly magma, altering the gradual and piecewise forms of epistemic sorting that have tangible long-term consequences for the scope, variety, and organization of disciplinary knowledge. Here ends the metaphor.

We can see this in a number of concrete cases. Peter, the young political scientist we met in chapter 3, found that being subject to evaluations did not directly change his intellectual concerns. A scholar of politics in the Arab world, Peter engages with literatures from across the globe—his work and interests span traditions, disciplinary boundaries, and networks of authors. His scholarly output is "the kind of thing," he noted, "that the REF is designed to exclude." In his own estimation, Peter's work does not really "fit with political science." In fact, he grumbled, "I often feel like I'm what the REF is designed to stop from happening." Still, live with the REF and its manifold expectations he must.

Peter reflected on how being quantified changed, even if only modestly, the tone of his intellectual conversations. "It's obvious to me that if I want to keep my job I have to do so," he said with a coffee in hand. "It wouldn't change the content of what I do, but it does change in some ways the *framing* of what I do. Not always for the worse, I would say—even though, in general, I don't agree with the exercise. You know, I probably should make more effort to talk to people that don't agree with my premises. And if . . . part of that means going to a more generalist disciplinary [journal], like trying to get into [the *American Political Science Review*] or something like that . . . if it fails, then at least it makes you think big. It's not always that bad." Musing momentarily on the prospect of submitting his work to the big-name journal, Peter added, "Having [these evaluation targets] in the back of my mind does make me think, 'Maybe I should.'"

Nothing in the research evaluations formally requires Peter to submit his work to the *American Political Science Review* nor to hastily adapt his research interests, styles, and matters of concern. If anything, the peer review built into the mechanisms of the Research Evaluation Framework theoretically means that publication venues are largely irrelevant—the scholars' work is ultimately read and graded by peers in British higher education, ostensibly without concern for the citation impact, status, or branding of its publishers. Research evaluations, however, necessarily foreground the forms of disciplinary prestige and merit that *can* affect how scholars frame their work and its value, imagine their craft, and chart their course in the literature. Submitting to the *American Political Science Review* requires talking to people "that don't agree with my premises," as Peter put it, but in rather specific ways. It beckons the "typical" British political science to establish conversations with audiences who may not share their training, sensibilities, and theoretical orientations. Of the 915 research articles published in the *American Political Science Review* since 2000, only twenty-seven were wholly produced by authors in Britain (if we include those with at least one author based in the United Kingdom, this number rises to a still underwhelming sixty-three). An effort to publish in this journal may not change researchers' concrete contributions, but it will fairly certainly transform the semantic universe in which they operate (if it does not, their work may be intellectually illegible to the journal's editors and network of trusted peer reviewers—grounds for summary dismissal). This is what Peter alludes to: the effort it takes to "talk" across academic traditions, while often positive and generative, is effort, at the end of the day. It subtly carves time away from other pursuits and shifts his approaches to pursuing and presenting knowledge. Like the small forces impressed by rivers upon sandy substrate, one nudge urges another, slowly changing the landscape.

MEASURING DISCIPLINARY CHANGE

So *how* did research evaluations change how social scientists wrote about the world? Answering this question is tricky. It requires distinguishing changes that occurred because of implementing evaluations from those that would have resulted in their absence. This imagined, counterfactual world—one without the RAE and REF, but with austerity and competition—is unavailable. Even comparing the British system with systems in Australia, the United States, France, or Germany is insufficient; at the end of the day, the processes that I examine are intertwined with the distinct organizational and academic cultures of the United Kingdom. Establishing a causal connection between the quantification of academic work and changes in the scholarly landscape is, nonetheless, possible, if not through the power of a single model and baseline reference, then through the extension over various forms of evidence, from personal and historical accounts to analyses of textual change. In the spirit of measuring, let's start with the latter—quantitative representations of how institutions reacted to the evaluation schemes and changed the types of texts that their scholars produced.

The first bit of evidence comes from observing how research evaluations are effectively tied to an institution's position in the field. If the outcomes of research evaluations are in any way entwined with what people write about, then they will necessarily create incentives to study and write about certain things—they create, in this sense, epistemic credentials of worth that are desirable in that they indicate membership in a particular academic community. Lacking these credentials leads to worse results, all things considered. This coupling between the type of work published by scholars and their university's standing in the assessments is, then, a product of the disciplining effect of the evaluations in general.

How is this the case? Recall that, in practice, research evaluations constitute a form of epistemic policing: they reward work that is deemed "internationally leading" by panels of disciplinary British scholars. In this way, the scoring systems reinforce global academic fields' ideals by enforcing specific stylistic, conceptual, symbolic, and epistemic boundaries.[4] The subpanels are not randomly constituted but are embodiments of normative positions regarding each discipline; Daniel Neyland, Véra Ehrenstein, and Svetlana Milyaeva keenly observe that the composition of the evaluative panels involves "a careful practice of deciding who and what ought to be represented in discussing and assessing the work of a discipline."[5] Neither internal mechanisms for allocating funding nor mere quality control practices (which happen to carry immediate practical and financial purposes), the evaluations are explicitly designed to provide, as official documentation explains, "benchmarking information and establish reputational yardsticks, for use within the Higher Education sector and for public information."[6] They are instruments of, and for, discipline.

By way of illustration, we can consider the key heuristics across which academic outputs were judged in the most recent framework, the REF 2021: originality, significance, and rigor. Their definitions ("important and innovative contributions," "capacity to influence" knowledge and practice, and "adopts robust and appropriate concepts," respectively) reveal these dimensions as anything but algorithmic, mechanistic measurements. They are not yardsticks in the same way as, well, a literal yardstick follows a defined practical schema for how it ought to be used and interpreted that is tied to a host of institutions— from land registries and local construction permits to bank loans and city ordinances. Their practical and explicit normativity is decidedly underdefined. Yet these three components of quality are framed in ways that promote distinct forms of disciplinary knowledge: the appropriateness of concepts and methods only makes sense when standing in a particular tradition (Should we talk about entropy in demography? Are robust estimators necessary for this particular model? Are two interviews enough to call this an "ethnography"? Is this social theory or philosophy? Do the causal claims hold with this evidence?), tying the measurement of quality to the "normal" practices, questions, and puzzles accepted by the field.[7] The "capacity to influence" only makes sense within each disciplinary paradigm (Do these concepts challenge our norms and push new avenues of research?). And the "importance" of contributions can only be evaluated on the basis of what subpanel members already consider important (Would I see this in a top journal in my part of the world?).

These yardsticks gain their performative consequences because they reinforce shared, visible, durable, and ostensibly legitimate standards that shape how institutions and individuals think about their actions, research, and careers. For instance, the evaluations assert the standards of rigorous science by realigning departments and their managers to the logic (or the assumed logic) of the subpanel's evaluators. In my interviews with social scientists, informants across disciplines often described internal job-search discussions in which their prospective colleagues are evaluated by the faculty with respect to the next national evaluation: is this potential hire's work legible for the evaluation ("Does this person have anything, really anything, we can submit to REF?" offered one interviewee) and does the candidate fit "somewhere within this sort of story [about the department and its relation to the discipline] that we're telling" in the department's REF narrative? Remember, this relatively brief narrative always accompanies submissions to the assessment panels. It is meant to frame the research outputs a department includes in its portfolio. In its few words, it is both sedimentary, reflecting years of accumulated colleagues and interests, and proactive, insofar as it is designed to present and substantiate a particular departmental profile to the subpanels' audience. By this path, evaluations change ideas about who is a valuable researcher and a valuable colleague by transforming the narrative possibilities available to actors in the field along distinct disciplinary lines. They change, in sum, the measures of the world.

The computational models that link careers, institutions, and scholarly texts (see chapter 3) also provide suggestive evidence of how research evaluations measure and reward those most proximal to disciplinary ideals. In modeling the careers of UK social scientists in the previous chapter, my research team innovated a measure of departmental typicality that reflects the degree to which institutions are central to their academic fields. This measure, folding in each institution's distributions of research publication topics by discipline, locates individual departments in the entire disciplinary network. In the organization that this process reveals, we define highly typical departments as those closer to the center of the network. These "exemplary" or "paradigmatic" departments share more topics with their proximal peers and thus represent the span of the discipline's thematic interests as well as the "average" department in each discipline. Institutions with low typicality, by contrast, are specialists in the sense that their distributions of interests, topics, and intellectual products are skewed from the center of the network. Their network marginality tends to become exponential as financial incentives attached to typicality are withheld, further marginalizing these atypical departments.

Although a blunt instrument, the measure of typicality we developed by quantifying the abstracts of research articles is surprisingly robust in predicting evaluation outcomes. By looking at the effect of typicality on institutions' standardized scores in the following round of assessments, we confirmed the greater payoffs for those institutions most central to their disciplinary networks. In figure 4.1, in addition to the stark differences across disciplines, we see a notable, positive relation between the degree of a department's typicality (that is, how well work by its affiliated scholars represented the overall literature in the discipline) and its standardized ratings (a fact made more surprising given that the model accounts for relative historical prestige). Even if all research outputs are read with care and consideration by panels of experts, in the aggregate, the assessment exercises operate as yardsticks through which disciplinary norms are rewarded and impressed upon the field. Instead of showing how innovation, originality, influence, and robustness are teased out of a multiplicity of complex outputs, our analysis

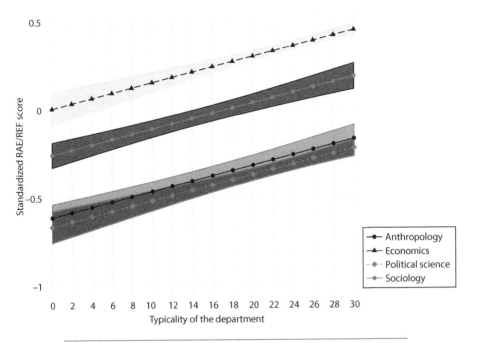

FIGURE 4.1 REF scores and typicality. The predicted values are estimated by controlling for the status, the number of citations across the period, and the size of the unit's submission.

of typicality provides evidence that the evaluations affect disciplines by rewarding departments that decline to stray far from their discipline's established traditions, both financially and with higher epistemic credentials.

The connection between an institution's typicality and its score in the research evaluations says nothing about how academic fields change over time; it just confirms a link between disciplinary conformity and positive peer evaluations. To observe the consequences of quantification, we need to visualize the piecewise shifts in typicality that, over time, add up to notable changes in the field's overall structure.

The data and computational methods to which we have access allow us to assess this possibility with remarkable results. Instead of focusing on typicality, the same techniques I described in the previous chapter can be used to examine how a structural feature of each discipline—something akin to the "degree of difference" between institutions—changed across evaluation periods. Because of how it is defined and calculated, the measure of typicality we have used so far captures the relative importance of an institution in the field without describing the institutions' relative positions. Considering how tightly or loosely institutions are interconnected within each discipline will take another measure—one that captures the similarity among departments. This gives us a better sense of how disciplinary heterogeneity changed over time and across fields.

The topic models used in the previous chapter are handy for this, too. Looking at the differences in the distribution of topics among departments, we built a measure to estimate their relative distance (this was, indeed, the first step in calculating typicality). Two departments with exactly the same distribution of topics have a distance of 0, while two departments with completely different topical investments will have the maximal distance of 1. Determining these distances for all department pairs gives us a sense of the degrees of difference between institutions across each field. If most distances are small, departments tend to be similar in terms of comparable academic staff, productivity, and thematic profiles. If, however, distances are larger, it would indicate that departments tend to specialize rather than emulate some ideal institutional and disciplinary distribution. Calculating these estimates for each period to determine the average distance between pairs of institutions yields a measure of an academic field's relative heterogeneity over time. Increases in the average distances over time are associated with rising heterogeneity, while decreases suggest greater field homogeneity.

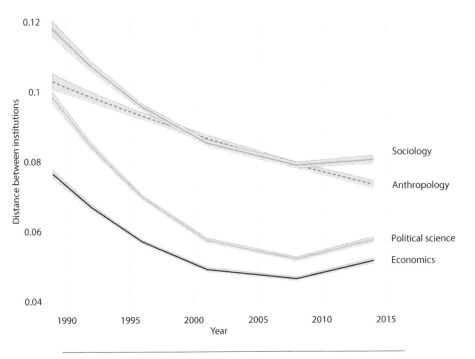

FIGURE 4.2 Average distance between departments as calculated using forty topics that describe the research interests of different institutions. The curves were obtained with a fractional polynomial fit of all pairwise distances between institutions in each period.

The results of this procedure, presented in figure 4.2, are startling. Over the years in which the research evaluations have been imposed, the British social sciences *have become more homogeneous.* *how can they bee 'extraordinary' or 'original'*

The process is noisy, yet the fact remains: the average department today is far less specialized than it was a few decades ago. Comparisons provide a sense of the scope of these changes. Contrast, for example, economics (a discipline often thought of as lacking in pluralism and epistemic diversity) and sociology (renowned for its fragmented, almost fractal organization).[8]

In our analysis, sociology in Britain today has the same degree of structural homogeneity as economics did in the mid-1980s. Put differently, when it comes to organizational forms, sociology today is not very different from what economics was a generation ago. Some of this convergence has to do with staff expansions: as departments grew in size and accommodated new scholars, their potential topical coverage expanded, ostensibly leading to more similar, "closer" institutions. Yet because our distance measure considers forty possible topics, staff expansion is unlikely to wholly explain the convergence. Because proximity is only attained when departments invest in the same topics, our data provide strong evidence of thematic convergence and overlap in the British social sciences.

These findings are supported by ample historical evidence. Histories of UK social sciences often start with the distinctly idiosyncratic founding of chairs and departments. Through time, these idiosyncrasies remained, perhaps as forms of organizational imprinting, only to be eventually diluted by the forces of growth and competition.[9] This is the overall narrative presented by John Scott who, in *British Sociology: A History*, identifies the shifting priorities of mid-twentieth-century sociology departments: some institutions, such as Birmingham, originally emphasized industrial sociology and social work, while others—such as Leicester, which was home to Illya Neustad and Norbert Elias—had a distinct international, theoretical orientation.[10] Individual scholars' inclinations created niches within institutions where research then flourished. The impressive strength of Birmingham's contributions to culture studies, for instance, resulted as much from the efforts and prowess of scholars such as Stuart Hall as from the serendipitous founding of the Center for Contemporary Cultural Studies in 1964 under Richard Hoggart (brought into the unit from English). The interpersonal structure of the discipline made for a world of many islets linked by common concerns and conversations but only loosely coupled by disciplinary norms. If anything, sociology seems to have emerged interstitially, through the efforts of the social work scholars, social philosophers, industrial relations students, historians, anthropologists, and sociologists who established the varied departmental landscape of their emerging field.

By the late 1980s, the interconnected archipelago of British sociology possessed clearly identifiable ecologies of specialization. The University Grants Committee's 1989 *Report of the Review Committee on Sociology*, for example, noted five self-declared areas of scholarly emphasis by sociology departments that reflected both long-standing histories of institutional buildup and path dependence and the emergence of new subfields of study (most notably, so-called science and technology studies). These specializations, however, clashed with the research assessments' pressures to conform "with the increasingly hierarchical organization of . . . departments" within their institutional hierarchies.[11] Rather than being associated with niches for exploration or spaces for the refinement of intellectual subfields, the thematic concentrations that defined the discipline's archipelago became sources of critique and potential depreciation when placed before subpanels of "peers."

A number of institutions' performance in the assessments fluctuated across evaluation periods, as demonstrated by Christopher Husbands's superb history of sociology at the London School of Economics and Political Sciences (LSE).[12] Although central to the structures of prestige and disciplinary development of the field in Britain (LSE's Department of Sociology was the country's first), sociology at LSE often came up unexpectedly short in the research assessment rankings, particularly when compared with other, consistently top-tier units in the school (notably, economics and anthropology). Husbands argues that some of this dissonance had to do with the specific way sociology was instituted at LSE. To some outside scholars/potential evaluators, the department lacked investments in key subfields. "In the eyes of many," LSE sociology had "made rather minimal contributions" to "rather important" research areas over the years.[13] Adding to its incommensurability, LSE sociology was decentralized, fragmented across numerous research centers on gender, social psychology, cities, human rights, and criminology—leading to a sense among outside evaluators that its scholarly community "lacked a central theoretical core or purpose."[14] Institutional status and prestige did not attenuate the disciplinary concerns of the evaluations and its assessors; they only made expectations of conformity more pressing and more consequential.

BUT WHAT ABOUT MEANING?

The evidence from the topic models is suggestive but not necessarily conclusive. At the end of the day, our study of similarities and distances within the British social sciences uses a rather blunt comparative measure of thematic profiles. The distribution of topics and areas of study is important, but it cannot help us assess whether disciplines converged in how they used specific concepts, relied on authors and literatures, and engaged with the empirical world. For a sociologist like myself, the question remains: Do the changes picked up by the topic models actually indicate an associated change in academic fields' webs of meaning?

I do not wish to abandon the computational techniques just yet. (They've been insightful thus far.) Rather, I want to "triangulate" different methods and types of evidence to make the case that research evaluations have affected the constitution of social scientific knowledge in Britain.

One method for assessing the convergence in concepts involves looking at the relative positions of words in texts. The topic models we have used so far involve a "bag of words" approach that uses the probabilistic distribution of terms within and across texts to produce classifications. In other words, the models look at how words co-occur in texts, irrespective of their relative position. This implies that topic models are unaware of syntax: the sentence "The cat is under the table" is indistinguishable from "table the The is under cat." We can avoid this near-total loss of meaning by recurring to a method that is slightly more attentive to the organization of words in texts. Computers cannot directly assess what terms "actually" stand for, but they can tell us how terms are associated with other terms in a particular universe of documents through a technique known as word embeddings. Leveraging the power of neural networks to reduce the complexity of problems, word embeddings create models that consider both the probabilistic features and the syntactic structures of large collections of texts.

Word embeddings are familiar to all of us through our interactions with a host of mundane technologies. The recommendation systems that populate most music and video streaming services are prime examples. They rely on models of user groups' preferences to guess what still-unheard, still-unwatched content might be relevant for individual users. Recommendation algorithms cannot account for cultural taste, yet by knowing which songs and videos are frequently watched together by users who share similar media consumption profiles, they can begin to guess what might appeal to, well, you or me. Beyond correlation, the systems predict future habits based on similarity of context: listening to songs by Britney Spears may be highly correlated to listening to songs by Taylor Swift, but across playlists, the sequence of play might present alternative suggestions varying from ABBA to Ziggy Marley. When applied to texts, these types of sequence-sensitive models offer representations of words as vectors (that is, points in space) that, while sensitive to variations in usage, distill information about which words are frequently found together in similar linguistic contexts and how they are semantically related to others in the textual field. Importantly, these techniques transform problems of meaning into problems of geometry; as Dustin Stoltz and Marshall Taylor note, cultural analysts can then use geometric relations like distance as correspondences to semantic relations.[15]

Word embeddings can be expanded to consider larger structures. If we are interested in assessing the similarity not of words but of paragraphs or documents, for example, we can use word embeddings to create vectorized representations and then, in turn, estimate the semantic similarities between writings. An expansion of word embeddings known as Doc2Vec performs this function by creating a model of the relations that define the terms in the data and then superimposing them onto a comparison between paragraphs in the text. This technique creates a "vector" representation of documents: two documents with very similar semantic structures (that is, similar ways of using words) will be closer, while documents that differ tremendously in their dictionaries and word usage will be farther apart. The proximity of documents reflects their similarity both in the use of terms (that is, words having similar meanings) and in the structure and organization of sentences (see figure 4.3).

With these two instruments—one that represents word similarities (Word2Vec) and one that represents document similarities (Doc2Vec)—we can conduct a more fine-grain analysis of

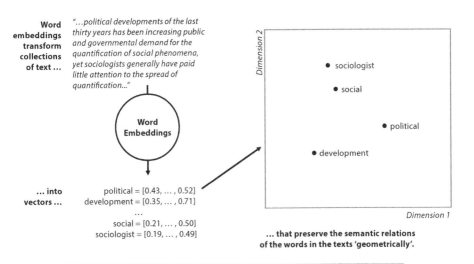

FIGURE 4.3 Word and document embeddings are powerful tools for representing the structure of language.

changes in the semantic universe of the British social sciences. Beyond simple topical convergences, we can look at how the webs of meaning and relations between words that structure a discipline's texts shifted over time, evincing changes in the thought and logic of countless authors bound by their vocations and the pressures of quantification. Because these techniques place all institutions in the same space, they permit the calculation and comparison of pairwise similarities that, collectively, speak to the organization of the discursive field. The average of these pairwise similarities for each period is an especially useful indicator of the degree of homogeneity in the use of concepts: lower average similarities entail more heterogeneity in the field and higher average similarities speak to more homogeneous conceptual universes. (As before, a technical note about this method is provided in the appendix.)

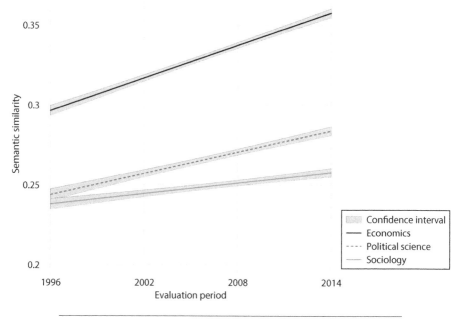

FIGURE 4.4 Semantic similarity among institutions
(anthropology is excluded).

As shown in figure 4.4, these techniques yield evidence that
the similarity among the publication outputs of different institutions increased over time. In politics and sociology, these
changes were statistically significant though modest, suggesting some degree of persistence in the way the disciplines' scholars used words. The semantic shifts were greater in economics
(anthropology is excluded due to the small size of the corpus).
The convergence across institutions during the era of research
evaluations is evident not only in the increasing thematic overlaps, as suggested by the topic models, but also in the ways
scholars used and combined concepts. Homogeneity rose both
in terms of departmental features (the themes that affiliated

scholars write about) and in terms of individual social scientists' conceptual repertoires.

This is not to say, of course, that academic disciplines converged to some unified, static theoretical framework. It would be a mistake to interpret the results of the document embeddings through a positivistic framework of incremental theoretical convergence. Topical and conceptual convergences do not suggest that social scientists were "getting closer" to some variety of truth over time. Quite the contrary: the picture conveyed by the computational representations of discursive shifts is one of constantly changing traditions and concerns, of changing paradigms and research programs.

Consider, for example, how terms changed with respect to others in each discipline's lexicon. While some terms were stable (their positions relative to other words did not change much over time), other terms' contexts of use were widely transformed. This is what table 4.1 shows. Between the mid-1980s and 2000, an era that saw the decline and dissolution of the Soviet Union and the rapid expansion of new forms of globalization and techno-political organization (the internet, global trade, the apogee of liberal economic policy), word embeddings suggest complicated patterns of intellectual shifts. In economics, words such as *value*, *method*, and *input* kept relatively stable positions within their constellations of meanings, while terms such as *growing*, *period*, and *capture* shifted contexts dramatically (think, for instance, of the emergence of "regulatory capture" as a distinct concept). During this same period, words such as *labor*, *equality*, and *success*, all reflecting distinct theories about the new world order, were also rapidly changing their context of use within sociological texts, counterbalanced by the stability of words such as *group*, *family*, and *male*.

Combined with disciplinary histories, these lexical shifts may be indicative of deeper epistemic transformations. This is

TABLE 4.1 EXAMPLES OF THE MOST UNSTABLE AND MOST STABLE WORDS ACROSS PERIODS FOR ECONOMICS, POLITICAL SCIENCE, AND SOCIOLOGY

ECONOMICS		POLITICAL SCIENCE		SOCIOLOGY	
1980–2000		1980–2000		1980–2000	
Most unstable	Most stable	Most unstable	Most stable	Most unstable	Most stable
growing	value	thought	factor	labor	group
period	method	point	group	equality	family
planning	input	meaning	war	success	treatment
attention	power	seek	opinion	framing	male
capture	comparative	positive	issue	attention	minority
reducing	good	professional	military	light	single
infrastructure	contrast	discussion	terrorist	low	black
area	equity	free	administration	capitalist	police
need	analysis	diversity	activity	act	role
	basis	deal	play	produce	sex
2000–2018		2000–2018		2000–2018	
Most unstable	Most Stable	Most unstable	Most Stable	Most unstable	Most Stable
management	effectiveness	right	war	change	student
housing	tax	decade	role	central	relationship
rate	extent	protection	shift	diversity	life
fundamental	model	growing	extent	attention	sample
link	intervention	discussion	area	market	experience
period	density	fundamental	dimension	animal	lesbian
convergence	root	negative	local	distribution	participant
regulation	function	core	term	activity	school
evolution	trade	poverty	planning	play	male
complex	power	view	elite	religious	people

particularly true of words that, owing to their conceptual importance, anchor conversations and research in their fields. In sociology, terms such as *race*, *class*, and *gender* constitute argumentative
pillars for the development of countless theories and studies

of our social world. They are strongly coupled to the multiple, pressing social problems that sociologists have studied for more than a century, so observing their changed positions with respect to other concepts over time produces a more targeted account of the patterns of epistemic shifts that characterized academic fields under quantification.

As an (admittedly abridged) example, let us focus on the central sociological concept of *class*. Scholars attempting to account for observed patterns of stratification have theorized class since at least the nineteenth century. Social class has been used to explain everything from inequalities, electoral politics, and religious practices to educational outcomes, the dynamics of social movements, and affinities in cultural consumption. Class is a complex, multifaceted, polysemous concept that has taken various forms and definitions throughout its history. Even at a single point in time, it has no definite operationalization, no unique way of being measured and understood, no simple and consensual meaning. It is, however, a fundamental part of the sociological theoretical repertoire, a useful site for evaluating possible shifts in a single concept's overall position in the field's constellation of concepts.

Class has, in fact, defined much of the sociological literature in Britain throughout the second half of the twentieth century.[16] Between the 1950s and the 1970s, as Mike Savage observes, sociological accounts of class tended to focus on "the working class as a harbinger of progressive social change." Indeed, Savage writes that the emergence and consolidation of British social science in the postwar period "depended on the dramatic mobilization of the question of class in British society," such that the concept was part and parcel of sociology's growth in the modernizing, public, "plateglass" universities created from the 1960s onward. In its orientation to a working class that was imagined as the counterpoint to British society's more gentlemanly upper sections, the literature was nevertheless "unsustainable." This was too narrow an emphasis, rendering the concept too wholly implicated in the model of white male workers. The literature, in a time of dramatic change to the composition of the UK's social and economic landscape amid deindustrialization and marketization, was soon undermined as the "cohesive worlds of the working class" and its shared consciousness fractured.[17]

In the 1980s, the concept of class within British sociology was reinterpreted around a novel, measurable, almost "scientistic" schema. Moving on from their previous emphasis on the solidaristic identities of working classes, scholars attended to class as a result of the distinct arrangements in employment relations (themselves reflections of profound recent transformations in the country's economy). The most prominent frame of analysis that emerged from this period came out of Nuffield via John Goldthorpe and colleagues. They introduced a taxonomy that distinguished employee classes in terms of contractual obligations: classes were defined by those employed via service contracts versus more "traditional" labor contracts. In addition to bypassing some of the political language that had embedded previous theories of class, Goldthorpe's schema proved methodologically useful. Analyses of occupational and employment statuses allowed for comparisons, projections, and near predictions of group behavior.

By the 1990s, critiques of Goldthorpe's schema redefined ideas of social class within British sociology. Inspired by a growing body of work that analyzed the cultural intersections of class with gender, consumption, identities, and mobility, a new generation of scholars moved discussions of social class away from the Goldthorpe's schema, thus cementing the "cultural turn" in the field that still defines much British sociological scholarship.

An important feature of this new critical literature was its theoretical links to the work of Pierre Bourdieu, who conceptualized class as the interaction between the social, economic, and cultural resources of social actors and their individual trajectories throughout the social space.

Our word embeddings models, perhaps not surprisingly, reflect this brief, bird's-eye view account of class in British sociology. The computational models reveal notable changes in the semantic neighborhoods in which the concept of class resided across evaluation periods. As table 4.2 shows, the words closest to *class* in the earlier periods (*consciousness, Goldthorpe, schema, formation, attribute*), tied to the analytical framework developed by Goldthorpe at Nuffield, have been more recently displaced by references of a more processual nature (*identity, mobility, inequality, mobility, position, meritocracy*) that come closer to Bourdieusian accounts of class as culturally constituted and experienced. This observable flux in semantic landscapes represents

TABLE 4.2 SEMANTIC SHIFTS FOR THE WORD *CLASS*

Pre-1996	1996–2002	2002–2008	2008–2014	2014–2018
formation	Goldthorpe	middle	middle	working-class
consciousness	schema	division	middle-class	middle
unit	latent	schema	mobility	class
middle	underclass	individualize	inequality	middle-class
conventional	study	formation	educational	inequality
hypothesis	validity	mobility	stratification	privilege
mobility	reconstruction	stratification	advantage	Bourdieusian
index	attainment	working-class	social	meritocracy
attribute	ability	middle-class	position	black
respondent	chance	identity	education	GBCS

movements in the scholarly conversations that shaped the concept of class over three decades. It also tallies the changing social and economic structures affecting the experiences, repertoires, and worldviews of the individual scholars interpreting social life.

MECHANISMS OF CHANGE

In the previous chapter, I stressed the importance of career mobility as a source of disciplinary change. By asserting conformist pressures, evaluation exercises create incentives for scholars to move across the employment space in ways that produce more organizational uniformity within academic disciplines. The relative flexibility of the labor market also offers opportunities for managers who, recognizing the symbolic and practical importance of evaluation outcomes, focus on creating centers of excellence that end up mirroring, more often than not, the "ideal" departmental organization.[18] This isomorphic convergence is both mimetic (hiring committees, department managers, and university administrators purposefully copying some form of ideal) and assortative (through mobility, scholars find positions that fit with their interests and concerns and where their expertise and specializations are valued), and it leads to what I have called epistemic sorting.

Alongside careers as scaffolds for disciplines, the quotidian pressures that scholars experience as they move across various institutional spaces are key in the disciplinary convergences we observe. As with any other form of labor, the lived experience of the academic workplace shapes how disciplinary pressures and the logic of quantification come to bear upon the knowledge we produce and the disciplines we collectively build. It is there, in the everyday experience of being a scholar, that slippages happen.

Peter, the political scientist described earlier, pointed to ways that evaluation regimes exert pressure on scholars' work, if not by defining their topics of study, then by inviting them to frame their research along specific lines. One of the salient points that Peter raised in our conversation was that this process of realignment occurred through publications. Scholars are compelled to submit their work to journals and publishers deemed adequately prestigious by their community of peers or risk poor evaluations. As a central part of the craft of the social scientist, the infrastructure of publications becomes a crucial mechanism for refashioning knowledge in response to quantification. To be blunt, publications are our production line and shop floor. Their structures and gatekeepers necessarily affect how we "make out" and reshape our fields.[19]

I discussed this with Mark, a mid-career sociologist from a large metropolitan university in London. Much like Peter, Mark had only encountered research evaluations when he was finishing his PhD. "I remember handing in the thesis," he said as we talked in his office, "and having not published anything, the examiners said, 'Now you've got to publish it because if you don't do it in the next six months, you won't get a job.'" Soon, Mark found a reputable UK-based publisher and released his dissertation as a book. In his estimation, the book "got [me] my first lectureship. That's when I realized REF was important."

The cultures of academia that Mark encountered in his first job were "contradictory" (a word he would use again and again in our conversation about the quantified academic workplace). He was fortunate, he confessed, to secure a lectureship in a well-regarded department associated with an innovative, progressive, left-leaning tradition of sociological scholarship. And yet, he described his workplace as having a "cutthroat culture." There was constant pressure not so much to generate ideas that linked and engaged with the local and broader community—a sense of discipline building through solidarity—but to get things done "on time." Indeed, the departmental expectations seemed to consider the contents of faculty research outputs peripheral. Everyone was expected to produce their best possible work, of course, but in adequate volume and venerable venues. As one of the assessments loomed, Mark recalled, his head of department was writing the narrative to accompany their institution's submission. "I remember s/he did a little interview to understand how I mattered," he said. "There was the book [I had just published] but also a journal I edited which contributed [to the submission], but the discussion didn't go beyond that."

Mark's institution was selective in its recruitment of faculty and students, and he did not remember that evaluations directly altering how he planned and conducted his research. He did, however, stress that the audit culture that came with being assessed for productivity made him more conscious of the *mechanics* of publishing:

> I didn't feel that the five years between cycles were so terrible. But now, for example, I have a book that is ready and am thinking of waiting on publishing it because I already have all that need for this cycle. There is a certain strategic calculus that influences the decision of when I publish. The exercise in and of itself hasn't affected what and how I write. Of course, if we didn't have REF, we probably wouldn't have the pressure to produce papers. And we all know that a good book takes many years to develop. People like [Theodor] Adorno, under REF, would probably not have a future.

Mark's personal incentives may not be explicitly tied to the formal mechanisms of the REF. By design, the REF aims to be as explicitly disconnected from institutional decisions on academic personnel as possible. But the incentives are very real for Mark's managers. Their evaluations of Mark as an employee, as I detail further in chapter 5, are linked to the language and expectations of the REF. His review, promotion, and reappointment all depend on how well Mark's work measures up to the yardsticks of the assessments, even if only in the haphazard approximations and interpretations of local managers (as we will see, this form of disciplinary discipline often comes in the simulations that institutions conduct to calibrate and prepare their submissions). Mark's reference to waiting to publish his next book is a hint of how the assessments figure into scholarly career strategies: having determined that he has "enough" to fulfill institutional expectations as a worthwhile department member for the next evaluation, Mark is considering whether to hold his next book for the following iteration of the assessment. It is a way to deal with uncertainties and try to guarantee that he will, once again, be seen as valuable to his discipline and his institution.

Apparently small strategic decisions about publishing are consequential because they both accede to and reinforce infra-structures of knowledge distribution (the journals, university presses, popular magazines, publishing houses, and other places our words are minted and travel) as gatekeepers and arbiters of disciplinary, epistemic worth. The hierarchies of value that disciplines build into these particular infrastructures become means for rewarding and punishing academics, so they influence decisions about which projects to pursue—they create an "economy of credit" that we adopt as a measure of our own worth against our interpretation of the assessment process.[20]

This presents a challenge for Mark, whose work as a social theorist stands somewhere between sociology and philosophy. His liminal position between fields makes Mark and the journals where he publishes less legible to subpanels of siloed representatives of a single discipline. "Everyone is talking about inter- and transdisciplinarity," he says in words that echo political scientist Peter's experience, "but the REF goes against that. You are defined by your disciplinary identity." When Mark is evaluated by peers, they often "have no idea of what they are reading," and he gets feedback that "'this isn't sociology, it's philosophy,' and vice versa." In consequence, "Social theorists think we've lost the battle. I have colleagues who publish a lot but aren't given a promotion." They are meeting the academic calls for synthetic, interdisciplinary research; they just aren't "REF-able."

These classification conundrums can lead, slowly but surely, to a transformation in the organization of disciplines and their schemas of thought and action.[21] Terry, a professor in sociology working at a large Scottish institution, noted in conversation that, when evaluating his peers' files as part of his department's preparations for the research assessments, distinguishing "true" social theory from "think pieces" can lead to placing a higher emphasis on specific qualities in the text. "If something is empirical, it's a bit easier to be totally confident and say, okay, well this is clearly research. Whereas if something is more theoretically minded, I guess there's a possibility you might shape that into think-piece territory." Terry is particularly fortunate in that his institution provides a protective environment for research—as discussed in the next chapter, quantification can be buffered through thoughtful institutional action—yet its scholars self-police to stay within the boundaries of what they imagine the elite peers who populate evaluation subpanels regard as legitimate social science. Matt, one of Terry's colleagues, explained that his work—influenced by a background in anthropology and an inflexion toward social theory—led him to rebrand his research and think more strategically about where he published. It was not because of the REF, he insisted, but because of its

"wider environment." Publishing in cross-disciplinary journals was "fine," Matt thought, but he couldn't shake the urge
to conform to the REF and frequently wondered whether he
"shouldn't . . . be publishing [in the *British Journal of Sociology*]
or whatever."

At the end of the day, when the infrastructures of publishing
become the gatekeepers of the discipline, they join the forces at
play in the concepts that we deploy to speak about the world
and the careers we embody. In their excellent study of publication patterns in sociology, Elisabeth Clemens and colleagues
suggest that the prestige of publications is partly tied to specific
genres and how these are valued by institutions.[22] Their study
focuses on American sociologists, finding that elite institutions
seem to have a stronger taste for employing scholars who write
books that are tied to the fostering of disciplinary conversations across subfields. Articles, on the other hand, are a more
punctual genre that allows comparing scholars along a more
uniform metric of citations. Another impressive study, by Misha
Teplitskiy and colleagues, underscores the point that the design
of these infrastructures of knowledge dissemination matters by
tallying citations. The most influential citations used in articles
(those considered by authors to be the most important for the
claims they are presenting) are disproportionately highly visible
papers from the leading journals in the field. As Teplitskiy and
colleagues document, these high-impact citations are frequently
found early in projects and through social connections who, in
a sense, reify their quality because of their impressive citation
counts—feeding back metrics into metrics, power onto power.[23]
The practical publication decisions of academics in general (and
British academics in particular) are also decisions about the
types of knowledge they should produce vis-à-vis their disciplinary visibility.

For all the pluralism and openness that science inspires, it also involves emphasis on standards of practice, authorship, genre, and style that constrain the scope and nature of our work through both self-monitoring and overt managerial interventions. Quantification nurtures a specific change in the "rules of the game" on the shop floor of academic work, in which deans, heads of school, and university administrators (the managerial staff) join doctoral students, instructors, and faculty in regarding journals and their hierarchies of prestige paramount indications of job and vocational success.

This is not to say that constraints are bad or should not exist. Disciplines are what they are in part because of their capacity for disciplining knowledge, for creating consensus and influencing the nature of conversations and research interests.[24] Yet what is particularly fascinating about the forms of quantification that have emerged in British academia is the degree to which they have strengthened these disciplinary forces. If anything, evaluations seem to kick existing disciplinary logic into a kind of overdrive.

A generation or two ago—when research evaluations were just starting their institutional life in Britain—the landscape of economics in the United Kingdom was relatively plural. The old hierarchies of status and prestige that had structured much of the higher education sector meant that institutions were relatively insulated from competition and could afford to have what would be seen today as rather quirky departments. For instance, well into the 1980s, the University of Cambridge employed numerous "heterodox" economists who, challenging the emerging canon of mainstream neoclassical economics, found it a productive space in which their research was protected by centuries of symbolic wealth. Even beyond those gothic walls, British economics was a rather epistemically diverse enterprise, with historians of

economic thought working a stone's throw from labor economists, post-Keynesian scholars, and operations researchers optimizing imagined utilities through intricate mathematical tricks.
As Marion Fourcade writes, economics in Britain was less organized and professionalized than its American counterpart, with
the identity of economists "shaped by their embeddedness in the
high-status, well-educated clerisy whose knowledge ought to be
put to the general service of society."[25]

As the discipline converged toward a more "American style
of doing economics, with increased emphasis on the publication
of journal articles," pluralism became a distinctly costly affair.
The logic and pressures produced by the research assessments
aligned with the increasingly standardized global economics profession and its shared conceptions of publication values.
For Roger Backhouse, the history of economic thought became
a casualty of quantification. Originally defended as a laudable
subfield, this specialty lost relevance amid the focus on technical sophistication in the discipline. In Backhouse's words, the
evaluation regime "clearly inhibits work" on the history of economic thought, particularly in the middle- to top-tier economics departments:

> [which] presumably [are] attempting to raise their ranking and
> [put] pressure on staff to direct their publication effort towards
> those journals that are believed to count for more with RAE
> panels. In economics, journals are so important that people even
> suggest (half seriously) that books should carry negative weight.
> Given that the most prestigious journals have little interest in [the
> history of economic thought], the result is pressure to work in
> other fields. At the same time, scholars in other fields (sociology,
> intellectual history, and philosophy) have begun to show greater
> interest in the history of economics.[26]

The late heterodox economist Frederick S. Lee was similarly emphatic in linking state-sponsored evaluations to the eventual dominance of neoclassical economic theory. In analyzing how departments presented themselves to the state's quality assurance bodies, Lee observed that none of the top-ranked institutions highlighted their investments in heterodox economics (even if, as at Cambridge, they had done so in the past). Instead, they stressed that their faculty provided their students with "a sound understanding of the central ideas, concepts, tools, models and methods of modern mainstream economic theory."[27] By means of peer review and the legitimization of research published by a hierarchy of journals, heterodox approaches were sidelined over time.[28] Indeed, for Lee, the national assessments are not "flawed in that [they] cannot ensure that quality research is funded, but only that [they fund] research that interest groups say is quality."

Decidedly more modest than the detailed work of scholars such as Fourcade, Backhouse, and Lee, the word embeddings modeling I have done confirms important shifts in the discourse of economics. Consider a term as central to our present understanding of the economy as *risk*. In contemporary disciplinary conversations, risk is often associated with distinctly monetary and financial concerns. There are "risks" in stock and derivatives markets, central banks, and the broader economic systems of our hyperlinked, financialized world. But a mere generation or two ago, finance was not the pinnacle of economic science that it is today, and risk was not primarily thought of in terms of complicated statistical models measuring the uncertainty of economic life through numerical methods and millions of simulations. Risk was actuarial, tied to the language of insurance, in which hazards and individual events mattered more than the optimization of investments under turbulent unpredictability. Table 4.3

TABLE 4.3 THE EVOLUTION OF *RISK* IN ECONOMICS

Pre–1996	1996–2002	2002–2008	2008–2014	2014–2018
aversion	hedging	portfolio	aversion	risky
premium	risky	aversion	downside	expect
hedging	adverse	exposure	averse	aversion
portfolio	premia	averse	risky	counterparty
premia	return	insurance	spread	equity
pound	hedge	assets	premia	riskiness
avoid	aversion	idiosyncratic	default	portfolio
obesity	time-varying	management	financial	financial
hedge	hazard	loss	credit	risk-taking
useful	death	swap	asset	return

shows this change. Whereas the context of *risk* in economic publications in the 1980s included terms that allude to individual forms of misfortune (*obesity, hazard, death*), in later periods, its semantic context was more closely associated with words we see as financial (*counterparty, portfolio, premia*). Like the profession, the language of economics financialized away from broad concerns transecting multiple understandings of risk and riskiness to more particular, technical understandings tied to the methods of financial management and calculation.

Again, we see that semantic convergences accord with a discipline ever more anchored to a recognizable "mainstream" paradigm, as Backhouse and Lee suggest. Economics is certainly notable, as it is arguably the most consensual of all social sciences (sociology shares patterns with political science, while anthropology remains quite distinct). Carl, a senior economist at a top institution in London, made the adherence of his discipline to its publication structures very clear: "we don't necessarily read all the papers for the REF submissions but trust the quality of the journals. There are very few borderline cases, and it is very clear what a four-star journal is for us. Getting in these is exceedingly difficult, so we trust the process that got these papers published." The evaluative heuristic of delegated trust may work well for many economists in a converging discipline, yet as Backhouse notes, it is disastrous for others. Heterodoxy and history, for instance, find few spaces (if any) in the top tier of economics publications.

Quantifications only come to matter when their weight is instituted through some organized, collective, bootstrapped force. Economists have taught us this lesson well. Sitting in his office, Carl explained the mechanics through which evaluations came to life in his department. Theirs is among the field's top institutions, so Carl and his colleagues feel that they can pay minimal attention to the REF. The department hires exceptional scholars, knowing that they will produce fine research without any need for audits or systems of surveillance. If anything, Carl insisted, his department plays the game of the REF as a means of signaling its faculty's worth to others in the discipline. Understanding its advantaged position as well as the logic of the evaluations, the institution takes part in the rituals of quantification, then reaps the expected benefits of being an exceptional, internationally competitive economics department. Indeed, the REF serves to chip status away from Oxbridge, letting the shiny modern buildings of London economics prove themselves intellectual equals to their gothic neighbors to the north.

In the lived experience of scholarly labor, none of us has a choice as to participating in quantified academia. Scholars and institutions can only determine the degree to which they will engage with or disengage from these exercises and their implied calculus of relative worth. The shifts in our language, theories, and practices are heterogeneous because quantification is experienced differently across the disciplinary space. It affords some power, others invisibility. Still others face intense precarity. It follows that disciplinary convergence is not necessarily coded into our professional vocations or the logic of discovery. Institutions and scholars can opt in or opt out of playing the game of evaluations, and those choices accrue in disciplinary inflections. Much like geological processes, the various forces of quantification generate a complex landscape. But unlike geological processes, this is a landscape we can (and perhaps should) better control.

5

HIERARCHIES OF
QUANTIFICATION

My conversation with Carl, the economist working at a top-ranked institution in London, was one of the most revealing interviews of this study. In addition to his generosity and candor, Carl had a perspective on research evaluations that stood apart from most other academics'. Rather than bureaucratic intrusions and scholarly distractions, Carl saw the assessments as malleable games played by institutions. REF did not really matter in the everyday labor of Carl and his colleagues, he thought. They were already excellent, selected into the institution through a meticulous hiring process and socialized into a shared departmental culture of rigorous research. The REF's standards seemed a bit low, in his estimation. Four publications? Check. Top-ranked journals? Check. Demonstrable policy impact? Check. If anything, any assessment-related accolades simply signaled to others on campus and outside of their discipline that Carl's department was, in fact, internationally competitive. Icing on the cake.

Placed in the context of the grievances I had heard about (and felt toward) research assessments, Carl's comments were an important reorientation (close to what ethnographers would call a "negative case"). However centralized, controlling, and exacting it may be, the quantification regime experienced by many British academics is not, in itself, powerful. Like other regimes of quantification, it is frequently accompanied by forceful consequences, yet its ratings, evaluations, and scores come to matter only when they are made meaningful in practice, affecting the everyday experiences of the workplace or defining the qualities of labor in the academic world. Individual scholars, institutions, and disciplines have tremendous flexibility in how they react to the logic of the REF and its various iterations. And, to a remarkable degree, they use it. In some places, in some disciplines, quantification is simply felt less than in others.

How are quantification regimes attenuated? How are they magnified? What goes into modulating the way numbers, metrics, scores, and rankings affect social life? An impressive number of scholars have addressed these and similar questions by focusing on the contours of the quantitative and algorithmic cultures that seem to define contemporary societies. The philosopher Ian Hacking famously described the proliferation of numbers as an "avalanche," characterizing the environment in the 1820s when statistical enthusiasm materialized in both bureaucracies and print media, as states and other social actors sought to measure, compare, and classify a rapidly changing social world in ever more quantified ways.[1] In studying the subsequent two centuries, many scholars have adopted similar language, reflecting a common sense of how we believe metrics operate in and on the world. Hacking's word *avalanche*, for instance, captures the public idea of quantification as an unstoppable force, overtaking everything in its path by virtue of sheer inertia. Once initiated, there was little to do but acquiesce, it seemed, with quantification mirroring markets and modernity as eminently remorseless social forces.

Recent, richer accounts presented by scholars in the sociology of quantification have instead reframed numbers and their social power as fickle, contingent, and contextual. Numbers are made to matter through ongoing institutional work. Their truthfulness is not fixed but maintained, their effects not presumed but performed into being. How are we to navigate such contrasting views?

COUNTING HIERARCHIES

A good entry point for this more recent literature comes in reconceptualizing quantification as a hands-on "social technology," a "means for managing events" that itself structures and gives sense to organizational practices.[2] It is because we do things with numbers that numbers accrue their power. We use them to attribute value, to compare, to rank, to enlist, to measure, to cut, to expand, to change our sociomaterial environments. As with any technology, the specifics of how and to what end we use numbers determine the forms of power that they come to hold with regard to our habits and actions. Regimes of quantification matter not because numbers have some magical character but rather because they are enmeshed with meaningful practices that are central to the reproduction of social life.

Quantifications such as those built into Britain's research assessments are altered by a pair of conflicting forms of power. In her impressive study of contemporary journalism, another industry defined by economies of analysis, regard, and prestige, Angèle Christin identifies two forms of power—bureaucratic and disciplinary—with importance for both the daily office operations of a digital newsroom and the distinct types of content it creates. Because the dynamics of attention and visibility that characterize contemporary digital newsrooms resemble the anxious economies of scholarly merit, Christin's ideal types are useful instruments for understanding quantification's effects on the academic workplace. In situations where *bureaucratic* power characterizes number making and interpretation, authority is centralized in a legible hierarchy. The rules of the evaluation are clear, as are the material sanctions associated with failure. Activity types are distinctly compartmentalized (research, for example, is clearly separated from teaching or impact) and associated with distinct parameters whose interpretation is determined by bureaucratic rulemaking. The notion of who and what is worthy, maintained by the higher managerial segments of the organization, is made visible through the metrics, standards, and requirements informing these performance measures. Power can also configure itself as the more decentralized *disciplinary* power. Here the center of authority is unclear and the mechanisms of reward and sanctioning are internalized rather than rationalized. Disciplinary power's weak, informal boundaries mean ambiguity but also flexibility, and metrics can be used in a more case-by-case, interpersonal, and tacit process of evaluation.

Scientific fields, like those studied in this book, are often defined by such disciplinary forms of power. The type of mutual dependencies that characterize scientific labor—seen in the degree to which scholars rely on fellow specialists to construct knowledge, have their contributions recognized, and gain resources and prestige—implies that power is diffused across the fields' cultures of training and practice.[3] Quantification may simply be a way of registering shared disciplinary standards rather than asserting central coordination. This possibility would fit with Carl's comments: by virtue of their training and the disciplining required to become competitive economists, "everyone" in Carl's field knows exactly which journals matter most. They have internalized both their community's standards and the task of policing those standards.

At the same time, research evaluations are patently *bureaucratic*. Peers conduct the assessments of scholars' work, but in a rationalized, organized manner. Hundreds, if not thousands, of participants discuss, review, and iteratively revise lengthy tomes full of the evaluative governing rules for each assessment. Institutions, managing their submissions, expand their organizational hierarchies in response, hiring research officers, coordinators, and managers to prepare and submit documents to the assessments. They also invest in information management systems to capture all their research-active scholars' "outputs" and craft the best possible submissions. Even the panels are carefully constructed, so that while the evaluators are peers, they are selected, high-status peers. The meticulous process of nominating, vetting, and confirming panel members inevitably reflects the formal hierarchies of higher education (lecturers, senior lecturers, and readers are, for instance, unlikely be chosen for the high-level panels). All these rationalized processes, these forms of bureaucracy, seem antithetical to the more open-ended, tacit, and self-policed logic of disciplinary power.

This tension is amplified but also made somewhat explicable when we recall that ideal types are just that—idealized representations of a messy social substrate. Bureaucratic and disciplinary power, in practice, are conceptual, incomplete simplifications of organizational life. In his terrific work on government-sponsored social credit scores in China, often represented as massive, bureaucratic interventions to control public life, for example, Chuncheng Liu gives us an exceptional demonstration of the difference between power in policy and power in practice. These omnipresent forms of quantification represent a bureaucratic aspiration, and their failure to actually yield a unified social credit score that is perfectly transferable across contexts reveals a host of disjunctures. The vast bureaucracies involved in collecting, processing, and aggregating all sorts of data associated with millions of individuals are, in fact, fragmented constellations of loosely interdependent units selectively interpreting and working with standards through mismatched patchworks of logic and practice. In the end, China's social credit score is an imperfect, malleable metric made sense of and used in different ways by different interfaces of public and private bureaucracies.[4]

Angèle Christin's work on the use of algorithms in the courts is a similar case. In exploring how judges and judicial bureaucracies make use of algorithmic risk assessments—controversial systems that, combining survey and secondary data, score a defendant's likelihood for recidivism—Christin and Sarah Brayne observe that decisions are rarely purely algorithmic. Something as material as how scores are printed and presented in case files (prominently at the top or buried somewhere within thousands of pages of legal documents) matters for the ways apparently mechanical quantifications are put into practice. If anything, quantification is modulated by discretion and choice, by the inevitable ambiguities of fickle bureaucracies.[5]

Returning to our academic evaluations, we can observe the ambiguity of numbers and situatedness of quantification in the mechanics of the enormous exercise. In my conversations with social scientists, it was clear that some panel members read their materials with greater care and detail than others. Confronted with hundreds of papers and books to assess, former peer panelists described performing a sort of triage. As in tackling a mountain of student papers at the end of the term, they tried to go through rapidly, focusing on broad strokes and key concepts. Others, by contrast, spoke of the task as onerous, tedious, and intensely detailed. They created and stuck to very specific daily schedules of focused reading over several months and paying close attention to each text's intellectual contributions to the discipline.[6] At the extreme ends, these panelists who shared the same "job," including its codes and expectations of behavior, and operated within the same disciplinary boundaries, demonstrated varying commitments and approaches to the assessment exercise and its hefty systems of rules.

Moreover, panelists' approaches to peer review were patterned by discipline. Each set of reviewers appeared to reflect their discipline's unique evaluation cultures. Economists, for instance, used journal rankings in a slightly more algorithmic way as they assessed the worth of scholarship, while anthropologists believed determining value required a slightly more contested process of discussion and deliberation. The rationalizing power of bureaucracy only goes so far: the results depend on how faithfully bureaucrats perform their utopias of rules into being.[7]

Of course, the same can be said about disciplinary power. While it would seem that disciplines are self-patrolled by shared understandings of worth and esteem—informal rankings of journals, recognized topics of interest, norms about the adequacy of methods, senses of innovativeness—the reality is that scientific fields are necessarily operationalized in organized settings, bureaucratizing the contours of disciplinary power. A key issue is that academics occupy awkward positions between the internal, administrative hierarchies of their institutions and the external logic of their discipline (explaining, in part, why a focus on careers is so fruitful). Heads (or chairs) of department are rather obvious examples, as they straddle administrative and disciplinary roles, enforcing processes around hiring, promotion, and merit reviews while being members of broader epistemic communities. Heads of departments guide their units' policies, interface with the administration, differentially support programs and initiatives, and play a central role in assessing and rewarding scholars *as employees*. Through and through, they are administrators. Simultaneously, they are interested academics and disciplinary disciples who live and work within the logics of vocation, reputation, and prestige unique to their fields. Indeed, disciplines as we know and assess them today do not exist as nebulous, invisible communities of scholars working in a vacuum; they, too, are made to matter through the institutional structures of the modern university. The dynamics of management and control cannot be detached from the reproduction of disciplines, just as the ambiguities of disciplines cannot be detached from the specificities of bureaucratic practice.[8]

Quantification regimes exist at the intersection of wobbly, practical forms of bureaucratic and disciplinary power. This in-betweenness was apparent in my conversations with social scientists across the UK, all of whom hinted at the importance of organizational context in shaping whether and how quantification was consequential to their professional lives. Specifically, the tension between bureaucracy and discipline played out in how departmental hierarchies of prestige within universities interacted with each field's hierarchies of institutional status: the experience of being a quantified scholar in a high-prestige department at a high-prestige institution was notably different from the experience in low-prestige departments (even in universities endowed with high public and disciplinary status).

Achieved prestige and ascribed status are so intensely crucial to the experience of scientific work because, as sociologist Richard Whitely insists in his formative study on the organization of the sciences, they are central to the reputational dynamics that ultimately structure academic fields.[9] In the early institutionalization of science, its practitioners had few means other than reputation by which to establish the boundaries of consensual knowledge and disciplinary belonging. Learned societies became sites of knowledge production as well as systems of prestige controlling the boundaries of emerging fields (like natural philosophy). Journals and their associated forms of peer review do something similar as they gatekeep the corpus of accepted and acceptable knowledge. In effect, the boundary work performed by scholars in evaluating knowledge and distinguishing "true" from "false" claims, "good" from "bad" science relies on shared reputational hierarchies and cultural repertoires—an apparent sense of within-field epistemic agreement. Given that science itself necessitates constant revisions to the contents of knowledge, these shared reputational hierarchies of people, claims, and institutions provide a sense of stability. They also, when instituted through organizations, carry distinct material effects, setting hard expectations about the genre, scope, and contents of valued scientific outputs. As the early Mertonian literature in the sociology of science stressed, prestige is epistemically consequential.[10]

Because science is structured through reputational dynamics, the way scientific outputs are evaluated and scholars are rewarded hinges on status. As in previous chapters, the specific link among quantifying practices, knowledge creation, and reputation is driven in my interview data by the employment conditions that tie metrics and assessments to career milestones, from hiring and review to promotion and overall evaluation.

In principle, this link should not exist. Research evaluations, from the start, were meant to be entirely decoupled from personnel decisions. Their aim was simply to standardize the allocation of austerity-level research funding. Yet given their obvious connection to prestige—in how their implied rankings of quality are used by gimlet-eyed researchers and strategic-minded administrators—research evaluations are almost unavoidably paramount to academics' employment strategies.

SIMULATING VALUE

The mechanisms through which these systemwide audits of scholarly output became punctual managerial interventions are telling, showing how broad quantification regimes can affect the work of individuals while also demonstrating how they are moderated by local organizational circumstances, buffers, and constraints.

When I spoke with my British colleagues for this book, I often started by asking about their first encounter with research evaluations, followed by how they thought the assessments shaped their intellectual concerns. Overwhelmingly, my informants claimed that research assessments had little effect on their practices and interests. They would pivot quickly to discussing the assessments as intrusive and bureaucratic, with one sociologist saying mildly that they were "not very productive" and a more cynical anthropologist dismissing them as an outright "waste of time." The actual effects of research evaluations tended to emerge in a lateral discussion, not of the periodic scores themselves but about the ways individual departments and institutions prepared for each iteration of the assessments. Here, focused on mundane organizational practices, I gathered repeated references to internal departmental practices that, given their connection to decisions on reward and promotion, were, in fact, visible mechanisms through which quantification shaped scholars' careers. Specifically, under the innocuous label of "mock" exercises, the organizational practice of preassessment simulations linked policy personal within departments.

Mock exercises are fascinating examples of how the might of quantification ultimately depends on how it is practiced, organized, and policed on the ground.[11] Some of my own personal experiences as an early-career scholar in British academia are telling. Like too many stories of auditing run amok, one of mine started with a seemingly harmless email from a management consultant in late 2011. The rules of the next assessment had been announced scarcely two months prior when all of the research-active staff at the LSE were invited to complete a short survey about the REF 2014. What did we understand by *impact*? Did we think research management structures were effective? Did we know how the REF worked? And more ominously, did we understand our "role and responsibilities [. . .] with respect to REF"? Revealingly, the email was sent by an employee of Binder Dijker Otte, an international consultancy hired to manage LSE's REF submission. One would have to be remarkably obtuse to miss the point: LSE was investing substantive organizational and financial efforts toward the REF, and the ultimate outcome for each department was explicitly the responsibility of its many scholars.

The survey was far from the only expansion of the campus's organizational structures aimed at the REF 2014. Two years ahead of the census date (set for November 2013), LSE's senior administrators created a dedicated, schoolwide REF Strategy Committee to coordinate the eventual submission to the panels. Each department created internal REF committees that, in collaboration with their own long-standing research committees, would collate, analyze, and give shape to their scholars' multiple submissions. Department meetings and away days dedicated increasing amounts of time and energy to discussions of "REF strategies"— what they meant and how they would work. Research officers were hired to email staff, collect scholarly outputs, document evidence of impact, and support the departmental REF coordinators. In hallways, meeting rooms, staff assemblies, pubs, and coffee shops, intense discussions about the collective approach to the impending evaluations unfolded with palpable anxiety.

The laborers, we research-active staff, understood that we had limited agency in terms of our "roles and responsibilities." It was, after all, *our* research being submitted, *our* research environment quantified, and *our* intellectual impact weighed, yet the school could "structure its submission in whatever way it thinks most appropriate and potentially beneficial for the institution," with administrators and senior academics "setting the research excellence quality threshold," deciding which units to submit, and how and where individual scholars were included in the assessment. The school's submission was, explicitly, "an institutional response, which is targeted both strategically and tactically," read a memorandum on LSE's REF Code of Practice circulated in May 2012.[12] The strategy was simple: Since only three- and four-star research counted toward quality-related funding, LSE decided to "aim for an average quality profile within the 3^* band across all units of assessment (internationally excellent in terms of originality, significance and rigor)." Those whose work fell short of this standard would be left out of the school's submission—and that meant mobilizing a self-policing apparatus full of hand-wringing comparison and paranoia.

The problem with this strategy (bolded and underlined in the original memorandum) was that it required departments to internally estimate the quality of their staff's potential submissions. Any sort of ad hoc, schoolwide committee would be adrift when it came to determining "internationally excellent" research across fragmented disciplines, idiosyncratic subfields, and work that fell at the boundaries of several fields. Indeed, I freely admit my crawling discomfort at the thought of being asked to decide what constitutes internationally excellent demography, gender studies, or work on immigration (among many, many other subfields). My own department was rather ahead of the game here. Having survived a historically poor result in the 2008 RAE—LSE sociology was the lowest-ranked unit across the entire school—we were prepared to approach the 2014 REF in the most serious, professional, and proactive way possible. As early as January 2011, the research-active staff in sociology were invited to submit and provisionally grade four of their scholarly outputs each. The move was meant to make "this process our own in a way that benefits us individually and benefits the department as a whole." Captured in a form (figure 5.1), our papers, books, and other contributions were to be read by the department's REF committee and moderated by two "external assessors" (one British, the other American), scored on the basis of how these readers understood that the 2014 REF would work.

Name:

Department of Sociology – REF preparations, January 2011

	Publication title ('output')	Your rating	Department rating	External rating	Broadly within Sociological discipline (UoA) (Y/N)?	Any other brief comments you might have, including regarding significance, originality, and rigour of the publication?
1						
2						
3						
4						

	Any other comments/possible reserves?	Department comments
1		
2		

External's comments

FIGURE 5.1 Standardized form used for indicating outputs that might potentially be submitted to REF 2014.

Over the following eighteen months, the research officer collected our work. As both the producers of this knowledge and
employees of the institution, we staff members had only partial
access to the process, though we were given the opportunity to
see external assessors' grades and comments regarding our outputs. At no point, however, did we partake in discussions about
which scholars and which works would be submitted to the
REF. Those strategies were the purview of the higher-ups.

Is this the case with us?

This process of grading and evaluating colleagues' work would
seem a familiar one, given its closeness to the accepted practice
of peer review. Soon, however, it became an object of conten-
tion. The internal evaluation forms and their outcomes were not
just about REF; increasingly, they became instruments of personnel management, a point that the school's upper administration was making explicit. In the future, the LSE was far less
likely to decouple the outcomes of these internal, assessment-
oriented mock exercises from very real discussions about staff
retention, review, promotion, and reward. In its Code of Conduct for the assessment exercise, the school declared that "those
staff who *potentially* may not be included in the School's REF
submission will first be notified by their Head of Department
(or Research Centre Director). Heads of Department will moni-
tor REF performance levels through 2012 and early 2013, and
where necessary will initiate conversations with members of staff
at risk of not being entered for REF2014." In other words, we
were to understand the discretionary choices about inclusion as
terrifying indicators of underperformance and, ultimately, dismissal. Later, in my interviews, I would learn that these type of
awkward conversations at LSE were proliferating across Britain's institutions of higher education. As the "mock" exercises got
underway, scholars began to feel nudges, if not shoves, toward a
very specific type of productivity—or toward the door.

In Carl's institution, the review of research outputs had been vastly rationalized since the previous assessment. His employer, he said, had since created a centralized repository of research outputs (notably, this is now explicitly incentivized by the assessments) to make it easier for departmental and university management to track staff productivity. "Everything has to be put in [the platform] and you have to score it, and it has to be transparent, so you see it," noted Carl. Every now and then, mock exercises use this platform to evaluate the institution's approximate standing in the upcoming assessments, providing "an indication [that you can] use it for any personnel decisions." Those showing modest productivity are suggested to "maybe [not] stay in the research track and maybe [move to the] kind of teaching track," Carl noted.

Mark, the London-based sociologist, mentioned, almost off-handedly, that scholars in his institution were required "to show publications once a year" in preparation for the assessments.

> A committee [of administrators] evaluates the quality of your publications. I have a cynical attitude towards them. Many times, the folks in the committees have no idea of what they are reading or doing. They also do it very fast. Five minutes per paper, looking at where it was published. We have an appeal procedure that allows us to check if the paper was properly judged. And we know it matters because it is a tool for increments and promotions.

The logic of research evaluations is so critical to the career paths of scholars in Mark's institution that their standards are explicitly cited in decisions about promotions. His employer frames its expectations about advancement in terms of "how many stars you need in your papers for promotion," and those who are periodically judged underperforming in the mock assessments are, as in Carl's, advised to "move . . . from research to teaching positions."

The internal assessments at William's large Scottish institution could equally result in what the anthropologist called "difficult conversations" should staff members fail to meet the criteria for evaluation inclusion in the mock exercises leading up to the REF. Historically, William's university had taken a decentralized approach, with individual units deciding how they ought to proceed with regard to submissions, but that changed over time. "The last time" the national evaluations came around, he noted, William was in an administrative position and "was enjoined to have a 'difficult conversation'" with staff who had not published enough to be included in the assessment submission. These conversations were "just excruciating, they're embarrassing because everyone kind of knew where they stood."

DISCIPLINE, IN-HOUSE

Research assessments are glaring examples of disciplining regimes, yet the lesson I derived from my interviews was that their mechanisms of action are not located in the assessment subpanels or the state's funding bureaucracies. The national results are surely consequential, as are the distributional politics of the assessments themselves, but what matters most to how scholars rethink their intellectual concerns is how they are evaluated by their line managers and employers in the context of career advancement. It is the local employment context that gives the evaluations the power to shape disciplines.

Back in 2011, when my colleagues and I were asked to indicate which of our outputs could potentially be considered for the assessment, we were invited to explain on the same standardized form how each work fell "broadly within the sociological discipline." This was an entirely reasonable request: even if constituted by four or five friendly colleagues, the department's REF committee would have found it difficult to evaluate every type and form of sociological scholarship, simply because of how specialized our work has become. Explaining how each paper, chapter, or book contributed to a broader sociological conversation seemed, at least at the time, a benign clarification and a chance for us to make our case for inclusion.

And with that, we're back to the start of this book—the moment when I realized that, in defining what falls "broadly within the discipline," by filling out this form to advocate for being counted, justify our belonging, and stake our claims to disciplinary identity, my colleagues and I were actively constructing the boundaries of our field. It was not an exercise in showcasing the diversity of sociology, its patchwork history, and its motley epistemologies, but a plea for the existence of diversity in the first place. (Is critical realism broadly sociological? Is demography distinct from sociology? How much philosophy makes a paper fall outside the boundaries of sociological traditions?) This modest, mundane, internal departmental form was a clear testament to the in-betweenness of bureaucracy and discipline in the research evaluations. It was not only a decidedly rationalizing instrument located within a larger apparatus of formal review and punishment but also a means for the epistemic (and embodied) implementation of both bureaucratic and disciplinary power.

There is nothing in the guidance of the research assessment that obligated institutions to adopt this particular variety of internal evaluation. Barring the stipulation for a code of practice, the evaluations' expectations about how institutions would approach the assessments via internal policy and practice were left open-ended. The form that we at LSE were required to fill out ahead of mock assessments was just one locally improved solution to the institutional politics of demonstrating our department's commitment to the process and our professionalism in making sure that we obtained the best outcome possible. (Remember, it was heavily inflected, in the case of our department specifically, by our perceived failure in the previous iteration of the assessments and how it had damaged our reputation within the broader scholarly community of our school.)

Elsewhere, departments adopted vastly different strategies. William, the anthropologist, recalled that "last time we basically . . . made the grades up in our heads" to appease the university's administration. Having participated in several assessments, sociologist Terry remembered that the exercise was conducted at his institution mostly by "looking at the outputs and having a team look at them and give a confidential ranking," rather than having individual conversations about expected productivity or revealing the implied ratings that came out of the internal assessment. "We've had discussions about that but decided it's not worth it," Terry said. And in Samuel's historically progressive sociology department in London, "we didn't do much of a mock REF," leaving the decisions about which scholars and work would be submitted to the evaluation to "a team of probably about three people." No matter how many similar themes emerged across my interviews with academics, I never found a single archetypical experience of quantification. There was no single device by which individuals or departments or institutions prepared or responded, nor was there any single way that numbers came to bear upon scholars' lives. It was all and always local, contextual, and variegated.

The pattern I did observe involves the three axes of prestige along which quantification regimes were implemented across

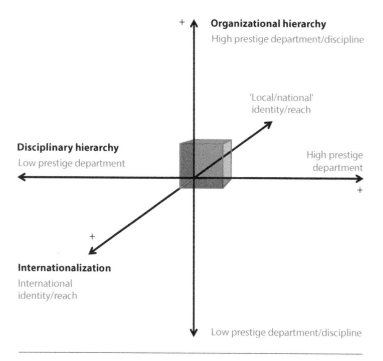

FIGURE 5.2 Hierarchies of prestige.

institutions (figure 5.2). Specifically, quantification was experienced in different ways depending on where units were located within the three-dimensional space created by internationalization, position in the national epistemic field, and position within the institution's internal hierarchies.

The first of these dimensions, internationalization, refers to the degree to which a field's infrastructure of knowledge production is coupled to international journals, standards, and labor markets. Because the evaluations' yardsticks place great worth on "international" quality, being highly internationalized affords a discipline more resources and power. At the same time, it means that universities and departments have less leeway to innovate and tinker with internal evaluations. This explains why economics departments—particularly those at the top of the heap—seem to be spared the strongest effects of research evaluations and rely so heavily on a list of journals in evaluating their scholars. Frank, an economist working in a large Scottish institution, reflected that the "center of gravity in economics [is in] the United States," so "we have effectively adopted U.S. academic values" regarding valued research areas and the organization of the labor market. Carl, Frank, and Frank's colleague John all highlighted the global character of recruitment in their institutions and alluded to this in explaining their relative degree of excellence and specialization. Indeed, for John, this international orientation was necessary, even if it led to difficulties in filling positions: "We actively try to recruit very good people. We see that as a sign of discipline. . . . You can grow in a haphazard and mediocre way, but you really don't want to do that. You want to preserve quality."

Internationalization was also apparent in my conversations with Charlotte, an early-career anthropologist working at a large research-intensive institution in London. She believed a long-standing fragmentation of the anthropological literature in Britain and its relative insularity from American schools of thought were giving way to a more integrated, transatlantic field. (William, the anthropologist based in Scotland, said similarly that, when he was a student, they spoke of American anthropology "in quite weirdly disparaging terms.") The status of American university presses and their role in maintaining the ethnographic monograph played a large part in the internationalization of anthropology. Charlotte noted that these monographs tend to be produced by younger scholars: "there's no way anyone gets a lectureship anymore without the book. . . . It's very conceivable that some of the more senior people at the department could have gone the last five years without producing a book. . . . The way of submitting books to the REF is through new early career hires." This organization of intellectual work, with younger anthropologists producing the books that get submitted to assessment subpanels, has the consequence of internationalizing the hierarchies of prestige in the field. PhD students, Charlotte thought, "know they have to aim high" when they try to get their books published, "so they go for Chicago or Duke. . . . I've seen people quite disappointed when they publish not with university presses and they feel like they've given away their gem." William put it differently: "There's books, and there's Books, and then there's the book published by Routledge," a so-called trade press with less cachet than the university presses, where he stipulated some of the books were "great but some of which are absolutely terrible." In both Charlotte's and William's institutions, anthropology's international orientation acts as a buffer, establishing a sense of worth about a department's standing in the field to external assessors and higher-ups in the administration while generating constraints in terms of the types of outputs they need to produce and the publishers they must court. Elsewhere, departments further removed from this international axis had a harder time gaining the evaluation's justificatory imprimatur. As Max, a Scottish anthropologist, told me, a university that "in my estimation has a fine department [that] produces really good graduates" but lacked the degree of internationalization that Charlotte's and William's schools had "didn't do nearly as well in the last REF as we thought [it would] and the ramifications have been quite severe for them."

The second dimension we see in figure 5.2 can provide insulation in similar ways. A department's position in the *national* epistemic field mirrors some of the logic of disciplinary power insofar as it reflects its own hierarchies of regard and epistemic worth. Scholars in departments associated with their discipline's main traditions, the professionalization of the field in the UK, or centrality (as recognized by their attendant epistemic communities) to the production of valuable knowledge accrued less managerial intervention than did those further down the ladder. Being a "top" department afforded them some independence and control. Conversely, scholars in departments that were struggling to find a presence and voice in the field endured greater pressures to justify their relevance and value, not only to the assessment subpanels but also to their university's administration.

The third axis, a unit's position within its university's particular hierarchy of prestige, moderated the degree to which a privileged position within a discipline's hierarchy afforded protection from the evaluations. This third axis evokes forms of bureaucratic power in which the intervention of managers and administrators is much clearer and takes the shape of ongoing evaluations, lists, and explicit performance criteria. Being at an elite institution saves a department from managerial interventions if—and only if—that department happens to be at the top of the pack within the university. Relative precarity with respect to other units could counterbalance external visibility, leading to more aggressive interventions by higher management. This was certainly our experience at LSE: despite our institution's visibility within the higher education sector, our past underperformance in the RAE implied more scrutiny, intervention, and oversight from the administration.

Hellen, a political scientist, saw asymmetries across institutions as a feature of her own career. Previously employed at an upward-oriented, mid-ranked university in northern England, when we spoke Hellen was working at a well-placed research-intensive institution in Scotland. Her move was lateral in rank

(it came without a promotion) but involved joining an institution with more prestige in the field (as she noted, "They wouldn't
give me a promotion because they already had six other [pres-
tigious] grants just like mine so they didn't treasure it as much
as my previous employer"). She recalled that the experience of
research assessments across these two settings was "qualitatively
different":

> [We are] a much wealthier university and, because of that, we
> also attract an incredible number of students and have never had
> recruitment problems. The REF ranking is important, but it's not
> as important as it is for a university that's poorer and struggles
> to recruit. Because of that, there was much more pressure [in
> my previous institution] to produce high quality research and
> to get very good scores in the REF. This is already a much more
> research-intensive university. People are already doing quite a lot
> of research. People have already internalized the standards and
> it's much more relaxed here than it is in a poorer university that
> depends on being placed high in the rankings in order to attract
> students.

Hellen also mentioned that the pressure to publish and orient
research along specific lines varied across these two settings. In
the research-intensive institution, Hellen heard repeated calls
from higher management to publish in "top" journals, which
research staff themselves regarded with a measure of skepticism.
"There is controversial data coming out directly from the REF
committee itself that says the journal doesn't really make a difference," research-minded Hellen mentioned. Some journals
are seen as particularly desirable by metrics-driven managers,
yet "there isn't so much a pressure to publish in what are considered [by the department] 'artificially top journals.'" Higher

management's expectations, in other words, were moderated by local departmental understanding of quality. In her previous university, however, Hellen and her colleagues were instructed to "'always go for the top American journals,' whatever American means." The problem, she figured, was not simply that scholars had to frame their research to target those specific journals (a theme raised by Peter, another political scientist, a couple of chapters back); it was that the institution's handling of the assessments meant that only particular *types* of political science were seen as holding intrinsically higher value and overall payoff: "There was a price put on large data sets and very complex statistical analyses in a way that made other people who are not doing that feel as lesser researchers and fear some sort of stigma or not being the big REF competition horses."

Hellen's example shows how prestige within the field of higher education can insulate scholars from some of the most overt forms of intervention from research assessments. Quantification comes with pressure at her current institution, but it is less keenly felt by scholars, who are perceived as having "already internalized" ideas about excellence, than in her previous workplace. Even so, the experiences of quantification are affected by the hierarchies of worth associated with a university's multiple units. Mark, the sociologist from London, alluded to this when he said that the pressure to produce along the lines of the research evaluations were "worse [here] than in other places I've worked at. Because we have a large business school, the parameters of the business school end up driving our departments. It's also not a very prestigious business school, so they sort of overcompensate. Somewhere like [Oxbridge] already has the prestige and they don't need to buy into the game of metrics and rankings." Surprisingly, this was even mentioned in relation to economists, who, in the context of the social sciences, tend to have more sway with administrators. "We have two economics departments, one in our school and another one in the business school," noted Mark, "and ours isn't really taken into account, valued. They almost closed the department because of its performance in the last REF. There's a very strong hierarchy in the institution."

Like other organizational interventions, mock exercises calcify over time, with their specific, contingent logic priming how scholars are evaluated not only in relation to the assessments but, more broadly, with respect to the institution's standards of review and promotion. They become a key part of the material culture of the evaluation of academics. This came across in a conversation with Sarah, who works at a midrange department within an otherwise elite institution. As in my own experiences at LSE sociology, Sarah's department was under administrative pressure to perform in line with the institution's other units. Part of this involved increased forms of monitoring and self-assessment. Like my department, hers was charged with producing a list of reputable discipline-specific journals to be used as part of the institution's mock exercise. As Sarah notes, some senior professors "even made a list and they gave it to the [administrators] with no intention of ever using it." But by its sheer existence, the list both performed epistemic work and acquired bureaucratic power. The list had since "gotten the power that everyone worried it would have, because it's now linked to promotion— you have to publish on the list." Although it was clear that the higher-ups were "forcing us to do this and it wasn't something that we could fight," an attempt to appease bureaucratic requests related to ostensibly mock exercises had gained internal cachet.

This patently bureaucratic device (a list, of all things) is now a routine form of disciplining in Sarah's department. Because of the qualities of her profoundly ethnographic research, Sarah explained, she published extensively in anthropology journals. Her work was cited and awarded by sociologists in Britain and beyond, yet the venues in which it appeared placed her in an awkward classification situation when it came to assessments. She remembered speaking to her head of department about one particular paper she had published in a leading journal not within her immediate discipline. Sarah recalled the conversation was not entirely amicable, though it ended with the department head recommending adding the journal to their department's list of upper-tier disciplinary outlets. The addition was presented not in the name of intellectual diversity but rather as a "big thing," an exception or a favor. In fact, she said, "I got annoyed by the idea that I needed a 'favor' for this to count." A few months later, her sense that the manager was in no way defending her research by including the journal was made far clearer. In her performance review, Sarah said, she was represented as "'really developing her career and profile in anthropology,' so it's gotten now stuck that I'm 'really not a sociologist.'"

In creating these environments, in becoming part of the material culture of the evaluation of academics, the calcification of mock assessments camouflages some forms of knowledge—particularly those at the boundaries, in trading zones and interdisciplinary spaces—so that they are less commensurable, less obviously valuable. The "categorical discount" means that some scholars must actively fight for and justify the worth of their research in the face of distinct, though often local, disciplinary norms.[13] In her large university in northern England, Mary saw a coauthored paper that she and a fellow sociologist had published in a top anthropology journal deemed two-star quality in her institution's mock exercise. Since it takes three stars to attract state funding through the REF, the mock grade meant that Mary's paper was unlikely to be included in her department's submission. When she questioned the ranking, Mary was told that her paper lacked rigor (specifically, because it didn't indicate "the number of interviews" that informed its conclusions, the evaluators believed it failed to "quantify the methods that made up the ethnography"). This apparent "lack of rigor" was entirely arbitrary, reflecting local politics of epistemic worth rather than actual disciplinary standards. Over time, all these internal politics have consequences. Mark said that the evaluation-inflected process in his department "creates resentment. Some people's work attracts more funding because it is applied, trendy, flavor of the month, but others' doesn't. They attain recognition within the discipline and department faster. And that seems to be stronger today than ever before."

WAYS OUT

Thinking about the local material cultures of evaluation, embodied in the forms, spreadsheets, internal documents, committee practices, and shared standards that operationalize quantifications in universities and departments, gives us a better understanding of how grades and rankings make collective structures like disciplines more uniform, homogeneous, paradigmatic systems over time. That is, they explain the patterns of epistemic sorting previously identified.

The bureaucratized trend toward uniformity was clear to William even in his relatively diverse field of anthropology. In fact, in assessing the work of others, he said that he only needed to "read enough to form a judgment . . . it's kind of normal science. It might be my age, my career stage, but I do feel we're a bit overwhelmed with normal science at the moment and not quite enough clever, interesting, risky type of things happening." The results of the previous chapter, which point to a narrowing of academic fields in Britain, echo William's words. There may not be a straightforward causal link between research evaluations in general and disciplinary convergence, yet my conversations with social scientists indicate that this is only because the pressure is not a single, omnipresent, state-imposed one but an array of compounding daily accommodations made by those working on the production lines of knowledge.

This is not all doom and gloom. Focusing on how the material cultures of academic assessment shape knowledge locally also provides an opportunity for understanding how quantification is reinterpreted, gamed, and resisted for the collective good. Culture is never predetermined. As much as it constrains our actions and frames our interpretations of the world, culture also enables intervention and provides a baseline for new structures of cooperation. This is the key point with which I close this chapter: because of their location, because of how they are constituted within organizational practices, because they require acceptance and adoption, cultures of quantification are hardly ever unavoidable. Nor are their effects on our worlds.

In that vein, there's a ready case that features scholars who creatively tackled research assessments to protect their intellectual community and their everyday workplace.[14] Almost by design, research assessments are peculiar types of games. Although there is a single formula governing the distribution of quality-related funding for every exercise, there are multiple ways in which institutions can compete for the more elusive reputational capital that underpins the evaluation. There are three ways an institution can argue it is among the "best" in the field, all based on the same data. Perhaps the most straightforward is relying on the grade point average calculated for each assessment. All you need to do is multiply the proportion of outputs for each grade (zero through four stars) and add them up for the entire submission (a unit would have the highest possible GPA if all of its submissions were graded four-star, while one that submits only ungraded outputs would shamefully claim a zero). Maximizing the GPA is relatively easy: all a unit has to do is submit only work of the highest possible grade, excluding any scholarship predicted to fall below "international excellence." This strategy is quite visible and transparent, which means it can invite incredulity, if not scorn, from disciplinary peers who see is as a too-obvious attempt to game the game.

Weighting the GPA by the percentage of full-time-equivalent staff submitted to the assessment produces a ranking that better reflects the relative strength of units. An institution in which all staff members produce excellent research that is submitted for the assessment will be in a better position than one that is highly selective in its submission and only includes the work of a handful of its employed scholars. To signal quality and repute, institutions can opt for this "intensity" score as their measure of excellence, but it is biased toward smaller, highly selective departments. Imagine a unit formed by a half-dozen scholars, all impressively productive and excellent in their outputs. Such a unit would outperform other, much larger departments producing a similar or even a greater amount of excellent work but, because of changes to the proportion of staff submitted across grades, would obtain a lower intensity score.

The third option is betting on the "power" score. This metric represents something akin to the absolute strength of the department, a product of multiplying the GPA by the total number of staff submitted to the assessment. This naturally benefits larger units in a way that does not necessarily affect their ability to obtain quality-related funding: adding a new staff member who has "just" an average research profile (or who is a "risky" scholar, working at the boundaries between fields) has minimal consequences but can significantly increase the position of the department in the national power ranking.[15]

Notably, these three ways of assessing departments' value are all born of the same exercise. None undermines the taken-for-grantedness of scholarly quantification in the way that some institutions' alternative measures might—they simply afford academics and administrators a degree of discretion within their institutional spaces. Their ambiguity allows for at least three ways of understanding and building arguments toward "quality" from the same data.[16] Deciding which of these three rankings matters, and which ought to direct an institution's strategy with regard to the evaluations, is, then, a choice about implementing specific organizational configurations to best balance bureaucratic logic and disciplinary investments. In some places, this choice emphasizes an evaluation culture of excellence and selectivity, creating incentives to remove "underperforming" scholars from the ranks of research-active staff. In others, it fosters growth, creating a form of safety in numbers that distributes the burden of excellence across every member of the unit. If intelligently played, these organizational forms can leverage the techniques of measurement in the service of "local, particularized knowledge." They can, in other words, be repurposed to create inclusiveness rather than selectivity.

In at least one institution, I saw this choice highlighted numerous times across several conversations. There, scholars repeatedly talked about how their institution's division of social sciences—encompassing all the departments that I study in this book along with others—entrepreneurially adopted the power strategy as a means of protecting its members of staff throughout the evaluations. In this institution's process of conducting simulations (of mocking worth, in more ways than one), the preparations became a community-building occasion more than a bureaucratic opportunity to discipline the ranks. There was, as one scholar noted, "pleasure the first time around . . . [in] discovering people that I hadn't realized were producing wonderful, imaginative things." The "general philosophical approach" of including all staff demonstrated a distinct ethics of community, which another senior scholar acknowledged "is both good in terms of the kind of communal effects of the process, but actually works strategically, which is, you know, [a] surprise." A third respondent confided that this inclusive strategy—which avoids penalizing research not deemed fundable—has survived across various iterations of the rules of the assessments: "definitely, the sort of 'bigger is better' idea has been one that's been consistent" since he joined the institution.

Obviously, this institution was not free from the pressures from quantification. Several informants across the four disciplines that I study in this book talked about the central administration's interest in obtaining the best result possible—which implied maximizing submissions at or above the three-star funding threshold. At the divisional level, however, the social scientists I spoke with nevertheless insisted that senior academics and local administrators had imposed a "strong rule" "to report everybody, even if some people's submissions are not that good." This particular local interpretation of the cultures of quantification had to be both explicit and consistent—the division, a scholar involved in the internal process noted, wanted "to be able to say we included everybody," "to make the claim about inclusiveness." Scholars were advised about their submissions and had conversations with the coordinators about what was expected, yet all knew that none would be excepted.

HIERARCHIES, DOMESTICATED

The stories of the scholars I talked to for this book, and my own experience as a worker in both British and American academia, underscore the centrality of hierarchies in shaping, producing, and evaluating knowledge.[17] Inhabiting a profession in which our vocation seems so inextricably tied to reputation, status, and prestige—of institutions, of journals, of scholars, of theories, of schools of thought—makes these ordinal systems seem almost inevitable. How else do you judge the worth and appropriateness of something as elusive as knowledge? In how these taken-for-granted hierarchies interact—within and across institutions, between and beyond the boundaries of national fields—they seem to modulate the on-the-ground effects of quantification in an almost naturalistic way, slowly changing the production of knowledge by disciplining scholars in the lower rungs and insulating those at the top. Whereas in some departments, privileged in their position, quantification is hardly felt, in others less fortunate it feeds into a distinct disenchantment with the profession and a complete "lack of democracy, a lack of collective vision."

Yet, as in any other social institution, the hierarchies of worth we inhabit in academia are bootstrapped kinds.[18] They do not exist independently of our labor. They are forged by the ways our work is assembled into specific configurations. These configurations and the value they actively attribute to structures of prestige are arbitrary choices. Hierarchies ultimately matter only insofar as we reify them, acquiesce in their delegated power, and reproduce them through our ways of acting and knowing. Think, for example, of how we transmit our vocation to new generations of scholars. In our interview, Hellen described research evaluations as a part of the job that she needed to prepare her PhD students to confront in their own careers. "On the one hand," she began, "I want them to be better prepared than I was. But on the other hand, I don't want to scare them completely and demoralize them and stifle their creativity. . . . It's a very fine line between preparing them and getting them ready and . . . depressing them." This is far from an exotic quirk of the British system. In American academia, the culture of prestige is equally intense, and students who have not been pushed to aim for and publish in the top journals in their fields will more likely than not have a harsher experience in what is already a cruel and brutal job market. The test of knowledge, the test of worth, is not only about the words smithed by scholars but, increasingly, about where they live in our disciplinary hierarchies of prestige.

That hierarchies may be convenient at times, serving as fast proxies for quality in moments of uncertainty or even as haphazard constellations for navigating a future career, must be balanced by the observation that they are also echo chambers for forms of accumulated prestige and frequently nonsensical inequalities. A surprising observation from the world of funding, where experiments have used lotteries rather than rankings to distribute resources, is that both methods result in similar amounts of high-quality research. Great knowledge is not the exclusive purview of institutions, scholars, and publications perched at the top of one list or another, a fact that speaks to the vacuity of these echo chambers.[19] Like the rankings selectively chosen by institutions as representations of their excellence, measuring the quality of knowledge is ultimately arbitrary. Rankings, hierarchies, and their attached paraphernalia speak only to a partial type of logic (which may not even comport with the logic of the broader discipline).

This is the crux of quantification. Numbers, in their avalanche, cannot dictate how the world ought to be ordered. Yet they often do. If numbers change knowledge, if they shape the lives of academics, if they reproduce the hierarchies of prestige in the organization of fields, it is by concatenated choices—the actions, delegations, and acquiescence that make them powerful through specific institutions of practice. Embedded within all sorts of constraints, the choices remain choices. They could always have been otherwise: quantification is not unavoidable; it is not irresistible; it is not unopposable. With that call for a counterpoint, I turn in the final chapter to solidarity, a frequently underappreciated potency of our vocation that offers a balm against the most pernicious effects of our self-imposed hierarchies of worth.

6

SOLIDARITIES

With the privilege to read and to think comes great responsibility.
—Tressie McMillan Cottom

T he forms of quantification that I have briefly studied in this book are just a tiny sliver of the many metrics, rankings, surveys, rubrics, and organized evaluations that suffuse and surround the work of contemporary academics.[1] In addition to standardized assessments of research outputs (such as journal articles, book chapters, and monographs), British scholars are evaluated on their societal impact, institutional environment, teaching quality, capacity to engage in "knowledge exchange," and success in obtaining external research funding (such as grants).[2] Around the world, in fact, academics are awash in countless metrics used to manage their workplaces in substantive and meaningful ways. As my colleagues in Britain think and talk about the impending assessment exercise, my California friends discuss which new publications, accolades, and teaching evaluations will affect their merit reviews, and my parents in Mexico assiduously track their citations to update their report to the national funding agency. Counting is everywhere.

If I have focused on research evaluations, it is largely because of their symbolic and practical proximity to the vocation of the contemporary scholar. Today more than ever, academics derive their repute and standing in their professional fields from the research they pursue and publish. Teaching and service remain central to the contractual relations and organizational expectations that regulate our working lives, but these do not garnish the same quality of projection, value, and visibility as does research (on the contrary, they compete with research for our scarce time, as we are often reminded). Ours is ultimately a profession of aspiring Matthews: we write to be read.

This does not mean, of course, that academics particularly covet celebrity or fame. Rather, we are habituated into a lifeworld that, like that of other craftspeople, involves recognizing our peers' efforts and contributions, emulating expertise and technique, and cherishing the rewards of a puzzle well solved.[3] Max Weber wrote of scholars as inhabiting a world that ultimately ends in their individual annihilation; their work is intended to be subsumed, surpassed, and abandoned by the findings of others. In our everyday lives, though, we do not think of this pathos. We are oriented toward the shorter-term satisfaction of reading, thinking, intervening, and writing for the recognition of our disciplinary peers—of accomplishing something through our specialized knowledge that, in Weber's words, "will truly last." On the assembly lines of social scientific knowledge, we do our research because we find it personally interesting, yet more crucially because we want to share our "strange intoxication" of the mind with others. In our merit-oriented training, our ways of mimicking the works of peers, and our emphasis on the value of disciplinary dexterity, we genuinely strive to produce the "best" work we possibly can, to achieve a form of mastery that speaks to our ostensibly shared ideals about knowledge. We evaluate our capacities relationally, through the sociality at the base of our vocation, which is maintained, increasingly, through outward, visible, "assessable" contributions demonstrating our commitment and devotion to our fields (and the practice of peer review that sustains a sense of scholarly give-and-take, approval, and internal disciplinary discipline).[4]

Quantification holds such sway in our hearts and minds because it is not merely an imposed, top-down form of power in which we are trained to self-discipline; quantification is, in fact, an imperfect but tantalizing reflection of our vocational call and the centrality that repute and prestige have in it. Despite the various accounts of discontent, cynicism, and incredulity about metrics' capacity to reflect scholarly value, few of the scholars I know personally or interviewed for this book actively contest or oppose quantification's creep into their disciplines and labors. Unwilling to publicly and vociferously fight to vanquish impact factors, citation metrics, and productivity indices from our language and that of our institutions, we prefer to manifest our concerns when necessary—only when these measures are corralled in the service of critical career decisions and hierarchical valuations ("We should hire this candidate, rather than the other, because her citations are exceptional"). There is a distinct sense in which these forms of evaluation, these devices of commensuration, are taken for granted in our craft. We accept, use, and deal with them because somehow scholars and our wholly incommensurable work have a deep need to be valued, to know where we stand and how we contribute to a Janus-faced intellectual tradition that stretches back into the past and will continue and evolve for the foreseeable future.

This lack of direct opposition was apparent just a few years ago, as teaching, research, and support staff in Britain mobilized to fight for their pensions, salaries, and working conditions. The issues were complex, but what became the most prominent

And again in 2022

mobilization—a strike distributed across four weeks in 2018—
was pegged to the widespread concern of drastic reductions in
higher education workers' retirement benefits. This strike and
similar actions marked a renewed moment of active pushback
in the sector that grew to encompass other important grievances. Research evaluations like the REF were critiqued, in particular, as symptoms of the inexorable marketization of higher
education and the related trend toward employment precarity in
most universities. Still, I noted that these mobilizations, which
coincided with my first days writing and researching this book,
criticized but never demanded the complete abandonment of
academic quantification in the form of research evaluations.[5]
Members of the University of Liverpool's union wrote in 2019,
"although few like it, we recognize it is a game we need to play."[6]
Rather than dismantle the evaluations, academic staff sought
revisions that might tame them, containing their effects to the
original purpose of funding distribution. "REF preparation is
not being used in ways that identify our strengths," they wrote,
"but is being used to undermine staff and drive an aggressive and
toxic management culture."

The scholars at Liverpool were ultimately correct. Uninventing quantification is a colossal, possibly insurmountable task. It
would require completely undoing much of the cultural, administrative, and evaluative structures of higher education. And
even if it could be accomplished, jettisoning the evaluations
would almost certainly fail to serve its intended equalizing purpose. Quantification's defenders point to the ways the evaluations have given many more scholars the opportunity to get in
on the game. Challenging the donnish past that made academia
so inaccessible to those without the benefits of racial and gender privilege, proponents suggest that, in its purest ideal form,
quantification is the type of impersonal, bureaucratic, rational

mechanism that imposes a measure of formal equality on otherwise closed systems driven by favors and interpersonal connections. The competition created by the quantified evaluation cultures of RAE and REF was not without positive implications. Scholars, especially underrepresented scholars, gained a way to prove their "value" and from there to join and move across their academic fields.

The problem, as we have seen, is that quantification in this context is being used to echo other long-standing forms of prestige and structural inequality. Complicated feedback loops enable some to play the game better than others (with definite consequences for the organization of knowledge). Whatever benefits it may bring, they come at the detriment of the working experiences of the scholars with whose vocational affinities it so cleverly fits. In other words, it is our vocational imaginations rather than the rituals of evaluation that call out for intervention. *How* we utilize metrics and other devices, *how* we engage with and make sense of quantification as either an instrument of equality or an echo chamber of prestige—these are choices made through the proactive institutional practices that fundamentally constitute and reconstitute our workplaces.

Recall that professional academics are charged not only with producing high-quality research but also with providing high-quality courses and serving our organizations and intellectual communities through tasks as varied as writing peer reviews, editing journals, organizing conferences, and serving on institutional committees of all sorts. These are not side gigs but key pillars of the twenty-first-century academic's lifeworld. How we choose to approach these tasks—whether in the interest of prestige or a sacrifice made to shore up our community—is mostly up to us. As reviewers, we may be harsh and acerbic or generous and constructive. As editors, we might be guided by the interests of tradition and gatekeeping or open to the serendipity of ambiguity and novelty. As organizers, we might promote star-studded panels or actively give voice to scholars who would otherwise go unnoticed (despite the quality of their work). And as evaluators of colleagues—for review, promotion, and tenure decisions—we can err on the side of generosity, giving our peers the benefit of the doubt, or punish them through their mismeasures of performance. We choose, in sum, how to use the instruments of quantification for or against ourselves. Indicating that a paper might be "widely cited"—a fanciful prognostication at best—does not speak directly to its intellectual merit but to its celebrity in numbers and the metrics of journals and references that are routinely used to assess our value. To evaluate a colleague as "merit worthy" is to actively accept one's role in policing standards of teaching, productivity, and service that we know are too often applied in haphazard and unequal ways. And to vote on ranked lists of journals, as my department did back on that unusually sunny day at the start of this book, is to reproduce, actively and decisively, the politics of prestige that ground the infrastructures of academic publication and epistemic organization of our fields.

Most of us bear the scars of these choices. We recall, in our experiences in the workplace, moments when colleagues—our comrades on the production lines of knowledge—chose to adopt prestige over compassion in their deliberations. In America, this is ever so clear in the gruesome process of tenure. As Craufurd Goodwin writes, such a moment of performance review "is not something that anyone but a masochist would endure voluntarily," yet it is accepted as a mechanism of control by academics and their self-governing institutions.[7] Tenure need not become a point of confrontation, contestation, and controversy, an acid test that profoundly burns and exhausts those who pass through it. It could be (and sometimes is) a moment to think carefully about potential and past contributions, about community, belonging, and the possibilities of change. But in story after story, tenure reviews emerge as the former: moments of shock, confusion, pain, and sorrow. They stand as traumas in many ways comparable to the capricious markets for tenure-track positions, so heavily patterned by chance. Managers, even in the age of austerity, are not to blame—more often than not it is our fellow academics who become our foes in the process, as if personifying guards in an imagined prison experiment.

When I submitted my tenure file in the United States, I was relatively at ease. This was not because of my standing in the landscape of my discipline (I admit my irrelevance); it was because I treated it as any other performance review. I'm an okay worker, and my previous experience of career reviews in Britain was that they were grueling but predictable (in a somewhat Weberian sense) in that I simply needed to measure up in terms of fairly transparent standards of bureaucracy known to most in the organization. So, as my tenure review loomed, I felt calm. My first book had just been published, and I had a new project underway (you are reading it now). The tenure "case" (as they are adversarially termed) should have been, as one colleague confided, "a slam dunk." Instead, while the administrators and dean's office staff were amenable, academics serving on the campuswide review committee for promotions and tenure evaluations lobbed a number of critiques. Quantification played a role in evaluating not my research but my teaching. A panel of people (most of whom I had never met) who had never sat in on one of my classes, who saw that I had but a handful of minor qualitative student criticisms, and who should have ample understanding of the documented shortcomings of teaching evaluations, found my file, in this respect, wanting. In a wearisome comment on their decision, they indicated various votes against awarding tenure (I was eventually tenured, though with caveats that don't necessarily matter for now). Being the entrepreneurial, number-friendly person that I have become, I followed my initial shock with a quick search of our campus's teaching evaluations records. As I had suspected, my teaching scores were above the average for those serving on the committee. Presented with a choice, my peers responded to an ambient sense of scarcity by complying with the interests and politics of prestige. Their choice was illogical, even cruel, but it was hardly deviant. We are punished not by numbers imposed from the outside but by those who share our vocation and embrace numbers as instruments for gatekeeping and oppression, becoming competitors rather than colleagues.

DISTRIBUTIONS OF KNOWLEDGE

The power of prestige and its effects on quantification is ultimately fragile, as are most social institutions. They are maintained by communitarian belief and practice. When these break down, so do their associated institutions. Sociologist Barry Barnes wrote in his study of power that "knowledge of society self-refers," so that observing how knowledge is distributed across people and artifacts, we can appreciate and understand how power is structured. To have power, argues Barnes, "an agent must be known to possess it. That distribution of knowledge which makes the discretionary activities of the agent possible is not an indicator of the power he possesses but the very embodiment of that power."[8]

I find Barnes's account compelling because it offers an off-ramp to some of our current predicaments. Like any other form of knowledge, the hierarchies of prestige and repute that are mirrored in the institutions of quantification are largely "self-referential," reinforced not by some underlying and unavoidable reality about the "actual" quality of knowledge but by their constant use and reenactment over time. Prestige is powerful because we *make* it powerful. This is not a "natural" zero-sum game, some intrinsic conservation principle of the universe, although we may treat it as such. Repute is our ultimate bitcoin, a form of capital produced through arbitrary scarcity, made valuable by collective agreement, sustained through the laborious institutions of our profession, and effectuated by uptake and use. Nevertheless, it cannot exist outside self-reference or the maintenance practices that give it weight. That is the core mechanism behind the Matthew effect, as well as our scholarly training, habituation, and professional practice.

There is a passage in Tressie McMillan Cottom's *Thick* that shows the extent of this logic. It resounds strongly with many of our collective experiences. Writing about attending an academic conference as a graduate student, McMillan Cottom recalls that "the most surefire way to get a real, minted academic to speak to you when you are just a graduate student is to introduce yourself by proxy," naming connections to other academics who these luminaries might "recognize as people." Conferences are, indeed, peculiar spaces. They physically manifest the status hierarchies of our fields, the sheer weight of prestige on how we configure our disciplines. At a recent event, a fellow attendee referred to "badge snobs," a depressingly accurate sobriquet for those who would dismiss or stigmatize another scholar based on the employer or institutional affiliation emblazoned on their name tag. Badge snobbery is endemic to the academic conference, where it is not uncommon to encounter small groups of early-career scholars assembling around senior figures in the field, as if Higgs bosons conferring them mass. As in our disciplines, in these situations we embody our positions in the hierarchy, our value given relationally by those who know us and are known to others (who are, McMillan Cottom would say, recognized as actual *people*). That is the embodied, performed, relational capital of prestige. The research we present and discuss in these meetings matters, but its value is partly comprised of the embodied recognition of those specific people who assign it worth—a tidy transference in which an estimation's provenance is every bit as key as a famous bauble's.

If our disciplinary value and ability to push our work forward by leveraging others' contributions are relational, there is a paradox: our work is also intensely individualized. All the milestones of our careers rely on individuating our work, recognizing the uniqueness of our scholarship (one cannot forget the strange exercise of attempting to parse out what percentage of the research, writing, and editing each coauthor contributed to a single publication for the sake of record keeping). The forms of disciplinary change that I have studied throughout this book—the epistemic sorting that responds to research evaluations—rely on monitoring individuals within their institutions. They involve shaping careers in the interest of quantified ends that, whether we want or even know about them, are tied to reputational as well as pecuniary forms of capital.

Individuals bear much of the brunt of demonstrating—and actively constructing—their worth beyond the odds and asymmetric dynamics of their professional fields. As Max Weber famously wrote, while "chance does not rule alone" our scholarly careers, it does so "to an unusually high degree." We know that fortune plays a disproportionate role in our career outcomes, yet we too often read academic worth through the lens of a naïve meritocratic framework. In other words, we know better, but we imagine that scholarly value is an almost mechanistic product of

our efforts, reflected in legible, quantified outputs. In the growing self-help literature for academics, such individuation is frequent, an attempt to empower would-be entrants to withstand
the arduous and uncertain university life. Success in obtaining
a job, for example, requires "having a *competitive* record" and
"presenting that record in a *competitive* way," Hitting the job
market in the first place requires building a "professional per-
sona," equipped with letters, statements, references, and ready-
made "elevator pitches." For graduate students barely finished
with their dissertations, this is a tall order (in fact, at that point,
even acquiring a suit appropriate to the job market is a hurdle).
Aspiring academics are encouraged to foster networks and
cultivate communities by developing both an outward and an
inward circle of scholarly acquaintances that, like a most strategic and economized form of social capital, may someday serve
as a resource for career progression and development. Amassing academic capital, as the French sociologist Pierre Bourdieu
remarked, inevitably demands "constant and heavy expenditure
of time," though the labor of some is dearer than that of others.
Invariably, in these calls to professionalize, to seek and build a
field of one's own, the onus falls upon the assiduous, entrepreneurial aspirant.

As Loraine Baxter and colleagues remind us in their *Academic
Career Handbook*, the costs of these efforts disproportionately
affect some more than others, reflecting the "prevailing gendered, ethnic, and class-based power relations within academic
life."[9] Suffice to say that those who do not demonstrate their
devotion to a particular form of "being an academic," those who
"make substantial family commitments . . . find that this com-
promises or postpones outwardly successful careers." Quantification can—sometimes—buy us just enough cache to overcome

some of the obstacles created by assumptions, suspicions, projections, and reputational prestige conferred (or not conferred) by our untended networks.

Scholars, as I wrote at the start, are akin to artists and craftspeople. Our personal, intimate lives are enmeshed with our professional personas. Peculiarly, we inhabit our professions. We live our disciplines. We derive pain and pleasure from our work, forming attachments and commitments that bleed into our evenings, weekends, vacations, and retirements. But unlike artists, scholars live by the commands of our disciplines and our employers. Sociology is not like cubism, and Max Weber was no Pablo Picasso. The scholar's labor is extracted, and it is inseparable from our names, identities, personas, and prestige, yet it is never entirely our own, because it is indebted to our epistemic communities in innumerable ways. The vocation of the scholar, at least in its classical sense, is to individuate while abiding by our disciplinary traditions and practices.

In this, we have power. Whatever authority we attribute to our disciplines—forms of power that, as explored in previous chapters, have wrought homogeneity in knowledge through quantification—that authority is no more than a product of our shared conventions. "Reflexive knowledge" of our work, of the institutions, feedback, distributions, asymmetries, and logic that animate our fields, inform our decisions, and constitute our cultures of evaluation, can thus be fruitfully reinvested in our scientific work, to paraphrase Bourdieu.[10] We are collectively privileged by this uncanny potential. We can deploy knowledge of our condition to change the distribution of rewards in our fields. We can bend the bars of our cage into slightly less unwieldy structures. If we so wish, we must simply know our little world and endeavor to build it into a more accommodating place.

REFLEXIVE SOLIDARITIES

Another privilege of the academic is that, unlike typical workers, we coregulate the spaces that contain our labor. The principles of "shared governance" that persist in contemporary higher education, however different across countries and institutions, mean that our academic peers are primarily responsible for evaluating performance and allocating rewards throughout our careers.[11] Even in the most controlled systems, academics recommend hires, promotions, and dismissals, not only by taking on managerial roles that control labor directly but also by the indirect ways we perform our disciplines into existence through reading, writing, and training. This is how we, like the assessments, contribute to making disciplines more or less homogeneous, more or less diverse.

In the previous chapter, I used the case of an unnamed institution to demonstrate the discretion afforded in these spaces. Constrained by quantification and the funding dictates of the state, scholars at that institution decided to participate in the assessments but with an inclusive logic, avoiding the types of awkward conversations and processes of demotion and devaluation that they observed elsewhere in the sector. This decision was anchored in the work of academics who chose to know and play the game in a particular way. It was, in its purest sense, reflexive knowledge: those coordinating the submissions were aware both of the status asymmetries in the field and their organization and of the specific mechanics of funding tied to the evaluation exercises. Together, they staged an informed intervention that fostered solidarity and community maintenance.

Mary Douglas, the always incisive anthropologist, reminded us that such commitments—when they are genuine—are never without a cost. As she wrote in *How Institutions Think*,

"Solidarity is only gesturing when it involves no sacrifice."[12] The scholars in the unnamed institution did not climb the rankings as much as they otherwise might have. Their decision cost them, perhaps, some reputational prestige that might have come in handy with their managers in times of crisis or when mobilized in service of a career move. They also received less quality-related funding than when they ran a counterfactual mock exercise in which they played the game of pure excellence. All of this was time-consuming; senior staff accepted that they would "take the hit" and lose time and attention that they could have directed toward their own packages in order to focus on the best strategy for the department as a whole. Their solidary was hardly a mere gesture.

These costs are unavoidable. Playing the game untruthfully is clearly penalized, whether the dishonesty is deliberate or simply perceived. Cris Shore and Susan Wright relate the attempts in anthropology to generate "disciplinary solidarity" in previous evaluations. In one of the periodic Teaching Quality Assessments performed by the British government, "all departments submitted bids claiming 'excellence.'" Peer assessors largely agreed, giving eighteen out of twenty departments an "excellent" standing. Scholars elsewhere found this suspicious, starting rumors that "anthropologists' solidarity extended to giving one another good results," even when results of the evaluation were confirmed by other assessments and assessors. The state agreed, refusing to recognize anthropology as a discipline in its own right. Anthropologists, according to an official quoted by Shore and Wright, "'shot themselves in the foot' by being too 'generous' to one another." If reflexive knowledge is to foster solidarities, it does so standing on a tightrope, acknowledging the managerial logic of modern, multidivisional universities as well as our potential agency, useful only when activated, coordinated, and deemed truthful by others. That is what the unnamed institution achieved so well—a form of truthful solidarity that protected from within, remaining legible as a valid input for quantification while also being practically meaningful for their unique workplace.

The problem with reflexive knowledge is that, as Douglas notes, resisting institutions and their classifications would require starting from an imaginary independent point o. Alas, the classifications we have for thinking about our organized worlds "are provided ready-made, along with our social life." This is, in some respects, the greatest barrier to reflexive interventions. In unsettled times, we challenge ourselves to imagine solutions that might guide our actions, but we lack the requisite conceptual repertoire. We can certainly "look at our own classifications just as we can look at our own skin and blood under a microscope," but how do we then transform these forms of reflexive knowledge, of introspection, into effective changes in the spaces we inhabit and the classifications that bring them into being? How are we to produce solidarity that is effective, transgressive, transformative?

I am a firm believer that metaphors are incredible tools for getting us past our own linguistic and intellectual tendencies. They provide us a way of challenging classifications and taken-for-granted institutions by affording ambiguity and opening lateral connections that spark our imaginations. Thus, in my scholarly work, I do my very best to mess things up. Of all the metaphors that matter for the problem of quantification, the most salient for disruption and intervention is that of vocation, both because it captures the affective intensity of our profession—we do not see filling blank sheets of paper with "knowledge" as *just* a job, however so it may be in practice—and speaks to our everyday experience on the epistemic shop floor, where we embody the academy as a quasi-mystical calling, our commitment to which is judged and evaluated by peers.

Like most other metaphors, the idea of a scholarly vocation illuminates and conceals complex aspects of our social life. In its most elementary form, it highlights the idealized pursuit of knowledge as requiring a certain abject commitment to hard work and the vicissitudes of research, with scholars becoming "wholly devoted to what [they] are studying." This is difficult to express to nonacademics. Scholarship is a calling, a lifeworld that overflows our public and private personas, our everyday conversations, our networks of acquaintances, our tastes and dispositions.[13] Research is central to this lifeworld, to the degree that scholars working in universities often complain about the lack of time they have for studying what they *truly* care about, with the demands of teaching, service, and administration taking too many of their working hours.

It is helpful, as we reimagine academia as a vocation, to dig into the various studies that document our time use. These studies not only normalize the vocation as requiring an investment of sixty hours of work per week—reaffirming a certain lifestyle and sociocultural acumen that is classed, gendered, and racialized toward the ideals of privilege—but they also frequently frame administration and meetings as unfortunate burdens that unfairly displace our "real" labor, research.[14] This complaint makes perfect practical sense. Research provides affective and intellectual satisfaction, plus it is the way we are evaluated within our institutions and allows us to demonstrate our value to disciplinary communities. But this often-parodied contempt for the bureaucratic, administrative, managerial (and, yes, sometimes pedagogic) components of the modern higher education establishment functions as a betrayal of the "bullshit" tasks that provide support and maintenance for our multilevel communities and help bring along the next generation of scholars to carry our work into the future.[15]

An abject focus on producing knowledge thus ignores other critical aspects of the scholar's career and their institutional ecology, constraining rather than liberating the possibilities of building lasting links of solidarity in the workplace and a richer, more diverse intellectual environment. Our traditional vocation, perfectly sound for the gentlemanly scientists of the eighteenth and nineteenth centuries, is out of date, unable to have anticipated the invisible forms of labor and maintenance so central to modern university life.

Moreover, the scholar's vocation is *internally* oppressive, transforming hierarchies of value and prestige into veritable articles of faith. It imposes on the individual scholar the expectation of a truthful surrender to the pursuit of knowledge "for its own sake"; it reduces the complex labor and commitment that they perform into a single form of devotion, disregarding the rest. In its emphasis on the discipline and autonomy of knowledge production, this vocational imagination is entirely contradictory. As we have been reminded in study after study, from the history of science to the economics of innovation, knowledge does not move through the efforts of lone geniuses, unconstrained by institutional contexts. It relies on the collective work of communities invested in understanding and acting in the world.

Knowledge will still happen, with or without us. But scholars have the potential to control much of our immediate world—the workplaces, conferences, classrooms, and collegial conversations we inhabit. We cannot anticipate our next source of inspiration or which finding will lead our discipline toward novel theoretical and empirical developments, but we know, quite practically, how to make our kindred lives immediately better, how to display and practice solidarity with peers and colleagues as a matter of principle. This is not part of our vocation, yet a vocation that places devotion entirely on what is otherwise a capricious component of our lives, ignoring those fellow travelers who are oppressed by our institutions, devalued by our hierarchies, erased through our value assessments, or ignored for their roles in the care and maintenance of our professions, is untenable. A vocation that takes into account reflexive solidarity starts with a recognition of "our own responsibility for the existence of unjust 'social mechanisms.'"[16] Building solidarity is not an intellectual exercise but a conversion. We must rededicate our depreciating vocation to a form of devotion keyed into the experiences of academic peers, staff, and students in modern higher education.

Indeed, the university system has changed enormously. Britain's higher education system grew in size and diversity in the second half of the twentieth century, coinciding with its designation as a site ripe for the imposition of those twin tormentors, austerity and precarity. A 2016 survey by the University and College Union 16 underlines some of the stakes, showing that 49 percent of the teaching staff and 54 percent of the academics in the UK were hired on insecure, temporary contracts. A 2018 report from the Education Support Partnership added to the unease by documenting increasing levels of stress, isolation, and mental health crises among academics. As one scholar noted, the system had "changed. . . . It used to be far more about the department, the team, but now it is more individualistic [with the result] that you become isolated, you feel isolated and this is not good for your sense of wellness." Precarity is not equally distributed, though. Research by Gianni De Fraja and colleagues, focused on the 2014 Research Excellence Framework, shows that, despite austerity, some institutions are capable of converting their prestige into higher salaries, particularly for senior professorial staff. At the other end of the spectrum, however, job insecurity is a common feature, with research staff having to adopt entrepreneurial personas constantly hustling for funding, seeking opportunities and applying for short-term contracts while, at the same time, demonstrating their intellectual worth through research and publications. If anything, regimes of quantification have been less useful in revealing quality than in revealing the inequities born of financialization in higher education.[17] The scholar's vocation cannot be ignorant of these conditions because, in the end, the knowledge we produce is only as worthy as the societies we decide to defend.

In this respect, cultivating reflexive solidarities is not an attempt to do less or to forego knowledge and specialization. It does not mean escaping work for leisure but, as Rebecca Solnit argues, for escaping "meaningless and exploitative work and overwork" in favor of "meaningful work, work that has a tangible benefit, that connects us to others, that has meaning."[18] That is what quantification gets wrong: it judges a single task in a plurality, a sliver of our actual working lives. It perpetuates the myth that scholars are somehow not workers, foreclosing possibilities for solidarities that may result in better working conditions for many. Research should be rewarded as one of the components in our lives, rather than the definitive encapsulation of our worth and prestige.

This was particularly poignant throughout the COVID-19 pandemic. In the early period of crisis, workers of all stripes, including scholars across the world, were forced to work from home. The sudden need to truly "do it all"—provide caregiving within the home, manage children's education, and continue to teach, research, and produce with more tenuous connections to the already meager support of our institutions—exacerbated the inequalities that already marked the education sector. Colleges and universities saw their enrollments and incomes drop precipitously, and on both sides of the Atlantic, planning for workforce reductions to balance budgets against this lost revenue. Many scholars' employment became more precarious than ever before.

That effect—the rising precarity—simply walloped some among us. Even those scholars with a certain level of job security faced a completely asymmetric landscape shaped by how care responsibilities modified some people's capacity to invest in the task that is most rewarded by their employers, research. Women, who sociologists have repeatedly proven bear the brunt of care responsibilities no matter how egalitarian their domestic relationships, saw their career prospects delayed as they added more and more uncompensated care work (in the home and the workplace), displacing any time they might have had for research and compounding long-standing gender biases in peer review, funding, and evaluation. Rather than adjust expectations, most institutions of higher education responded to the crisis by allowing academics to defer review—that is, to effectively retard their careers by a year or more "without punishment." In doing so, and as Jessica Malisch and colleagues argue, the coronavirus crisis increased "gender and racial inequity in teaching and service" without changing expectations of productivity. As austerity has always commanded, scholars were forced to do more with less—and they continued to judge each other against a baseline in which research holds paramount value.[19]

The coronavirus crisis could have spurred productive solidarity, giving us a moment to reflect on how to build better workplaces using the insights of a robust and growing literature on inequalities in academia and beyond.[20] Instead, most academics and academic institutions demonstrated their commitments to an untenable vocation by pausing rather than rethinking and restructuring our practices of evaluation. It was not that, as the late anthropologist David Graeber wrote, the "caring value of work would appear to be precisely that element in labor that cannot be quantified."[21] What a strange sentiment, revealing the tight grip of a narrow vocation strangling the social scientific imagination! We quantify elusive concepts constantly (if imperfectly), through standardized evaluations, citation metrics, impact factors, h-indices, peer observations, surveys, clicks, time spent watching videos, and all sorts of novel altmetrics. What these pages have stressed is that the problem of quantified scholars is not that they are quantified in the first place, but that they are quantified *in particular ways* that reproduce a vocation fashioned at a time when scholarly work was not a job but a calling.[22]

Numbers can be equally liberating and oppressive. The institutions we bootstrap into existence around their use are what determine whether they are instruments of empowerment or instruments of torture. Our academic institutions are built around ideals of merit, prestige, and individualization that are out of date and out of step with the urgent intrusions of inequality throughout academic life. We could evaluate care if we so wished, for example, asking committees to take into account (with forms, practices, training, and deliberation, perhaps) our colleagues' demonstrated contributions in that vein; we could hire, reward, and promote on the basis not only of exceptional and prestigious research but also of disciplinary involvement and community orientation; we could create metrics that weight maintenance and repair as much as hierarchies of status; we could show commitment to the penuries that our colleagues face, a form of reflexive solidarity that errs on the side of generosity without demolishing the rationalized logic of knowledge making; we could recognize that scientific labor is labor in the fullest sense, involving tasks that seem far removed from intellectual work but that are nevertheless critical for making our institutions habitable; we could be more modest, less grandiose, more aware that, in our intense specialization, our contributions will invariably fade, making care and the lives of others more precious to our professional lives than sheer productivity. But this seems antithetical to our current vocation. Our unwillingness to reclaim imagination is our collective sin.

EVALUATIVE DIVERSITY

What, then, does quantification do to the knowledge we produce? Motivated by this question, this book has sought to explore the way the evaluative exercises in the United Kingdom have reshaped the social sciences. The key finding, from both our models of career mobility and analysis of textual shifts over time, is that the social sciences have become more homogeneous through a slow process of epistemic sorting. Like a somewhat conservative market mechanism, with producers vying for the attention of a small number of consumers with limited taste for innovation, quantification begets homogeneity, castigating diversity in organizational forms and linguistic repertoires that might otherwise be positioned as wellsprings of new forms of thinking and engaging with the world. Quantification produces, in this sense, more paradigmatic, disciplinary knowledge with fewer and fewer deviations from some epistemic core.

Still, throughout this book, I have argued that we must turn our ire not on quantification but on its practices of implementation—the decisions we take that, over time and through institutional mechanisms, make knowledge more similar and less diverse. This is a hopeful point, however, because it indicates that academics have a choice in the matter. We can continue to follow a path on which we adhere to a scholarly vocation tied to hierarchies that individuate our work as if the product of isolated effort, rewarding and punishing on the basis of rather arbitrary definitions of value, or we can veer onto a radically different path where, by recognizing academic labor as multidimensional and necessarily diverse, we foster inclusive solidarities, reduce inequalities, and encourage adventuresome thought.

In *No Exit*, French philosopher, author, and playwright Jean-Paul Sartre presented a unique take on human suffering. Escorted by a valet and arriving one after the other into a drawing room decorated in the lavish and almost kitschy Second Empire style, his three characters (Garcin, Inez, and Estelle) realize that they are, in fact, dead. They are in a hell of their own making, where their suffering comes not from pains inflicted on their souls but from each acting "as the torturer of two others." Taking to their corners, ignoring the others, proves a failure, as does deploying violent devices such as knives, poison, and ropes. There is no escape, because they are condemned to the words, glances, and dispositions they inflict upon each other and, by reflection, themselves.

Academia is not Sartre's imagined drawing room, but it certainly can be. In our decidedly livelier worlds, quantification furnishes the rooms we inhabit, shaping our experiences, careers, and the knowledge we attach to these in distinct ways. I hope to have convinced you that quantification changes the quality, contents, and distribution of social scientific knowledge by fostering convergence, homogeneity, and increasingly similar framings of big problems and tough questions. Through how we and our institutions react to quantification, we all become a little bit more similar. Quantification is, after all, a technology of the workplace, be it a pristine lab bench, a busy library, a shared office, or a laptop on an otherwise silent midnight kitchen table. And as a technology that affects how we work—how we are valued and value others—it invariably changes the objects we deliver to the world.

From the outset, I have been careful to avoid promising a solution to the problem of quantification. That's because, well, there isn't one. If anything, what matters is how quantification reflects the forms of prestige, status, worth, and merit that we carry (and carry out) in our professions. Through the voices of individual scholars, I have tried to uncover the role that prestige plays in our vocation, presenting quantification not as an external force dictated by a bureaucratic state or a neoliberal organization but as resonance box invited into our workplace, where our virtues and vices are too often amplified.

The argument we must make, in any case, is not epistemic. It is moral. In his vocational lectures, Max Weber made a still salient point: in the collective institutions of science, we are all individually and ultimately insubstantial. Our specialized findings, however internationally recognized, however cited and engaged with, however extolled by our peers, will fade with time. What ultimately matters are the experiences of our labor and lives. This is where we have the power to soften our Second Empire–style rooms. Staying in our corners, focused on the task of "making knowledge" for knowledge's sake, is not enough when confronted with the inequalities and precarities reproduced by the institutions where we practice our ostensible vocation. Unlike Garcin, Inez, and Estelle, we are agentic, able to wrangle our world into a different, more accepting form, playing the games of quantification while challenging their basic assumptions.

Academics have the privilege of writing and reading, of being reflexive, and we choose to produce knowledge in these conditions. Solidarity and change are not unimaginable in principle, they are simply weighted down by inertia. Why, then, choose a vocation oriented to so brittle an object when we can foster a different one, orienting our grounds and actions to common, lived experiences of the strife, precarity, and achievements of others? Why choose a vocation of the individual when we can build one of solidarity?

In the end, we ought to focus not on resisting numbers and their pretense of authority but on the scaffolding we knowingly, willingly construct and then defer to. I am no Max Weber. I cannot offer any details of some alternate vocational vision beyond what I have observed and suggested herein. To that end, I offer my evidence and insights as steppingstones laid in the road toward making ours a fairer form of science.

APPENDIX

STUDYING SOCIAL SCIENTISTS

I n conducting research for this book, I combined both quantitative and qualitative evidence to understand how research evaluations shaped the careers and knowledge of British social scientists. My process for collecting evidence was thoroughly iterative, using results from each module of the project to make methodological choices for subsequent modules. Elsewhere, I have called this the "extended computational case study," a mixed methodology that allows me to weave the findings together in a manner similar to how the ethnographer transforms experience and observation into dense cultural narratives. Like other forms of comparative, interpretative, grounded research, the extended computational case study seeks to uncover patterns by moving back and forth between computational and qualitative analyses.

This study is situated within a large, recent literature on the sociological dynamics of scientific knowledge. This flourishing owes a great deal to the increased availability of both machine-readable data related to scientific publications, policies, and institutions and the creation and refinement of computational techniques for data processing and classification. Studies of scientific change, once the province of historical and ethnographic work,[1] can now involve quantitative analyses of giant data sets in order to tackle central questions about the constitution of knowledge.[2] Captured under the umbrella "Science of Science," this research genre has already advanced important sociological claims about the production of knowledge.[3] Because they often deal with tens of thousands of data points, the contributions in the science of science have the potential to yield generalizable claims about what matters for scientific research, a possibility wholly unavailable to the earlier qualitative, interpretive studies published by earlier generations of researchers.

In this study, I have tried to strike a balance between the logic of "large N" studies, such as those that characterize the science of science, and more traditional, interpretative approaches. In this, I am inspired by two methodological positions. The first, linked to sociologist Michael Burawoy, involves thinking about the study of science as part of an extended case method in which reflexivity, participation, and comparison are part and parcel of the research design. This may involve computational techniques to observe science "through the outside, interrogating [it] through intermediaries" such as abstracts and bibliographic records (as in my textual analysis) as well as qualitative iterations that create new knowledge in response to quantitative findings. The second approach, abductive analysis as proposed by sociologists Iddo Tavory and Stephan Timmermans, involves taking each iterative step in the research process as a moment to interrogate and construct sociological theories of science.[4]

Further, my approach is directly linked to Laura Nelson's pioneering contributions in computational social science.[5] As a scholar attentive to both the possibilities of computer-aided text classification and the importance of expert-based hermeneutic interpretation, Nelson combines in her computational grounded theory both structural understandings of texts (which see automated coding as a sensible means for scaling sociological analyses and are consistent with the logic of the science of science) and humanistic forms of theory building and claims making (which, in their most radical form, are critical of *any* possibility of valid scientific coding). Departing slightly from Nelson's approach, which aims to help "researchers discover new ideas, codes, or concepts while remaining grounded in the data,"[6] my path in this book has meant moving between the computational data set and its reference group (social scientists) to build my account, letting the findings from one domain abductively elicit questions in the other.

Part of the difference between this book and other science-of-science studies stems from the way I think of data more generally. Instead of basing my account only on the quantitative data set of careers, I treat that data set as an artifact that must itself be queried in conversation with the groups that I study. This is more consistent with an "ethnographic" approach, in which claims are constantly tied to the particularities of the data, its attendant data structures, and their associated practices of infrastructuring, maintenance, and reinscription. In effect, the bibliographic records contained in data sets like Clarivate's Web of Science—perhaps the most central and authoritative bibliographic infrastructure for contemporary research on science—are not science itself. They are the traces, the fragments that come at the end points of a complex, unequal, and globally distributed activity. Should the research analyze only what is contained within a data set, it would be impossible to take the data's own features into account. Research has to be extended. This necessarily requires iteratively querying the data's significance, meaning, interconnections, and representativeness: it calls, in other words, for the extended computational case that continuously reviews boundaries as part of the production of knowledge.

The extended computational case at hand included four distinct empirical modules. The first used data from the Social

Science Citation Index, particularly the corresponding author information, to reconstruct the career trajectories of British social scientists across evaluation periods. In the second module, our research team used computational techniques for text classification in order to compare scholars and departments, and in the third, we applied computational techniques for natural language processing to distinguish changes in the textual features of publications over time. The final module involved obtaining oral histories from scholars themselves, pursuant to understanding the sociological processes behind the linkage the data established between the imposition of research evaluation schemes and epistemic shifts in disciplinary fields.

CONSTRUCTING CAREERS

The quantitative component of this study's career analysis was inspired by the work of Floriana Gargiulo and Timoteo Carletti, who used the American Physical Society's publication records to produce a longitudinal data set of career mobility among that population of researchers.[7] Combining this research design with work on the disambiguation of author information from Web of Science records allowed us to approximate the career paths of 16,531 individual scholars in four fields (2,208 anthropologists, 6,384 economists, 4,271 political scientists, and 3,668 sociologists).[8] These 16,500 individuals correspond to a total of about 150,000 bibliographic records, manually obtained through queries of the Clarivate's Web of Science search engine such as this one, used for economics:

AD=(england OR scotland OR wales OR United Kingdom) AND WC=(economics NOT sociology NOT anthropology) for

DOCUMENT TYPES: (Article OR Book OR Book Chapter), Timespan: 1970–2018. Indexes: SCI-EXPANDED, SSCI.

We focused our efforts on disambiguating the authors and institutional affiliations associated with these 150,000 records. This first revision of the data required us to develop further familiarity with how the Social Science Citation Index stands as both a constructed object and a proxy for scholarly work. In the process, we discovered, for example, that standards of archiving differed over time, affecting our ability to identify individual authors as we constructed our longitudinal data set. Initially, one of the fields denoting author (AF) was presented in the format "LAST NAME, INITIAL." By 2005, this had changed to an extended format of "LAST NAME, First Name." A potential source of fuller information, in a practical sense, this development produced any number of complications. Data on institutional affiliation was inconsistent, not matching the order of authors in field AF nor that in AU (an older, original field that kept the format "LAST NAME, INITIALS"), in which two individuals with similar names had higher odds of being confused (Adam Smith and Agnes Smith, for instance). Affiliation data (coded in fields C1, for addresses, and RP, for reprint author information) were temporally inconsistent, with standards changing considerably over time, both in terms of how addresses were associated with listed authors (in some periods mirroring the order) and how the data were presented.

Disambiguating authors and their institutions took repeated revisions to the code, accuracy checks, and deeper dives into the data and the python script. Eventually, we combined data from several fields to validate records across articles by the same author (using data from AF when available, AU when not), which required us to standardize reported institutional affiliation using a mix of manual and automated text classification for listed institutions (Is "Univ of London" the same as "University of London"?) and manual checks for cases in which academic careers identified by our workflow seemed overly erratic. Our gold standard for disambiguation was the strength of the link between an author and a discipline over several evaluation periods. If an author was seen as having a foot in too many disciplines (or changing areas of publication as described in the WC field in Web of Knowledge), we knew to look at the specific case and make corrections accordingly.

To infer the gender of our disambiguated author data set, we used the distribution of first names from the 1991 United Kingdom Census. Our cutoff point was 0.5, which meant that some ambiguous names were misclassified (for example, Alison). A manual inspection of two hundred randomly selected results of the classification nonetheless indicated a 92 percent accuracy of attribution. Combined with our author and affiliation data, we had a unique, longitudinal data set that captured the institutional affiliation of scholars in four disciplines who published research articles, books, and book chapters indexed by the Social Science Citation Index from 1979 to 2018. Given that we possessed complete bibliometric data for each author, we could calculate their citations, number of publications, reported grant funding (coded as either British, European, or other), and average journal impact, cumulatively and by individual evaluation period.

At this point, we were able to assess whether and when scholars changed jobs, consistent with studies in the broader literature on academic careers. Unlike the data used in other studies, however, our data set lacked information on rank and salaries, which are not available for the United Kingdom (where scholars' complete CVs are seldom posted on institutional websites and salary information is fiercely protected). Still, we could test several of the standard hypotheses about productivity and mobility documented by a previous generation of studies of scientists.[9] Importantly, these data made it possible to evaluate productivity and reputational dynamics associated with both the outcomes of research evaluations and the established hierarchies of status (with Oxford and Cambridge occupying the top of the heap and newer institutions the bottom). A complete table of descriptive statistics is presented in table A.1.

TABLE A.1 DESCRIPTIVE STATISTICS OF THE MAIN VARIABLES

Variable	Mean	Standard deviation	Minimum	Maximum	Number of observations
Mobility	0.1312749	0.3377029	0	1	79,284
Gender	0.3508036	0.4772266	0	1	47,471
Active age	4.987299	7.596054	0	42	79,284
Cumulative number of articles	4.163791	6.331331	0	182	79,284
Articles per evaluation period	2.504251	3.361689	0	43	79,284
Cumulative average journal impact factor during period	0.9328543	1.152946	0	13.0829	79,284
Average journal impact factor during evaluation period	0.7025544	0.8815296	0	7.863	79,284
Cumulative citations	7.607828	30.43311	0	2,279	79,284
Citations over period	5.126759	18.50763	0	1,089	79,284
UK funding	0.1367111	0.3435442	0	1	79,284
EU funding	0.0212527	0.1442265	0	1	79,284
Other reported funding sources	0.0140634	0.117753	0	1	79,284
Standardized RAE/REF score	0	0.9999504	−4.060072	2.427367	40,325

MEASURING KNOWLEDGE

In deciding how to approach the epistemic production of scholars, we chose to focus on abstracts rather than citations as our basis of analysis. Traditionally, studies about changes to scientific fields have made robust use of citation networks as a way of showing varying levels of engagement and disengagement in the literature. For our purposes, mapping changes in the use of concepts or the thematic organization of fields was less useful, though we included citation data in our final model as a proxy for productivity (but not of disciplinary organization).

Our data were constrained by the design and organization of Clarivate's Web of Science, which contained full abstracts only for those articles published after 1992. The Web of Science contains older abstract records for a number of journals, but by no means all. The data we worked with, furthermore, referred only to research articles. These are but one kind of social scientific output, and they are encouraged to different degrees in different disciplines. At the extremes, anthropology's heavy epistemic work takes place not in research articles but in monographs, while the opposite is true for fields like economics (table A.2). This unbalanced corpus required the exclusion of anthropology in some of our analyses. We chose

TABLE A.2 NUMBER OF PAPERS AND ABSTRACTS PER DISCIPLINE

Discipline	Number of papers	Number of abstracts
Anthropology	17,303	7,808
Economics	64,657	44,891
Political science	35,153	15,253
Sociology	24,383	13,225

Latent Dirichlet Allocation topic models as the most appropriate means for classifying and analyzing the themes contained in the scholarly abstracts over time.[10]

Topic models have gained traction within sociology since their introduction to the study of cultural formations almost a decade ago.[11] In the context of our project, the Latent Dirichlet Allocation, as developed by Blei and coauthors, was a particularly good fit for working with the type of texts available to us (abstracts rather than full-length papers). Our first task was to identify an adequate number of topics to represent the literature over time. After preprocessing the abstracts, we produced solutions ranging from fifteen to sixty topics, in intervals of five, using the Gensim library for Python. This generated a solution for every field (modeling disciplines in isolation). The challenges of topic modeling involved balancing statistical and semantic fit: combining a close inspection of the model and of changes with perplexity by varying parameters, we identified a forty-topic solution as an adequate representation of the disciplinary diversity of each field.[12] Other segmentations of the data were tried, including the calculation of topics per period and by balancing the number of publications. These robustness checks did not reveal problems with the original strategy. If anything, modeling the entire corpus created more interpretable models than strategies that, while attentive to changes in the volumes of publication, were less intelligible to an expert reader.

In turn, we used the results of the topic model estimations to calculate three measures. The first was the topical distribution of the aggregate work of every individual academic i over every period t. To represent the distribution of topics across individual academics' oeuvre within evaluation periods, we constrained the sum of topics so that it was equal to 1.

$$Individual\_Topics_{i,t} = \left[t_{i,t}^1, \cdots, t_{i,t}^{40} \right],$$

$$\sum_{j=1}^{40} t_{i,t}^j = 1$$

where *Individual_Topics* is a vector over the forty possible topics indicated by our models. Second, using a similar technique, we calculated the topical distribution of departments, aggregating all publications associated with each institution in each period and determining their topical profiles:

$$Departmental\_Topics_{i,t} = \left[t_{i,t}^1, \cdots, t_{i,t}^{40} \right],$$

$$\sum_{j=1}^{40} t_{i,t}^j = 1$$

Third, we calculated the topical distribution of each department, excluding the target scholar. This involved estimating the topic distributions for department *j*, excluding work by scholar *i*.

$$Department\_Author\_Topics_{i,t}^j = \left[t_{i,t}^1, \cdots, t_{i,t}^{40} \right],$$

$$\sum_{j=1}^{40} t_{i,t}^j = 1$$

We defined the similarity of author *i* with respect to department *j* in period *t* as a cosine similarity between the vectors for Department_Author_Topics and Individual_Topics, as follows:

$$Similarity_{i,j,t} = \frac{Department\_Author\_Topics_{i,t}^j \cdot Individual\_Topics_{i,t}}{\| Department\_Author\_Topics_{i,t}^j \| \cdot \| Individual\_Topics_{i,t,} \|}$$

The measure of departmental typicality presented in the text was constructed by determining the pairwise distances between their topical vectors. Formally, the distance was calculated as:

$$Distance\,(i,j) = \left| Department\_Topics_{i,t} - Department\_Topics_{j,t} \right|$$

The pairwise distances for all departments were used to define a graph $G(t)$ over all institutions at a set point in time. Using Python's NetworkX package, we defined typicality as the eigenvector centrality of departments at time t. The descriptive statistics for both similarity and typicality are presented in table A.3.

TABLE A.3 DESCRIPTIVE STATISTICS OF THE TWO COMPUTATIONAL VARIABLES

Variable	Mean	Standard deviation	Minimum	Maximum	Number of observations
Similarity	0.1320621	0.0491929	0	0.831371	44,048
Typicality	20.26517	5.389539	2.602462	29.48124	60,427

MODELING MOBILITY

Our dependent variable, mobility, was determined as being 1 when scholars changed affiliations between evaluation periods and 0 otherwise. The structure of our data—longitudinal panel data with individual-level covariates across time—led to our selection of a random effects panel logistical regression for modeling. We included fixed effects for disciplines (groups) and evaluation periods (time) in all regressions.

We ran various models to test for associations between our outcome (mobility) and our covariates. We ran several models, which show varying combinations of control variables and those produced by our computational analysis. These models are presented in table A.4. The first model concerns the role of resources and productivity in mobility and speaks to the literature on academic labor markets. These were approximated by the number of publications produced over a period, the cumulative publication

TABLE A.4 PANEL LOGISTIC MODELS WITH
INDIVIDUAL SCHOLAR RANDOM EFFECTS

	Model 1	Model 2	Model 3	Model 4	Model 5	Model 6
	Interinstitutional mobility					
Age (log)	-0.158***	-0.135***	-0.120**	-0.0802*	-0.181***	-0.186***
	(-5.93)	(-4.08)	(-2.64)	(-2.22)	(-3.94)	(-4.05)
Number of publications (log)	0.0336	0.264**	0.448***	0.438***	0.221	0.236
	(0.48)	(2.75)	(3.38)	(4.12)	(1.66)	(1.77)
Cumulative publications (log)	0.0602	-0.221*	-0.343*	-0.374**	-0.134	-0.120
	(0.75)	(-2.05)	(-2.32)	(-3.14)	(-0.89)	(-0.80)
Number of citations (log)	0.117	0.170	0.355*	0.240*	0.356*	0.360*
	(1.53)	(1.66)	(2.42)	(2.13)	(2.53)	(2.55)
Cumulative citations (log)	-0.141	-0.174	-0.404**	-0.248*	-0.355*	-0.359*
	(-1.86)	(-1.71)	(-2.77)	(-2.21)	(-2.53)	(-2.55)
Average journal impact factor	0.00602	-0.0965	-0.0350	-0.0804	-0.132	-0.127
	(0.09)	(-1.24)	(-0.36)	(-1.01)	(-1.45)	(-1.39)
Cumulative journal impact factor	-0.0795	-0.0146	0.0243	-0.0240	-0.0149	-0.0102
	(-1.37)	(-0.22)	(0.30)	(-0.36)	(-0.20)	(-0.13)
UK funding	-0.0482	-0.0464	-0.0417	-0.0617	-0.0605	-0.0460
	(-0.74)	(-0.63)	(-0.45)	(-0.82)	(-0.75)	(-0.57)
European Union funding	0.719*	0.934*	0.979*	0.915*	0.696	0.654
	(2.24)	(2.56)	(1.99)	(2.46)	(1.77)	(1.67)
Anthropology	0	0	0	0	0	0
	(.)	(.)	(.)	(.)	(.)	(.)
Economics	-0.0619	-0.0780	-0.0333	0.180	-0.125	0.0966
	(-0.99)	(-0.98)	(-0.29)	(1.53)	(-1.13)	(0.65)
Politics and IR	0.0298	0.0167	0.0357	0.190	0.0239	0.247
	(0.45)	(0.20)	(0.32)	(1.76)	(0.21)	(1.81)
Sociology	0.262***	0.177*	0.131	0.151	0.176	0.148
	(3.94)	(2.16)	(1.13)	(1.68)	(1.55)	(1.30)
1986	0	0				
	(.)	(.)				
1989	0.133	0.185				
	(1.54)	(1.38)				
1992	0.128	0.0478		0	0	0
	(1.50)	(0.36)		(.)	(.)	(.)

TABLE A.4 (CONTINUED)

	Model 1	Model 2	Model 3	Model 4	Model 5	Model 6
1996	0.198*	0.144	0	0.416*	0.0607	0.250
	(2.54)	(1.22)	(.)	(2.15)	(0.12)	(0.50)
2001	0.250***	0.211	0.113	0.583**	0.199	0.436
	(3.33)	(1.92)	(0.92)	(2.92)	(0.41)	(0.86)
2008	-0.303***	-0.517***	-0.673***	-0.0796	-0.543	-0.287
	(-4.41)	(-5.19)	(-5.83)	(-0.39)	(-1.11)	(-0.56)
2014	-0.438***	-0.562***	-0.783***	-0.146	-0.607	-0.380
	(-6.10)	(-5.45)	(-6.31)	(-0.71)	(-1.24)	(-0.74)
Male		0	0	0	0	0
		(.)	(.)	(.)	(.)	(.)
Female		0.272***	0.188**	0.241***	0.283***	0.296***
		(5.23)	(2.75)	(4.31)	(4.39)	(4.59)
Standardized evaluation rating			-0.0684* (-2.11)			
Departmental typicality				-0.0304*** (-3.50)		-0.0233* (-2.15)
Similarity					1.385* (2.41)	1.146* (1.98)
Structural coherence						0.333*** (5.03)
Constant	-0.640***	-0.459***	-0.506***	-0.476**	-0.635	-0.656
	(-8.61)	(-4.22)	(-3.71)	(-2.66)	(-1.27)	(-1.31)
lnsig2u _cons	0.339***	0.196	0.416*	0.330**	0.144	0.131
	(4.14)	(1.71)	(2.51)	(2.59)	(0.78)	(0.69)
N	24,745	15,362	9,393	13,502	9,456	9,456

Note: *** p>0.99, ** p>0.95, * p>0.90

volumes, and the self-reported access to funding. Variables related to visibility were also included, proxied through the average impact factor of the journals in which a scholar published and the citations (cumulative and by period) they attained.[13]

Model 2 added the inferred gender of the author in the regression and was subsequently used as the baseline for analysis as more covariates were included. The covariates for productivity, visibility, and gender are thus part of all further models.

Model 3 included the standardized evaluation in the previous evaluation period to account for the effects of quality, as perceived by the evaluation panel, on the outcome. Model 4 is similar, but tests whether departmental typicality plays a role in mobility. Both of these variables relate to institutional-level characteristics (the typicality and GPA scores obtained in the evaluation are of the department/unit of assessment, not the individual). Individual-level characteristics associated with the relative position of the scholar (similarity and structural coherence) are included in models 5 and 6.

Model 6 serves as our full model. Note that structural coherence and the presence of a standardized evaluation are colinear, leading to the exclusion of the second variable from the model.

ORAL HISTORIES

The results from the full model (expanded in chapters 3 and 4) suggested the operation of a process of epistemic sorting associated with research assessments. At this point, our model could not provide further information regarding the causes of epistemic convergence, so we augmented the study with an additional layer of data collection: oral histories. Unlike structured interviews, oral histories are closer to the narrative interviews of an extended case study.[14] By accessing and then opening up the situated experiences of scholars, these oral histories involved using a guided conversation to allow academics to dynamically make sense of their own epistemic and organizational practices.[15]

In total, I conducted thirty-six interviews with scholars working across seven institutions. Interviewees were selected through a convenience sample informed by the results of our quantitative model, capturing scholars at institutions that were both highly typical and highly atypical in their respective disciplines across recent evaluation periods. Scholars and institutions were coded and anonymized to the extent possible.

Importantly, the oral history data were not intended to serve as a primary pillar for building claims about the transformation of the social sciences but were designed to speak to the patterns observed in the initial stage of quantitative modeling. They were, in this sense, geared at corroborating observations, extending the data into the field and vice versa (this is a feature of the extended computational case study that I trialed in this book, creating claims by bridging multiple, interconnected domains of evidence).

The conversations were loosely structured to include a set of standard prompts and then introduce initial findings from our models in order to elicit scholars' narratives. Disciplinary changes are difficult for those within a field to observe; they are tied to notably slow forms of institutional and organizational change and require a broad analytical frame that clashes with the more fine-grain analysis of trajectories of specialization in academic disciplines. Our models, however, suggested a convergence toward thematic homogeneity. Presented with the evidence from our models, interviewees were asked to reflect on whether and how they had experienced forces of isomorphism in their own careers. There was no assumption of evidentiary isolation in this strategy, of avoiding "contamination" across the components of our research project (this differs from traditional research designs in which "triangulation" seeks to create then compare across different and fully independent sources of evidence). Making our computational results part of the conversational dynamics of the oral history interviews allowed me to gauge the extent to which early findings exaggerated or failed to identify dimensions of epistemic matching.

This method of extending results into the field, while not clearly applicable to all research designs, creates concrete analytical and explanatory possibilities. Since we had no control case, for example, assessing causal mechanisms among evaluations, individual researchers' behaviors, and the structure of their epistemic fields was fraught with difficulties. Oral histories helped narrow this gap by giving us a sense of how researchers reacted to and made sense of evaluations. In particular, presenting the findings problematized the academics' initially naïve accounts (academics did not describe the evaluations as imposing much weight on the topics of their research) and highlighted the slow mechanisms of action that might explain some of the disciplinary shifts we observed (thus, academics saw whether and how the incentives that accrued to publishing in particular venues and formats had indirectly affected their work).

WORD EMBEDDINGS

In addition, the oral histories suggested supplementary analyses of the original corpus that could further qualify our claims. One concern raised by the original workflow, for example, was that it identified topical rather than semantic shifts. Changes in topics could be explained by structural transformation in the organization of universities or discipline-wide realignments around research trends. Our research design lacked an analysis addressing *semantic* changes—shifts in the use of key terms that would represent shifts in the culture of knowledge—that might help interpret the evidence at hand. This is why we turned to word embeddings.

A growing technique of text analysis, word embeddings allow researchers to reduce a large universe of concepts into dense vectors contained in a low-dimensional space.[16] In this transformation, word embeddings preserve semantic similarity as spatial proximity: two words that are used in the same context and ostensibly have similar meanings will be represented as two vectors that are relatively close to each other. This transformation, which mirrors the distributional hypothesis of language, moves problems of semantic similarity from a frequentist ("how often were certain terms used?") to a geometric framework ("how close are certain terms with respect to their contexts of sematic use?").[17] The process is "cartographic,"[18] identifying similarities in the use of the tokens in a corpus rather than "actual" meanings. It is, however, powerful for describing how linguistic units evolve over time in their context of use.[19] Importantly, our research team did not initially intend to use word embeddings in our workflow. It was an innovation elicited by the responses we got collecting the oral histories. This research choice would not have occurred absent our iterative approach to amassing and utilizing evidence in the production of further evidence.

In particular, word embeddings allowed us to identify important contextual changes for concepts in the four focal fields. Using a skip-gram Gensim implementation of word embeddings with a window of five words (word2vec) and segmenting our corpus by periods of evaluation, we estimated not only changes in the immediate semantic universe of key terms identified by the first iteration of topic models but also those subsets of terms that had experienced the greatest shifts with respect to others in the corpus. The latter involved calculating a weighted Kendall tau for the cosine similarities between every term across consecutive periods. Through this technique, we could "navigate" the corpus as a process of linguistic change and confirm our initial hypothesis about changes in the structure of meaning of disciplinary language.

An extension of word embeddings, document embedding, provided further evidence of disciplinary changes. Built on top of a word-embedding model, doc2vec transforms texts into comparable dense vectors in which proximity equates semantic similarity at the paragraph level (a particular larger textual unit). Document-embedding models can discriminate between different texts, even when they are mostly identifiable by ambiguous words. The word *culture*, for example, is important for several sociological subfields, yet it performs different roles in each: the "culture" of an economic or political sociologist does not fully match the "culture" of a cultural sociologist.[20] Document-embedding models allow identifying these different contexts of use by taking into account a representation of language as well as subunits of texts such as sentences and paragraphs.[21] As such, they are a more appropriate instrument for evaluating textual similarity than our initially naïve comparison of topic distributions.

Calculated using the texts produced by institutions over each period as our segmentation of the corpus, the document-embedding models allowed estimating the similarity among the work of scholars across institutions and evaluating its evolution over time. Consistent with the findings from the topic models, and despite a growing number of academics in every field over the periods, we identified a secular increase in the semantic similarity of papers among institutions, providing further evidence of field-level epistemic convergence.

NOTES

1. CHAINS OF KNOWLEDGE

1. British lecturers are roughly the equivalent of tenure-track assistant professors in the United States.
2. Unlike in the United States, where faculty is a distinct group, academics in the United Kingdom are referred to as "academic staff." I will use this terminology throughout the book.
3. Strathern, *Audit Cultures*.
4. Wilsdon, *The Metric Tide*.
5. To use the term introduced by Wendy Espeland and Michael Sauder in their classical study of rankings and law schools. Espeland and Sauder, *Engines of Anxiety*.
6. Espeland and Stevens, "A Sociology of Quantification"; Porter, *Trust in Numbers*.
7. Lepenies, *The Power of a Single Number*; Özgöde, "Institutionalism in Action"; Bland, "Measuring 'Social Class'"; Goldthorpe and McKnight, "The Economic Basis of Social Class"; Bukodi and Goldthorpe, "Decomposing 'Social Origins'"; Verhulst, Eaves, and Hatemi, "Correlation Not Causation"; Norpoth and Lodge, "The Difference Between Attitudes and Nonattitudes in the Mass Public"; Vaisey, "The 'Attitudinal Fallacy' Is a Fallacy"; Vaisey and Lizardo, "Cultural Fragmentation or Acquired Dispositions?"; Jerolmack and Khan, "Toward an Understanding of the Relationship Between Accounts and Action"; Himmelfarb, "Measuring Religious Involvement."

8. The Journal Impact Factor is a proprietary metric developed by the Institute for Scientific Information (now Clarivate Analytics) that tries to approximate the visibility of publications by calculating the "average" frequency of citations of papers published in peer-reviewed journals.
9. "How to Improve the Use of Metrics."
10. Wouters, *The Citation Culture*, 4.
11. Lotka, "The Frequency Distribution of Scientific Productivity," 317.
12. Godin, "On the Origins of Bibliometrics"; Godin, *Measurement and Statistics on Science and Technology*; Abramo, D'Angelo, and Caprasecca, "Allocative Efficiency in Public Research Funding"; Cronin and Sugimoto, *Beyond Bibliometrics*; Gingras, *Bibliometrics and Research Evaluation*.
13. Hacking and Hacking, *Representing and Intervening*.
14. Espeland and Sauder, *Engines of Anxiety*.
15. DiMaggio and Powell, "The Iron Cage Revisited."
16. "Assessment Criteria and Level Definitions."
17. Espeland and Sauder, "Rankings and Reactivity."
18. Hacking and Hacking, *Representing and Intervening*; Hacking and Hacking, *The Social Construction of What?*; Barnes, Bloor, and Henry, *Scientific Knowledge*; Latour, *Science in Action*; Latour, *The Pasteurization of France*; Kuhn, *The Structure of Scientific Revolutions*; Lakatos, *Proofs and Refutations*; Feyerabend, *Against Method*; Popper, *The Logic of Scientific Discovery*.
19. I owe this observation to Judy Wajcman and her pioneering work and always generous conversations.
20. Goffman, *Asylums*, 127.
21. Long, "Productivity and Academic Position in the Scientific Career."
22. Foster, Rzhetsky, and Evans, "Tradition and Innovation in Scientists' Research Strategies"; Evans, Gomez, and McFarland, "Measuring Paradigmaticness of Disciplines Using Text"; Shwed and Bearman, "The Temporal Structure of Scientific Consensus Formation."
23. Weber, "Science as a Vocation."
24. Shapin, *The Scientific Life*, 251.
25. Shapin, *The Scientific Life*.
26. Whitley, *The Intellectual and Social Organization of the Sciences*.
27. Gelber, *Grading the College*.
28. Gelber, *Grading the College*.

29. Espeland and Sauder, *Engines of Anxiety*; Espeland and Sauder, "Rankings and Reactivity."

30. Rankings, scores, and other metrics are often coupled to specific national settings. They are all ultimately specific, in the sense that they are meaningful within bounded contexts. The *U.S. News & World Report* rankings, for example, match only partly ideas of institutional prestige about the U.S. system held overseas; the international QS Rankings matter little to decisions and strategies in countries like Mexico or Brazil; and, while used, teaching evaluations that rank academic staff have different weights and practical implications across the world. These variations invite a comparative analysis of rankings; this, however, is beyond the scope of this short book.

31. Berman and Hirschman, *The Sociology of Quantification*.

32. "Ratings Games."

33. Burrows, "Living with the H-Index?"

34. I thank Nara França for this key observation, which inspired much of this book.

35. Mills, "On Intellectual Craftsmanship (1952)," 46.

36. Lupton, *The Quantified Self*.

37. Much of *The Quantified Scholar* is inspired by Michèle Lamont, *How Professors Think*, which highlights the tensions in interdisciplinary spaces (like grant- and award-review panels) where evaluations of quality and excellence are made across distinct and relatively insular academic fields. Fortunately, what I study here are mostly contained disciplinary struggles, which allows approximating in a slightly more idealized way the disciplinary cultures that characterize different fields. The reader should understand that these are always typifications of a much messier reality, and that while some commonalities may be present within fields, they are not by consequence defining.

38. A recent paper by Tolga Yuret confirms different mobility rates for academics across disciplines, with higher overall turnover in fields that have larger infrastructural investments. See Yuret, "Tenure and Turnover of Academics in Six Undergraduate Programs in the United States."

39. Parish, Boyack, and Ioannidis, "Dynamics of Co-Authorship and Productivity Across Different Fields of Scientific Research"; Henriksen, "The Rise in Co-Authorship in the Social Sciences (1980–2013)"; Pontille, "Authorship Practices and Institutional Contexts in Sociology."

40. Fourcade, *Economists and Societies*; Fourcade, "The Construction of a Global Profession."

41. Strathern, *Audit Cultures*.

2. MEASURES OF AUSTERITY

1. Strathern, *Audit Cultures*.

2. An interesting study of class dynamics by Gregory Clark and Neil Cummins using the distribution of elite medieval surnames at these two institutions shows their class insularity over time. See Clark and Cummins, "Surnames and Social Mobility in England, 1170–2012"; Clark, *The Son Also Rises*.

3. Collini, *What Are Universities For?*, 28.

4. Robbins report.

5. Shattock, *The UGC and the Management of British Universities*, 5–11.

6. Collini, *What Are Universities For?*, 29; Shattock, *The UGC and the Management of British Universities*.

7. Mayhew, Deer, and Dua, "The Move to Mass Higher Education in the UK."

8. Shattock, *The UGC and the Management of British Universities*, 34.

9. Kogan and Hanney, *Reforming Higher Education*.

10. Shattock, *The UGC and the Management of British Universities*, 37.

11. Shattock, *The UGC and the Management of British Universities*, 57.

12. Whitley, Gläser, and Engwall, *Reconfiguring Knowledge Production*.

13. Great Britain, Department of Education and Science, *The Development of Higher Education Into the 1990s*, 31.

14. Shore et al., "Audit Culture Revisited."

15. Kogan and Hanney, *Reforming Higher Education*; Berman, *Creating the Market University*; Strathern, *Audit Cultures*.

16. Anderson, "Research Gradings Stir Emotions."

17. Phillimore, "University Research Performance Indicators in Practice," 258–59.

18. Nield, "A 4m Nonsense to Rate University Research," 17; Brown, "Restore the Equilibrium," 30.

19. Johnes and Taylor, "The 1989 Research Selectivity Exercise."

20. MacLeod, "Universities Fear Cuts in Humanities Funding," 8.

21. MacLeod.

22. These were later known as units of assessment, roughly encompassing all departments, centers, and units active in a particular academic discipline.
23. Pugh, "Empires of Hype," E6.
24. McBain, "Paper Mountain to Climb in Ratings Bid."
25. Lamont, *How Professors Think*.
26. Bence and Oppenheim, "The Evolution of the UK's Research Assessment Exercise."
27. Celeste, Griswold, and Straf, *Furthering America's Research Enterprise*; Lewis, "Research Policy as 'Carrots and Sticks'"; Haddow and Hammarfelt, "Quality, Impact, and Quantification"; Cave, *The Use of Performance Indicators in Higher Education*.
28. Recent work by Zack Griffen and Aaron Panofsky on the use of value-added modeling in education provides an important counterpoint. In VAM, the techniques of assessment were thoroughly individualized, and while they were initially seen as means for leading to more efficient outcomes in public education by creating transparency and incentives among schoolteachers, they soon became mechanisms for contesting the work stability afforded to teachers and more directly controlling their workplace; see Griffen and Panofsky, "Ambivalent Economizations."
29. Bence and Oppenheim, "The Evolution of the UK's Research Assessment Exercise."
30. Sayer, *Rank Hypocrisies*, 90.
31. Angermuller and Hamann, "The Celebrity Logics of the Academic Field."
32. Wright, "A Guide to the REF for the Shameless Academic."
33. "Academic Estimates 'Real' Cost of REF Exceeds £1bn"; Farla and Simmonds, "REF Accountability Review."
34. Thomas, "Universities Under Attack."
35. Halsey and Halsey, *Decline of Donnish Dominion*.
36. Neyland, Ehrenstein, and Milyaeva, *Can Markets Solve Problems?*
37. Salganik and Watts, "Leading the Herd Astray"; Salganik, Dodds, and Watts, "Experimental Study of Inequality and Unpredictability in an Artificial Cultural Market."
38. By the time this book is published, the most recent evaluation will be REF 2021, but data on this latest round will not be available until 2022.

39. While the REF is a UK-wide exercise, funding allocations and decisions are delegated to the four national funding bodies corresponding
to England, Scotland, Wales, and Northern Ireland. Some national
allocation models are more egalitarian than others.

3. SORTED BY WORK

1. All work is based on knowledge, of course. The skill of the carpenter, the
awareness of the nurse, and the sweat of the gardener are profoundly
based on knowledge of materials, bodies, treatments, approaches, and
possibilities of intervention. What distinguishes academic labor is, perhaps, the emphasis on knowledge as a product, an endgame in itself,
however disingenuous this may factually be.

2. Celeste, Griswold, and Straf, *Furthering America's Research Enterprise*;
Wilsdon, *The Metric Tide*; Abramo, D'Angelo, and Caprasecca, "Allocative Efficiency in Public Research Funding"; Cronin and Sugimoto,
Beyond Bibliometrics. Wildson, in particular, provides an extensive and
impressive account of how metrics are used in research evaluation as
well as an analysis of how this transposes onto the UK's system.

3. McKiernan et al., "Meta-Research."

4. Kogan and Hanney, *Reforming Higher Education*.

5. MacKenzie and Spears, "'The Formula That Killed Wall Street.'"

6. Consider, as a very brief example, the works by Gingras, *Bibliomet-
rics and Research Evaluation*; de Rijcke et al., "Evaluation Practices
and Effects of Indicator Use"; Ràfols, "S&T Indicators in the Wild";
Hammarfelt and de Rijcke, "Accountability in Context"; de Rijcke and
Rushforth, "To Intervene or Not to Intervene"; Cronin and Sugimoto,
Beyond Bibliometrics; David and Frangopol, "The Lost Paradise, the
Original Sin, and the Dodo Bird."

7. Hammarfelt and de Rijcke, "Accountability in Context"; de Rijcke et
al., "Evaluation Practices and Effects of Indicator Use"; de Rijcke and
Rushforth, "To Intervene or Not to Intervene"; Csiszar et al., *Gaming
the Metrics*.

8. Krefting, "Intertwined Discourses of Merit and Gender"; Gill, "Academics, Cultural Workers and Critical Labour Studies"; Roemer and Schnitz,
"Academic Employment as Day Labor"; Enders and Teichler, "A Victim
of Their Own Success?"; Burgess and Strachan, "Academic Employment."

9. Goffman, *Asylums*.
10. Smith-Doerr et al., "Gender Pay Gaps in US Federal Science Agencies"; Woolston, "Scientists' Salary Data Highlight US$18,000 Gender Pay Gap."
11. Kleven et al., "Child Penalties Across Countries."
12. Merton, "The Matthew Effect in Science."
13. Koppman and Leahey, "Risk and Reputation"; Koppman and Leahey, "Who Moves to the Methodological Edge?"
14. Bol, de Vaan, and van de Rijt, "The Matthew Effect in Science Funding."
15. We can see similarities here with the larger education sector where tracking individual students can become a signal that transforms the life chances of individual pupils.
16. Azoulay, Fons-Rosen, and Graff Zivin, "Does Science Advance One Funeral at a Time?"
17. Weber, "Science as a Vocation"; Sauder, "A Sociology of Luck."
18. Strathern, *Audit Cultures*; Power, *The Audit Society*.
19. Wilsdon, *The Metric Tide*.
20. McCulloch, "The Importance of Being REF-able"; Kinsey, "Understanding the REF and TEF, and What They Mean for Postgraduate Students."
21. McCulloch, "The Importance of Being REF-able."
22. For this phase of the project, Renan Sallai-Iwayama provided absolutely invaluable support, along with Prithviraj Pahwa who joined the project at a later stage. I am infinitely indebted to their generous, patient, meticulous contributions.
23. Clark, "The Many Pathways of Academic Coordination," 261–62.
24. Fernández-Zubieta, Geuna, and Lawson, "Productivity Pay-Offs from Academic Mobility", 93.
25. Langton and Pfeffer, "Paying the Professor"; Rosenfeld and Jones, "Institutional Mobility Among Academics"; Rosenfeld, "Job Mobility and Career Processes"; Ault, Rutman, and Stevenson, "Mobility in the Labor Market for Academic Economists"; Roemer and Schnitz, "Academic Employment as Day Labor."
26. For all the talk of "digital traces" in computational social science, researchers are most often confronted with multifarious digital fragments that reflect the buildup in archiving standards, digital tools, and the changing logic of organizations (see Lewis, "Three Fallacies of

Digital Footprints"; Gitelman, *Raw Data Is an Oxymoron.*). We navigate between plain text files and PDFs, work across encodings, bridging legacy applications as we go along. The work is more reconstructive archeology than tracing, more intervention than pure observation.

27. These estimates were determined using a fixed-effects logistic model with inferred gender as the outcome variable. More precisely, the proportions in the graph represent the probability that an author was female during each evaluation.

28. Henriksen, "The Rise in Co-Authorship in the Social Sciences (1980–2013)."

29. The publication patterns were estimated using a fixed-effects negative binomial regression for the number of publications per evaluation period, constraining the data to scholars with at least five years of documented activity (this eliminates biases that might be introduced by early career scholars that leave academia shortly after obtaining their doctorates).

30. Note that, as an outcome, mobility is neither positive nor negative. Mobility occurs for a number of reasons, but whenever it happens, it is associated with reconfiguring scholarly communities. As such, mobility tells us something about the instability of scholarly careers and, consequently, of academic fields. This is, indeed, the perspective that I take when thinking about mobility: it is good for some, forced for others, but in both cases involves a change in the organization of academic communities.

31. There is evidence, of course, that prestige is important in mediating how academic markets are formed. Think here, for example, of Val Burris's now classic study of hiring in American sociology departments (Burris, "The Academic Caste System."). By examining data on the exchange of students through placements, Burris found that the subjective prestige of departments is associated with the strength and number of connections that they have with other prestigious institutions—a social capital that accounts for the types of relations they establish with their peers. Departments maintain these prestige networks through how they hire freshly minted PhDs: students in high-status institutions are much more likely to be recruited by high-prestige peers whereas those who studied in departments endowed with less social capital have much

lower chances of ending up at the top of the field, resulting in a highly stratified "caste system" among scholars and institutions. These forms of preferential matching in academic careers are not constrained to sociology. In an impressive study of more than 19,000 scholars, Aaron Clauset, Samuel Arbesman, and Daniel Larremore identified similar hierarchies of placement and mobility across multiple disciplines (Clauset, Arbesman, and Larremore, "Systematic Inequality and Hierarchy in Faculty Hiring Networks"). As they demonstrate, the prestige of a scholar's PhD was a key predictor of higher productivity, better placement, and citations overall, echoing the logic of visibility and status of the Matthew effect.

32. Rosenfeld, "Job Mobility and Career Processes."

33. Rosenfeld and Jones, "Institutional Mobility Among Academics"; Long, "Productivity and Academic Position in the Scientific Career"; Long, Allison, and McGinnis, "Rank Advancement in Academic Careers"; Fuller, "Job Mobility and Wage Trajectories for Men and Women in the United States."

34. Barbezat and Hughes, "The Effect of Job Mobility on Academic Salaries."

35. Barbezat and Hughes, "The Effect of Job Mobility on Academic Salaries."

36. Allison and Long, "Interuniversity Mobility of Academic Scientists."

37. Blei and Lafferty, "A Correlated Topic Model of Science"; Blei, Ng, and Jordan, "Latent Dirichlet Allocation."

38. White and Borgatti, "Betweenness Centrality Measures for Directed Graphs."

39. The concept of epistemic sorting we have arrived at alludes not only to the role of labor markets in "matching" employees to jobs according to their complementary resources and skills (scholars may be more likely to be hired in departments where they are less redundant) but also to a growing body of studies that show how imprinting in academic careers lead to organized, "partially deliberate" forms of matching in scientific careers. See Coleman, "Matching Processes in the Labor Market"; Azoulay, Liu, and Stuart, "Social Influence Given (Partially) Deliberate Matching"; Roth and Sotomayor, "Two-Sided Matching."

40. Allison and Long, "Interuniversity Mobility of Academic Scientists."

4. SHIFTING WORDS

1. Radkau, *Max Weber*; Cassidy, "Interview with Eugene Fama"; Bourdieu, *Homo Academicus*; Haraway, *The Companion Species Manifesto*; Hall, *Familiar Stranger*.
2. Eribon, *Returning to Reims*; Cottom, *Thick*.
3. Frickel and Gross, "A General Theory of Scientific/Intellectual Movements."
4. Lamont, *How Professors Think*; Lamont and Molnár, "The Study of Boundaries in the Social Sciences."
5. Neyland, Ehrenstein, and Milyaeva, *Can Markets Solve Problems?*, 86.
6. Traag and Waltman, "Systematic Analysis of Agreement Between Metrics and Peer Review in the UK REF", 2.
7. Here, I am using the framework offered by Thomas Kuhn's concept of "normal science." Kuhn, *The Structure of Scientific Revolutions*.
8. Abbott, *Chaos of Disciplines*.
9. Stinchcombe, "Organizations and Social Structure."
10. Scott, *British Sociology*.
11. Scott, *British Sociology*, 133.
12. Husbands, "Sociology at the London School of Economics and Political Science, 1904–2015."
13. Husbands, "Sociology at the London School of Economics and Political Science, 1904–2015," 375. Husbands notes weakness in race and ethnic relations, quantitative sociology, gerontology, and studies of families.
14. Husbands, "Sociology at the London School of Economics and Political Science, 1904–2015," 378.
15. Stoltz and Taylor, "Cultural Cartography with Word Embeddings," 2021.
16. Mills, "Social Status, Social Position and Social Class in Post-War British Society"; Scott, *British Sociology*.
17. Savage, "The Fall and Rise of Class Analysis in British Sociology, 1950–2016." See also Acker, "No-Woman's-Land"; Duke and Edgell, "The Operationalisation of Class in British Sociology"; Arnot, "Male Hegemony, Social Class and Women's Education"; Whitty, "Education, Social Class and Social Exclusion."
18. Similar processes of status/differentiation, which are tied to inequalities in outcomes among worker salaries, productivity, and other outcomes,

have been studied elsewhere, notably in Wilmers, "Job Turf or Variety"; Zuckerman, "Optimal Distinctiveness Revisited"; Phillips, Turco, and Zuckerman, "High-Status Conformity and Deviance."

19. Burawoy, *Manufacturing Consent.*
20. Heesen and Bright, "Is Peer Review a Good Idea?"
21. Csiszar et al., *Gaming the Metrics.*
22. Clemens et al., "Careers in Print."
23. Teplitskiy et al., "Status Drives How We Cite."
24. Whitley, Gläser, and Engwall, *Reconfiguring Knowledge Production*; Whitley, *The Intellectual and Social Organization of the Sciences*; Abbott, *Chaos of Disciplines.*
25. See Fourcade, *Economists and Societies.*
26. Backhouse, "History of Economics, Economics and Economic History in Britain, 1824–2000."
27. Lee, "The Research Assessment Exercise, the State and the Dominance of Mainstream Economics in British Universities."
28. There is ample evidence of this in the recent work of Danielle Guizzo, James T. Walker, Marina Della Giusta, and Rita Fontinha, who document ways in which the RAE/REF have shifted the nature of macroeconomics as practiced in the United Kingdom.

5. HIERARCHIES OF QUANTIFICATION

1. Hacking, "Biopower and the Avalanche of Printed Numbers."
2. Porter, *Trust in Numbers.*
3. Whitley, *The Intellectual and Social Organization of the Sciences.*
4. Liu, "Multiple Social Credit Systems in China."
5. Christin, "Algorithms in Practice"; Brayne and Christin, "Technologies of Crime Prediction"; Brayne, *Predict and Surveil.*
6. Neyland, Ehrenstein, and Milyaeva, *Can Markets Solve Problems?*
7. Du Gay, *In Praise of Bureaucracy*; Auyero, *Patients of the State*; Neyland, Ehrenstein, and Milyaeva, *Can Markets Solve Problems?*; Salter and Tapper, "The Politics of Governance in Higher Education."
8. Abbott, *Chaos of Disciplines*; Whitley, *The Intellectual and Social Organization of the Sciences.*
9. Whitley, *The Intellectual and Social Organization of the Sciences.*

10. Merton, *The Sociology of Science.*

11. Emily Bosk's work offers an important parallel. See Bosk, "Iron Cage or Paper Cage?"

12. Concerns with inequities in the policies for submissions after the 2008 Research Assessment Exercise, HEFCE, the regulator for higher education in the UK, asked institutions to develop individual codes of practice about how the REF would be managed. As far as I can tell from Derek Sayer's account in *Rank Hypocrisies*, LSE's code of conduct was unexceptional, placing the responsibility and power to submit scholars to the assessment in the hands of an ad hoc, institution-wide committee.

13. Zuckerman, "The Categorical Imperative."

14. To preserve the anonymity of the institution and its scholars, I have chosen to leave them completely unidentified both geographically and reputationally.

15. Power comes at a cost. Given that the REF is explicitly a quality assessment linking funding to research at or above 3* grades, an institution could play the game of maximizing both its income and its position in the ranking by submitting only scholars whose predicted grade was at or above the cutoff. The way the assessments work means that larger departments are expected to demonstrate more exceptional "impact," documenting in laborious case studies how research has had transformational effects on society.

16. Sauder and Espeland, "Strength in Numbers?"

17. Hermanowicz, *Lives in Science.*

18. Barnes, "Social Life as Bootstrapped Induction."

19. Gross and Bergstrom, "Contest Models Highlight Inherent Inefficiencies of Scientific Funding Competitions"; D'Ippoliti, *Democratizing the Economics Debate*; Smaldino, Turner, and Contreras Kallens, "Open Science and Modified Funding Lotteries Can Impede the Natural Selection of Bad Science."

6. SOLIDARITIES

1. Csiszar et al., *Gaming the Metrics.*

2. Wilsdon, *The Metric Tide.*

3. Sennett, *The Craftsman.*

4. There is an intriguing contradiction between our vocational interest in sharing knowledge yet devaluing—in relative terms—teaching as a key component of the profession. Increasingly, some of this contradiction has been dealt with through quantification. In addition to student evaluations, for example, the United Kingdom now has a Teaching Excellence Framework that seeks to value this part of our professional lives. Ironically, this only creates further tensions in already anxious careers and does little to erode the prominence of research as the normative core of the modern university. I thank Letta Page for this keen observation.

5. Mackenzie, "Uninventing the Bomb?"

6. UCU Branch Solidarity Network, "Why We Will Strike Against REF."

7. Goodwin et al., *The Academic's Handbook*, 175.

8. Barnes, *The Nature of Power*.

9. Baxter, Hughes, and Tight, *Academic Career Handbook*.

10. Bourdieu, *Homo Academicus*.

11. As Charlie Eaton and Mitchell Stevens argue, universities are peculiar organizations in contemporary societies for their quasi-sovereign capacity to control internal boundaries, categories, and hierarchies and practices, even when these have implications for external credentialization and labor market signaling; see Eaton and Stevens, "Universities as Peculiar Organizations." Degrees of sovereignty vary across countries, though, and both the United States and the United Kingdom are characterized by greater independence from the state in terms of how they set educational, financial, and organizational criteria. See Westerheijden, "University Governance in the United Kingdom, the Netherlands and Japan"; Taylor, "Shared Governance in the Modern University"; Leach, "Shared Governance in Higher Education."

12. Douglas, *How Institutions Think*, 4.

13. Bourdieu, *Homo Academicus*.

14. Link, Swann, and Bozeman, "A Time Allocation Study of University Faculty"; Suitor, Mecom, and Feld, "Gender, Household Labor, and Scholarly Productivity Among University Professors"; Malisch et al., "Opinion."

15. Graeber and Cerutti, *Bullshit Jobs*.

16. Gutiérrez, *We Drink from Our Own Wells*.

17. Eaton et al., "The Financialization of US Higher Education."

18. Solnit, foreword to *Pandemic Solidarity*, xiv.
19. Malisch et al., "Opinion."
20. Zambrana, *Toxic Ivory Towers*; Deo, *Unequal Profession*.
21. Graeber and Cerutti, *Bullshit Jobs*.
22. Shapin, *The Scientific Life*.

APPENDIX: STUDYING SOCIAL SCIENTISTS

1. Ben-David and Collins, "Social Factors in the Origins of a New Science"; Ben-David and Sullivan, "Sociology of Science."
2. Azoulay et al., "Toward a More Scientific Science."
3. McMahan and Evans, "Ambiguity and Engagement"; Foster, Rzhetsky, and Evans, "Tradition and Innovation in Scientists' Research Strategies"; Teplitskiy et al., "Status Drives How We Cite."
4. Tavory and Timmermans, *Abductive Analysis*.
5. Nelson, "Computational Grounded Theory"; Nelson, "To Measure Meaning in Big Data, Don't Give Me a Map, Give Me Transparency and Reproducibility"; Nelson et al., "The Future of Coding."
6. Nelson, "Computational Grounded Theory."
7. Gargiulo and Carletti, "Driving Forces of Researchers Mobility."
8. Wu and Ding, "Author Name Disambiguation in Scientific Collaboration and Mobility Cases."
9. Long, "Productivity and Academic Position in the Scientific Career"; Allison and Long, "Interuniversity Mobility of Academic Scientists"; Long, Allison, and McGinnis, "Rank Advancement in Academic Careers"; Leahey, "Not by Productivity Alone," 2007.
10. Blei, Ng, and Jordan, "Latent Dirichlet Allocation."
11. DiMaggio, Nag, and Blei, "Exploiting Affinities Between Topic Modeling and the Sociological Perspective on Culture"; Mohr and Bogdanov, *Introduction—Topic Models*; Bohr and Dunlap, "Key Topics in Environmental Sociology, 1990–2014"; Roose, Roose, and Daenekindt, "Trends in Contemporary Art Discourse"; Bail, "Lost in a Random Forest."
12. Nelson et al., "The Future of Coding"; Marshall, "Defining Population Problems."
13. Leahey, "Not by Productivity Alone," 2007; Long, Allison, and McGinnis, "Rank Advancement in Academic Careers."

14. Burawoy, "The Extended Case Method."
15. Laslett, "Personal Narratives as Sociology."
16. Stoltz and Taylor, "Cultural Cartography with Word Embeddings," 2020; Kozlowski, Taddy, and Evans, "The Geometry of Culture."
17. Kozlowski, Taddy, and Evans, "The Geometry of Culture."
18. Stoltz and Taylor, "Cultural Cartography with Word Embeddings," 2020.
19. Hamilton, Leskovec, and Jurafsky, "Diachronic Word Embeddings Reveal Statistical Laws of Semantic Change"; Bizzoni et al., "Grammar and Meaning"; Garg et al., "Word Embeddings Quantify 100 Years of Gender and Ethnic Stereotypes."
20. Liu et al., "Task-Oriented Word Embedding for Text Classification."
21. Navigli and Martelli, "An Overview of Word and Sense Similarity"; Haj-Yahia, Sieg, and Deleris, "Towards Unsupervised Text Classification Leveraging Experts and Word Embeddings."

BIBLIOGRAPHY

Abbott, Andrew. *Chaos of Disciplines*. Chicago: University of Chicago Press, 2010.

Abramo, Giovanni, Ciriaco Andrea D'Angelo, and Alessandro Caprasecca. "Allocative Efficiency in Public Research Funding: Can Bibliometrics Help?" *Research Policy* 38, no. 1 (2009): 206–15.

"Academic Estimates 'Real' Cost of REF Exceeds £1bn." *Times Higher Education (THE)*, February 12, 2015. https://www.timeshighereducation.com /news/academic-estimates-real-cost-of-ref-exceeds-1bn/2018493.article.

Acker, Sandra. "No-Woman's-Land: British Sociology of Education 1960–1979." *Sociological Review* 29, no. 1 (1981): 77–104.

Allison, Paul D., and J. Scott Long. "Interuniversity Mobility of Academic Scientists." *American Sociological Review* 52, no. 5 (1987): 643–52.

Anderson, Alun. "Research Gradings Stir Emotions." *Nature* 322 (1986): 299.

Angermuller, Johannes, and Julian Hamann. "The Celebrity Logics of the Academic Field: The Unequal Distribution of Citation Visibility of Applied Linguistics Professors in Germany, France, and the United Kingdom." *Journal for Discourse Studies* 1 (2019): 77–93.

Arnot, Madeleine. "Male Hegemony, Social Class and Women's Education." *Journal of Education* 164, no. 1 (1982): 64–89.

"Assessment Criteria and Level Definitions." REF 2014. Accessed December 14, 2020. https://www.ref.ac.uk/2014/panels/assessmentcriteriaandlevel definitions/.

Ault, David E., Gilbert L. Rutman, and Thomas Stevenson. "Mobility in the Labor Market for Academic Economists." *American Economic Review* 69, no. 2 (1979): 148–53.

Auyero, Javier. *Patients of the State: The Politics of Waiting in Argentina*. Durham, NC: Duke University Press, 2012.

Azoulay, Pierre, Christian Fons-Rosen, and Joshua S. Graff Zivin. "Does Science Advance One Funeral at a Time?" *American Economic Review* 109, no. 8 (2019): 2889–2920.

Azoulay, Pierre, Joshua Graff-Zivin, Brian Uzzi, Dashun Wang, Heidi Williams, James A. Evans, Ginger Zhe Jin, Susan Feng Lu, Benjamin F. Jones, and Katy Börner. "Toward a More Scientific Science." *Science* 361, no. 6408 (2018): 1194–97.

Azoulay, Pierre, Christopher C. Liu, and Toby E. Stuart. "Social Influence Given (Partially) Deliberate Matching: Career Imprints in the Creation of Academic Entrepreneurs." *American Journal of Sociology* 122, no. 4 (2017): 1223–71.

Backhouse, Roger E. "History of Economics, Economics and Economic History in Britain, 1824–2000." *European Journal of the History of Economic Thought* 11, no. 1 (2006): 107–27. https://doi.org/10.1080/0967256032000171524.

Bail, Christopher A. "Lost in a Random Forest: Using Big Data to Study Rare Events." *Big Data & Society* 2, no. 2 (2015). https://doi.org/10.1177/2053951715604333.

Barbezat, Debra A., and James W. Hughes. "The Effect of Job Mobility on Academic Salaries." *Contemporary Economic Policy* 19, no. 4 (2001): 409–23.

Barnes, Barry. *The Nature of Power*. Cambridge: Polity, 1988.

——. "Social Life as Bootstrapped Induction." *Sociology* 17, no. 4 (1983): 524–45.

Barnes, Barry, David Bloor, and John Henry. *Scientific Knowledge: A Sociological Analysis*. Chicago: University of Chicago Press, 1996.

Baxter, Lorraine, Christina Hughes, and Malcolm Tight. *Academic Career Handbook*. London: McGraw-Hill Education (UK), 1998.

Bence, Valerie, and Charles Oppenheim. "The Evolution of the UK's Research Assessment Exercise: Publications, Performance and Perceptions." *Journal of Educational Administration and History* 37, no. 2 (2005): 137–55.

Ben-David, Joseph, and Randall Collins. "Social Factors in the Origins of a New Science: The Case of Psychology." *American Sociological Review* 31, no. 4 (1966): 451–65.

Ben-David, Joseph, and Teresa A. Sullivan. "Sociology of Science." *Annual Review of Sociology* 1, no. 1 (1975): 203–22.

Berman, Elizabeth Popp. *Creating the Market University: How Academic Science Became an Economic Engine*. Princeton, NJ: Princeton University Press, 2011.

Berman, Elizabeth Popp, and Daniel Hirschman. *The Sociology of Quantification: Where Are We Now?* Los Angeles: Sage, 2018.

Bizzoni, Yuri, Stefania Degaetano-Ortlieb, Katrin Menzel, Pauline Krielke, and Elke Teich. "Grammar and Meaning: Analysing the Topology of Diachronic Word Embeddings." In *Proceedings of the First International Workshop on Computational Approaches to Historical Language Change*, 175–85. Florence, Italy: Association for Computational Linguistics, 2019.

Bland, Richard. "Measuring 'Social Class': A Discussion of the Registrar-General's Classification." *Sociology* 13, no. 2 (1979): 283–91.

Blei, David M., and John D. Lafferty. "A Correlated Topic Model of Science." *Annals of Applied Statistics* 1, no. 1 (2007): 17–35.

Blei, David M., Andrew Y. Ng, and Michael I. Jordan. "Latent Dirichlet Allocation." *Journal of Machine Learning Research* 3 (2003): 993–1022.

Bohr, Jeremiah, and Riley E. Dunlap. "Key Topics in Environmental Sociology, 1990–2014: Results from a Computational Text Analysis." *Environmental Sociology* 4, no. 2 (2018): 181–95.

Bol, Thijs, Mathijs de Vaan, and Arnout van de Rijt. "The Matthew Effect in Science Funding." *Proceedings of the National Academy of Sciences* 115, no. 19 (2018): 4887–90.

Bosk, Emily A. "Iron Cage or Paper Cage? The Interplay of Worker Characteristics and Organizational Policy in Shaping Unequal Responses to a Standardized Decision-Making Tool." *Social Problems* 67, no. 4 (2020): 654–76.

Bourdieu, Pierre. *Homo Academicus.* Stanford, CA: Stanford University Press, 1988.

Brayne, Sarah. *Predict and Surveil: Data, Discretion, and the Future of Policing.* New York: Oxford University Press, 2021.

Brayne, Sarah, and Angèle Christin. "Technologies of Crime Prediction: The Reception of Algorithms in Policing and Criminal Courts." *Social Problems* 68, no. 3 (2021): 608–24.

Brown, Roger. "Restore the Equilibrium." *Times Higher Education Supplement*, March 28, 2013.

Bukodi, Erzsébet, and John H. Goldthorpe. "Decomposing 'Social Origins': The Effects of Parents' Class, Status, and Education on the Educational Attainment of Their Children." *European Sociological Review* 29, no. 5 (2013): 1024–39.

Burawoy, Michael. "The Extended Case Method." *Sociological Theory* 16, no. 1 (1998): 4–33.

———. *Manufacturing Consent: Changes in the Labor Process Under Monopoly Capitalism.* Chicago: University of Chicago Press, 1982.

Burgess, John, and Glenda Strachan. "Academic Employment: Current Pressures, Future Trends and Possible Responses." *Australian Universities' Review* 39, no. 2 (1996): 28.

Burris, Val. "The Academic Caste System: Prestige Hierarchies in PhD Exchange Networks." *American Sociological Review* 69, no. 2 (2004): 239–64.

Burrows, Roger. "Living with the H-Index? Metric Assemblages in the Contemporary Academy." *Sociological Review* 60, no. 2 (2012): 355–72. https://doi.org/10.1111/j.1467-954X.2012.02077.x.

Cassidy, John. "Interview with Eugene Fama." *New Yorker*, January 13, 2010. https://www.newyorker.com/news/john-cassidy/interview-with-eugene-fama.

Cave, Martin. *The Use of Performance Indicators in Higher Education: The Challenge of the Quality Movement.* London: Jessica Kingsley, 1997.

Celeste, Richard F., Ann Griswold, and Miron L. Straf. *Furthering America's Research Enterprise.* Washington, DC: National Academies Press, 2014.

Christin, Angèle. "Algorithms in Practice: Comparing Web Journalism and Criminal Justice." *Big Data & Society* 4, no. 2 (2017). https://doi.org/10.1177/2053951717718855.

Clark, Burton R. "The Many Pathways of Academic Coordination." *Higher Education* 8, no. 3 (1979): 251–67.

Clark, Gregory. *The Son Also Rises: Surnames and the History of Social Mobility.* Princeton, NJ: Princeton University Press, 2015.

Clark, Gregory, and Neil Cummins. "Surnames and Social Mobility in England, 1170–2012." *Human Nature* 25, no. 4 (2014): 517–37.

Clauset, Aaron, Samuel Arbesman, and Daniel B. Larremore. "Systematic Inequality and Hierarchy in Faculty Hiring Networks." *Science Advances* 1, no. 1 (2015): e1400005.

Clemens, Elisabeth S., Walter W. Powell, Kris McIlwaine, and Dina Okamoto. "Careers in Print: Books, Journals, and Scholarly Reputations." *American Journal of Sociology* 101, no. 2 (1995): 433–94.

Coleman, James S. "Matching Processes in the Labor Market." *Acta Sociologica* 34, no. 1 (1991): 3–12.

Collini, Stefan. *What Are Universities For?* London: Penguin UK, 2012.

Cottom, Tressie McMillan. *Thick: And Other Essays.* New York: New Press, 2018.

Cronin, Blaise, and Cassidy R. Sugimoto. *Beyond Bibliometrics: Harnessing Multidimensional Indicators of Scholarly Impact*. Cambridge, MA: MIT Press, 2014.

Csiszar, Alex, Yves Gingras, Michael Power, Paul Wouters, James R. Griesemer, Barbara M. Kehm, Sarah de Rijcke, Tereza Stöckelová, Daniele Fanelli, and Sergio Sismondo. *Gaming the Metrics: Misconduct and Manipulation in Academic Research*. Cambridge, MA: MIT Press, 2020.

David, Daniel, and Petre Frangopol. "The Lost Paradise, the Original Sin, and the Dodo Bird: A Scientometrics Sapere Aude Manifesto as a Reply to the Leiden Manifesto on Scientometrics." *Scientometrics* 105, no. 3 (2015): 2255–57.

Deo, Meera E. *Unequal Profession: Race and Gender in Legal Academia*. Stanford, CA: Stanford University Press, 2019.

de Rijcke, Sarah, and Alexander Rushforth. "To Intervene or Not to Intervene: Is That the Question? On the Role of Scientometrics in Research Evaluation." *Journal of the Association for Information Science and Technology* 66, no. 9 (2015): 1954–58.

de Rijcke, Sarah, Paul F. Wouters, Alex D. Rushforth, Thomas P. Franssen, and Björn Hammarfelt. "Evaluation Practices and Effects of Indicator Use: A Literature Review." *Research Evaluation* 25, no. 2 (2016): 161–69.

DiMaggio, Paul, Manish Nag, and David Blei. "Exploiting Affinities Between Topic Modeling and the Sociological Perspective on Culture: Application to Newspaper Coverage of U.S. Government Arts Funding." *Poetics* 41, no. 6 (2013): 570–606.

DiMaggio, Paul J., and Walter W. Powell. "The Iron Cage Revisited: Institutional Isomorphism and Collective Rationality in Organizational Fields." *American Sociological Review* 48, no. 2 (1983): 147–60.

D'Ippoliti, Carlo. *Democratizing the Economics Debate: Pluralism and Research Evaluation*. London: Routledge, 2020.

Douglas, Mary. *How Institutions Think*. Syracuse, NY: Syracuse University Press, 1986.

Du Gay, Paul. *In Praise of Bureaucracy: Weber-Organization-Ethics*. London: Sage, 2000.

Duke, Vic, and Stephen Edgell. "The Operationalisation of Class in British Sociology: Theoretical and Empirical Considerations." *British Journal of Sociology* 38, no. 4 (1987): 445–63.

Eaton, Charlie, Jacob Habinek, Adam Goldstein, Cyrus Dioun, Daniela García Santibáñez Godoy, and Robert Osley-Thomas. "The Financialization of U.S. Higher Education." *Socio-Economic Review* 14, no. 3 (2016): 507–35.

Eaton, Charlie, and Mitchell L. Stevens. "Universities as Peculiar Organizations." *Sociology Compass* 14, no. 3 (2020): e12768.

Enders, Jürgen, and Ulrich Teichler. "A Victim of Their Own Success? Employment and Working Conditions of Academic Staff in Comparative Perspective." *Higher Education* 34, no. 3 (1997): 347–72.

Eribon, Didier. *Returning to Reims*. London: Penguin UK, 2018.

Espeland, Wendy Nelson and Michael Sauder. *Engines of Anxiety: Academic Rankings, Reputation, and Accountability*. New York: Russell Sage Foundation, 2016.

——. "Rankings and Reactivity: How Public Measures Recreate Social Worlds." *American Journal of Sociology* 113, no. 1 (2007): 1–40.

Espeland, Wendy Nelson, and Mitchell L. Stevens. "A Sociology of Quantification." *European Journal of Sociology/Archives Européennes de Sociologie* 49, no. 3 (2008): 401–36.

Evans, Eliza D., Charles J. Gomez, and Daniel A. McFarland. "Measuring Paradigmaticness of Disciplines Using Text." *Sociological Science* 3 (2016): 757–78.

Farla, K., and P. Simmonds. "REF Accountability Review: Costs, Benefits and Burden." *Report by Technopolis to the Four UK Higher Education Funding Bodies*, 2015.

Fernández-Zubieta, Ana, Aldo Geuna, and Cornelia Lawson. "Productivity Pay-Offs from Academic Mobility: Should I Stay or Should I Go?" *Industrial and Corporate Change* 25, no. 1 (2016): 91–114.

Feyerabend, Paul. *Against Method*. London: Verso, 1993.

Foster, Jacob G., Andrey Rzhetsky, and James A. Evans. "Tradition and Innovation in Scientists' Research Strategies." *American Sociological Review* 80, no. 5 (2015): 875–908.

Fourcade, Marion. "The Construction of a Global Profession: The Transnationalization of Economics." *American Journal of Sociology* 112, no. 1 (2006): 145–94.

——. *Economists and Societies: Discipline and Profession in the United States, Britain, and France, 1890s to 1990s*. Princeton, NJ: Princeton University Press, 2009.

Frickel, Scott, and Neil Gross. "A General Theory of Scientific/Intellectual Movements." *American Sociological Review* 70, no. 2 (2005): 204–32.

Fuller, Sylvia. "Job Mobility and Wage Trajectories for Men and Women in the United States." *American Sociological Review* 73, no. 1 (2008): 158–83.

Garg, Nikhil, Londa Schiebinger, Dan Jurafsky, and James Zou. "Word Embeddings Quantify 100 Years of Gender and Ethnic Stereotypes." *Proceedings of the National Academy of Sciences* 115, no. 16 (2018): E3635–44.

Gargiulo, Floriana, and Timoteo Carletti. "Driving Forces of Researchers Mobility." *Scientific Reports* 4, 4860 (2014). https://doi.org/10.1038/srep04860.

Gelber, Scott M. *Grading the College: A History of Evaluating Teaching and Learning*. Baltimore: Johns Hopkins University Press, 2020.

Gill, Rosalind. "Academics, Cultural Workers and Critical Labour Studies." *Journal of Cultural Economy* 7, no. 1 (2014): 12–30.

Gingras, Yves. *Bibliometrics and Research Evaluation: Uses and Abuses*. Cambridge, MA: MIT Press, 2016.

Gitelman, Lisa. *Raw Data Is an Oxymoron*. Cambridge, MA: MIT Press, 2013.

Godin, Benoît. *Measurement and Statistics on Science and Technology: 1920 to the Present*. London: Routledge, 2004.

——. "On the Origins of Bibliometrics." *Scientometrics* 68, no. 1 (2006): 109–33.

Goffman, Erving. *Asylums: Essays on the Social Situation of Mental Patients and Other Inmates*. London: AldineTransaction, 1968.

Goldthorpe, John H., and Abigail McKnight. "The Economic Basis of Social Class." In *Mobility and Inequality: Frontiers of Research in Sociology and Economics*, ed. Stephen L. Morgan, David B. Grusky, and Gary S. Fields, 109–36. Stanford, CA: Stanford University Press, 2006.

Goodwin, Craufurd D., A. Leigh DeNeef, Jerry G. Gaff, Samuel Schuman, and Stanley Hauerwas. *The Academic's Handbook*. Durham, NC: Duke University Press, 2007.

Graeber, David, and Albertine Cerutti. *Bullshit Jobs*. New York: Simon & Schuster, 2018.

Great Britain. Department of Education and Science. *The Development of Higher Education Into the 1990s*. London: HMSO, 1985.

Griffen, Zachary, and Aaron Panofsky. "Ambivalent Economizations: The Case of Value Added Modeling in Teacher Evaluation." *Theory and Society* 50, no. 3 (2021): 515–39. https://doi.org/10.1007/s11186-020-09417-x.

Gross, Kevin, and Carl T. Bergstrom. "Contest Models Highlight Inherent Inefficiencies of Scientific Funding Competitions." *PLoS Biology* 17, no. 1 (2019): e3000065.

Gutiérrez, Gustavo. *We Drink from Our Own Wells: The Spiritual Experience of a People*. London: SCM, 2013.

Hacking, Ian. "Biopower and the Avalanche of Printed Numbers." In *Biopower: Foucault and Beyond*, ed. Vernon W. Cisney and Nicolae Morar, 65–81. Chicago: University of Chicago Press, 2015.

Hacking, Ian, and Jan Hacking. *Representing and Intervening: Introductory Topics in the Philosophy of Natural Science*. Cambridge: Cambridge University Press, 1983.

——. *The Social Construction of What?* Cambridge, MA: Harvard University Press, 1999.

Haddow, Gaby, and Björn Hammarfelt. "Quality, Impact, and Quantification: Indicators and Metrics Use by Social Scientists." *Journal of the Association for Information Science and Technology* 70, no. 1 (2019): 16–26.

Haj-Yahia, Zied, Adrien Sieg, and Léa A. Deleris. "Towards Unsupervised Text Classification Leveraging Experts and Word Embeddings." In *Proceedings of the Fifty-Seventh Annual Meeting of the Association for Computational Linguistics*, 2019, 371–79.

Hall, Stuart. *Familiar Stranger: A Life Between Two Islands*. Durham, NC: Duke University Press, 2017.

Halsey, Albert Henry, and A. H. Halsey. *Decline of Donnish Dominion: The British Academic Professions in the Twentieth Century*. Oxford: Clarendon, 1992.

Hamilton, William L., Jure Leskovec, and Dan Jurafsky. "Diachronic Word Embeddings Reveal Statistical Laws of Semantic Change." ArXiv Preprint ArXiv:1605.09096, 2016.

Hammarfelt, Björn, and Sarah de Rijcke. "Accountability in Context: Effects of Research Evaluation Systems on Publication Practices, Disciplinary Norms, and Individual Working Routines in the Faculty of Arts at Uppsala University." *Research Evaluation* 24, no. 1 (2015): 63–77.

Haraway, Donna Jeanne. *The Companion Species Manifesto: Dogs, People, and Significant Otherness*. Chicago: Prickly Paradigm, 2003.

Heesen, Remco, and Liam Kofi Bright. "Is Peer Review a Good Idea?" *British Journal for the Philosophy of Science* 72, no. 3 (2021): 635–63.

Henriksen, Dorte. "The Rise in Co-Authorship in the Social Sciences (1980–2013)." *Scientometrics* 107, no. 2 (2016): 455–76.

Hermanowicz, Joseph C. *Lives in Science: How Institutions Affect Academic Careers*. Chicago: University of Chicago Press, 2010.

Himmelfarb, Harold S. "Measuring Religious Involvement." *Social Forces* 53, no. 4 (1975): 606–18.

"How to Improve the Use of Metrics." *Nature* 465 (2010): 870–72. https://doi .org/10.1038/465870a.

Husbands, Christopher T. *Sociology at the London School of Economics and Political Science, 1904–2015*. Cham, Switzerland: Palgrave Macmillan, 2019.

Jerolmack, Colin, and Shamus Khan. "Toward an Understanding of the Relationship Between Accounts and Action." *Sociological Methods & Research* 43, no. 2 (2014): 236–47.

Johnes, Jill, and Jim Taylor. "The 1989 Research Selectivity Exercise: A Statistical Analysis of Differences in Research Rating Between Universities at the Cost Centre Level." *Higher Education Quarterly* 46, no. 1 (1992): 67–87.

Kinsey, Debbie. "Understanding the REF and TEF, and What They Mean for Postgraduate Students." In *A Guide for Psychology Postgraduates*, ed. Emma Norris, 96. British Psychological Association, 2019.

Kleven, Henrik, Camille Landais, Johanna Posch, Andreas Steinhauer, and Josef Zweimüller. "Child Penalties Across Countries: Evidence and Explanations." In *AEA Papers and Proceedings* 109 (2019):122–26.

Kogan, Maurice, and Stephen Hanney. *Reforming Higher Education*. London: Jessica Kingsley, 2000.

Koppman, Sharon, and Erin Leahey. "Risk and Reputation: How Professional Classification Signals Drive the Diffusion of New Methods." In *Academy of Management Proceedings* 2016, no. 1 (2016). https://journals .aom.org/doi/10.5465/ambpp.2016.11676abstract.

——. "Who Moves to the Methodological Edge? Factors That Encourage Scientists to Use Unconventional Methods." *Research Policy* 48, no. 9 (2019): 103807.

Kozlowski, Austin C., Matt Taddy, and James A. Evans. "The Geometry of Culture: Analyzing the Meanings of Class Through Word Embeddings." *American Sociological Review* 84, no. 5 (2019): 905–49.

Krefting, Linda A. "Intertwined Discourses of Merit and Gender: Evidence from Academic Employment in the USA." *Gender, Work & Organization* 10, no. 2 (2003): 260–78.

Kuhn, Thomas S. *The Structure of Scientific Revolutions*. Chicago: University of Chicago Press, 2012.

Lakatos, Imre. *Proofs and Refutations: The Logic of Mathematical Discovery.* Cambridge: Cambridge University Press, 2015.

Lamont, Michèle. *How Professors Think.* Cambridge, MA: Harvard University Press, 2009.

Lamont, Michèle, and Virág Molnár. "The Study of Boundaries in the Social Sciences." *Annual Review of Sociology* 28, no. 1 (2002): 167–95.

Langton, Nancy, and Jeffrey Pfeffer. "Paying the Professor: Sources of Salary Variation in Academic Labor Markets." *American Sociological Review* 59, no. 2 (1994): 236–56.

Laslett, Barbara. "Personal Narratives as Sociology." *Contemporary Sociology* 28, no. 4 (1999): 391–401.

Latour, Bruno. *The Pasteurization of France.* Cambridge, MA: Harvard University Press, 1993.

——. *Science in Action: How to Follow Scientists and Engineers Through Society.* Cambridge, MA: Harvard University Press, 1987.

Leach, William D. "Shared Governance in Higher Education: Structural and Cultural Responses to a Changing National Climate." *SSRN Electronic Journal*, 2008. https://ssrn.com/abstract=1520702.

Leahey, Erin. "Not by Productivity Alone: How Visibility and Specialization Contribute to Academic Earnings." *American Sociological Review* 72, no. 4 (2007): 533–61.

Lee, Frederic S. "The Research Assessment Exercise, the State and the Dominance of Mainstream Economics in British Universities." *Cambridge Journal of Economics* 31, no. 2 (2007): 309–25.

Lepenies, Philipp. *The Power of a Single Number: A Political History of GDP.* New York: Columbia University Press, 2016.

Lewis, Jenny M. "Research Policy as 'Carrots and Sticks': Governance Strategies in Australia, the United Kingdom and New Zealand." In *Varieties of Governance*, ed. G. Capano, M. Howlett, and M. Ramesh, 131–50. London: Palgrave Macmillan, 2015.

Lewis, Kevin. "Three Fallacies of Digital Footprints." *Big Data & Society* 2, no. 2 (2015). https://doi.org/10.1177/2053951715602496.

Link, Albert N., Christopher A. Swann, and Barry Bozeman. "A Time Allocation Study of University Faculty." *Economics of Education Review* 27, no. 4 (2008): 363–74. https://doi.org/10.1016/j.econedurev.2007.04.002.

Liu, Chuncheng. "Multiple Social Credit Systems in China," SocArXiv Papers, July 25, 2019. doi:10.31235/osf.io/v9frs.

Liu, Qian, He-Yan Huang, Yang Gao, Xiaochi Wei, Yuxin Tian, and Luyang Liu. "Task-Oriented Word Embedding for Text Classification." In *Proceedings of the Twenty-Seventh International Conference on Computational Linguistics*, 2018, 2023–32.

Long, J. Scott. "Productivity and Academic Position in the Scientific Career." *American Sociological Review* 43, no. 6 (1978): 889–908.

Long, J. Scott, Paul D. Allison, and Robert McGinnis. "Rank Advancement in Academic Careers: Sex Differences and the Effects of Productivity." *American Sociological Review*, 58, no. 5 (1993): 703–22.

Lotka, Alfred J. "The Frequency Distribution of Scientific Productivity." *Journal of the Washington Academy of Sciences* 16, no. 12 (1926): 317–23.

Lupton, Deborah. *The Quantified Self*. Hoboken, NJ: Wiley, 2016.

Mackenzie, Donald. "Uninventing the Bomb?" *Medicine, Conflict and Survival* 12, no. 3 (1996): 202–11.

MacKenzie, Donald, and Taylor Spears. "'The Formula That Killed Wall Street': The Gaussian Copula and Modelling Practices in Investment Banking." *Social Studies of Science* 44, no. 3 (2014): 393–417.

MacLeod, Donald. "Universities Fear Cuts in Humanities Funding." *The Independent*, October 10, 1991.

Malisch, Jessica L., Breanna N. Harris, Shanen M. Sherrer, Kristy A. Lewis, Stephanie L. Shepherd, Pumtiwitt C. McCarthy, Jessica L. Spott, Elizabeth P. Karam, Naima Moustaid-Moussa, and Jessica McCrory Calarco. "Opinion: In the Wake of COVID-19, Academia Needs New Solutions to Ensure Gender Equity." *Proceedings of the National Academy of Sciences* 117, no. 27 (2020): 15378–81.

Marshall, Emily A. "Defining Population Problems: Using Topic Models for Cross-National Comparison of Disciplinary Development." *Poetics* 41, no. 6 (2013): 701–24.

Mayhew, Ken, Cécile Deer, and Mehak Dua. "The Move to Mass Higher Education in the UK: Many Questions and Some Answers." *Oxford Review of Education* 30, no. 1 (2004): 65–82.

McBain, Barclay. "Paper Mountain to Climb in Ratings Bid." *The Herald* [Glasgow], June 25, 1992.

McCulloch, Sharon. "The Importance of Being REF-able: Academic Writing Under Pressure from a Culture of Counting." *Impact of Social Sciences Blog*, February 9, 2017.

McKiernan, Erin C., Lesley A. Schimanski, Carol Muñoz Nieves, Lisa Matthias, Meredith T. Niles, and Juan P. Alperin. "Meta-Research: Use of the Journal Impact Factor in Academic Review, Promotion, and Tenure Evaluations." *ELife* 8 (2019): e47338.

McMahan, Peter, and James Evans. "Ambiguity and Engagement." *American Journal of Sociology* 124, no. 3 (2018): 860–912.

Merton, Robert K. "The Matthew Effect in Science: The Reward and Communication Systems of Science Are Considered." *Science* 159, no. 3810 (1968): 56–63.

——. *The Sociology of Science: Theoretical and Empirical Investigations.* Chicago: University of Chicago Press, 1973.

Mills, C. Wright. "On Intellectual Craftsmanship (1952)." *Society* 17, no. 2 (1980): 63–70.

Mills, Colin. "Social Status, Social Position and Social Class in Post-War British Society." In *The History of Sociology in Britain*, ed. Plamena Panayotova, 161–90. Cham, Switzerland: Palgrave Macmillan, 2019.

Mohr, John W., and Petko Bogdanov. "Introduction—Topic Models: What They Are and Why They Matter." *Poetics* 41, no. 6 (2013): 545–69.

Navigli, Roberto, and Federico Martelli. "An Overview of Word and Sense Similarity." *Natural Language Engineering* 25, no. 6 (2019): 693–714.

Nelson, Laura K. "Computational Grounded Theory: A Methodological Framework." *Sociological Methods & Research* 49, no. 1 (2020): 3–42.

——. "To Measure Meaning in Big Data, Don't Give Me a Map, Give Me Transparency and Reproducibility." *Sociological Methodology* 49, no. 1 (2019): 139–43.

Nelson, Laura K., Derek Burk, Marcel Knudsen, and Leslie McCall. "The Future of Coding: A Comparison of Hand-Coding and Three Types of Computer-Assisted Text Analysis Methods." *Sociological Methods & Research* 50, no. 1 (2021): 202–37. https://doi.org/10.1177/0049124118769114.

Neyland, Daniel, Véra Ehrenstein, and Sveta Milyaeva. *Can Markets Solve Problems?: An Empirical Inquiry Into Neoliberalism in Action.* London: Goldsmiths, 2019.

Nield, Ted. "A 4m nonsense to rate university research." *The Independent*, Science and Technology, November 13, 1989.

Norpoth, Helmut, and Milton Lodge. "The Difference Between Attitudes and Nonattitudes in the Mass Public: Just Measurements." *American Journal of Political Science* 29, no. 2 (1985): 291–307.

Özgöde, Onur. "Institutionalism in Action: Balancing the Substantive Imbalances of 'the Economy' Through the Veil of Money." *History of Political Economy* 52, no. 2 (2020): 307–39.

Parish, Austin J., Kevin W. Boyack, and John P. A. Ioannidis. "Dynamics of Co-Authorship and Productivity Across Different Fields of Scientific Research." *PloS One* 13, no. 1 (2018): e0189742.

Phillimore, A. J. "University Research Performance Indicators in Practice: The University Grants Committee's Evaluation of British Universities, 1985–86." *Research Policy* 18, no. 5 (1989): 255–71.

Phillips, Damon J., Catherine Turco, and Ezra W. Zuckerman. "High-Status Conformity and Deviance: Pressures for Purity Among U.S. Corporate Law Firms." Unpublished Working Paper, Sloan School of Management, Massachusetts Institute of Technology, 2010. http://citeseerx.ist.psu.edu /viewdoc/download?doi=10.1.1.368.8703&rep=rep1&type=pdf.

Pontille, David. "Authorship Practices and Institutional Contexts in Sociology: Elements for a Comparison of the United States and France." *Science, Technology, & Human Values* 28, no. 2 (2003): 217–43.

Popper, Karl. *The Logic of Scientific Discovery*. London: Routledge, 2005.

Porter, Theodore M. *Trust in Numbers: The Pursuit of Objectivity in Science and Public Life*. Princeton, NJ: Princeton University Press, 1996.

Power, Michael. *The Audit Society: Rituals of Verification*. Oxford: Oxford University Press, 1997.

Pugh, Martin. "Empires of Hype." *The Guardian*. November 10, 1992.

Radkau, Joachim. *Max Weber: A Biography*. Hoboken, NJ: Wiley, 2013.

Ràfols, Ismael. "S&T Indicators in the Wild: Contextualization and Participation for Responsible Metrics." *Research Evaluation* 28, no. 1 (2018): 7–22.

"Ratings Games." *Nature* 436, no. 7053 (2005): 889–90. https://doi.org/10.1038 /436889b.

Roemer, Robert E., and James E. Schnitz. "Academic Employment as Day Labor: The Dual Labor Market in Higher Education." *Journal of Higher Education* 53, no. 5 (1982): 514–31.

Roose, Henk, Willem Roose, and Stijn Daenekindt. "Trends in Contemporary Art Discourse: Using Topic Models to Analyze 25 Years of Professional Art Criticism." *Cultural Sociology* 12, no. 3 (2018): 303–24.

Rosenfeld, Rachel A. "Job Mobility and Career Processes." *Annual Review of Sociology* 18, no. 1 (1992): 39–61.

Rosenfeld, Rachel A., and Jo Ann Jones. "Institutional Mobility Among Academics: The Case of Psychologists." *Sociology of Education* 59, no. 4 (1986): 212–26.

Roth, Alvin E., and Marilda Sotomayor. "Two-Sided Matching." *Handbook of Game Theory with Economic Applications* 1 (1992): 485–541.

Salganik, Matthew J., Peter Sheridan Dodds, and Duncan J. Watts. "Experimental Study of Inequality and Unpredictability in an Artificial Cultural Market." *Science* 311, no. 5762 (2006): 854–56.

Salganik, Matthew J., and Duncan J. Watts. "Leading the Herd Astray: An Experimental Study of Self-Fulfilling Prophecies in an Artificial Cultural Market." *Social Psychology Quarterly* 71, no. 4 (2008): 338–55.

Salter, Brian, and Ted Tapper. "The Politics of Governance in Higher Education: The Case of Quality Assurance." *Political Studies* 48, no. 1 (2000): 66–87.

Sauder, Michael. "A Sociology of Luck." *Sociological Theory* 38, no. 3 (2020): 193–216.

Sauder, Michael, and Wendy Nelson Espeland. "Strength in Numbers? The Advantages of Multiple Rankings." *Indiana Law Journal* 81 (2006): 205.

Savage, Mike. "The Fall and Rise of Class Analysis in British Sociology, 1950–2016." *Tempo Social* 28, no. 2 (2016): 57–72.

Sayer, Derek. *Rank Hypocrisies: The Insult of the REF.* Los Angeles: Sage, 2014.

Scott, John. *British Sociology: A History.* Cham, Switzerland: Palgrave Macmillan, 2020.

Sennett, Richard. *The Craftsman.* New Haven, CT: Yale University Press, 2008.

Shapin, Steven. *The Scientific Life: A Moral History of a Late Modern Vocation.* Chicago: University of Chicago Press, 2009.

Shattock, Michael. *The UGC and the Management of British Universities.* Bristol, PA: Society for Research Into Higher Education and Open University Press, 1994.

Shore, Cris, Susan Wright, Vered Amit, Judy Brown, Casper Bruun Jensen, Mark Maguire, Sally Engle Merry, Michael Sauder, Wendy Espeland, and Gavin Smith. "Audit Culture Revisited: Rankings, Ratings, and the Reassembling of Society." *Current Anthropology* 56, no. 3 (2015): 431–32.

Shwed, Uri, and Peter S. Bearman. "The Temporal Structure of Scientific Consensus Formation." *American Sociological Review* 75, no. 6 (2010): 817–40.

Smaldino, Paul E., Matthew A. Turner, and Pablo A. Contreras Kallens. "Open Science and Modified Funding Lotteries Can Impede the Natural Selection of Bad Science." *Royal Society Open Science* 6, no. 7 (2019): 190194.

Smith-Doerr, Laurel, Donald Tomaskovic-Devey, Sharla Alegria, Kaye Husbands Fealing, and Debra Fitzpatrick. "Gender Pay Gaps in U.S. Federal

Science Agencies: An Organizational Approach." *American Journal of Sociology* 125, no. 2 (2019): 534–76.

Solnit, Rebecca. Foreword to *Pandemic Solidarity: Mutual Aid During the Covid-19 Crisis.* Ed. Marina Sitrin and Colectiva Sembrar. London: Pluto, 2020.

Stinchcombe, Arthur L. "Organizations and Social Structure." *Handbook of Organizations* 44, no. 2 (1965): 142–93.

Stoltz, Dustin S., and Marshall A. Taylor. "Cultural Cartography with Word Embeddings." ArXiv Preprint ArXiv:2007.04508, 2020.

——. "Cultural Cartography with Word Embeddings." *Poetics* 88 (2021). https://doi.org/10.1016/j.poetic.2021.101567.

Strathern, Marilyn. *Audit Cultures: Anthropological Studies in Accountability, Ethics and the Academy.* London: Routledge, 2003.

Suitor, J. Jill, Dorothy Mecom, and Ilana S. Feld. "Gender, Household Labor, and Scholarly Productivity Among University Professors." *Gender Issues* 19, no. 4 (2001): 50–67.

Tavory, Iddo, and Stefan Timmermans. *Abductive Analysis: Theorizing Qualitative Research.* University of Chicago Press, 2014.

Taylor, Mark. "Shared Governance in the Modern University." *Higher Education Quarterly* 67, no. 1 (2013): 80–94.

Teplitskiy, Misha, Eamon Duede, Michael Menietti, and Karim R. Lakhani. "Status Drives How We Cite: Evidence from Thousands of Authors." ArXiv E-Prints, 2020, arXiv-2002.

Thomas, Keith. "Universities Under Attack." *London Review of Books* 33, no. 24 (2011): 9.

Traag, V. A., and L. Waltman. "Systematic Analysis of Agreement Between Metrics and Peer Review in the UK REF." *Palgrave Communications* 5, no. 1 (2019): 1–12. https://doi.org/10.1057/s41599-019-0233-x.

UCU Branch Solidarity Network. "Why We Will Strike Against REF." March 19, 2019. https://ucubranchsolidaritynetwork.wordpress.com/2019/03/19/why-we-will-strike-against-ref/.

Vaisey, Stephen. "The 'Attitudinal Fallacy' Is a Fallacy: Why We Need Many Methods to Study Culture." *Sociological Methods & Research* 43, no. 2 (2014): 227–31.

Vaisey, Stephen, and Omar Lizardo. "Cultural Fragmentation or Acquired Dispositions? A New Approach to Accounting for Patterns of Cultural Change." *Socius* 2 (2016). https://doi.org/10.1177/2378023116669726.

Verhulst, Brad, Lindon J. Eaves, and Peter K. Hatemi. "Correlation Not Causation: The Relationship Between Personality Traits and Political Ideologies." *American Journal of Political Science* 56, no. 1 (2012): 34–51.

Walker, James, Marina Della Giusta, and Rita Fontinha. "Initial Findings from the Consultation on the Impact of Research Metrics on the Work of Academic Economists 2020," Unpublished Working Paper, Henley Business School, University of Reading, UK, 2020.

Weber, Max. "Science as a Vocation." *Daedalus* 87, no. 1 (1958): 111–34.

Westerheijden, Donald F. "University Governance in the United Kingdom, the Netherlands and Japan: Autonomy and Shared Governance After New Public Management Reforms." *Nagoya Journal of Higher Education* 18 (2018): 199–220.

White, Douglas R., and Stephen P. Borgatti. "Betweenness Centrality Measures for Directed Graphs." *Social Networks* 16, no. 4 (1994): 335–46.

Whitley, Richard. *The Intellectual and Social Organization of the Sciences*. 2nd ed. Oxford: Oxford University Press, 2000.

Whitley, Richard, Jochen Gläser, and Lars Engwall, eds. *Reconfiguring Knowledge Production: Changing Authority Relationships in the Sciences and Their Consequences for Intellectual Innovation*. Oxford: Oxford University Press, 2010.

Whitty, Geoff. "Education, Social Class and Social Exclusion." *Journal of Education Policy* 16, no. 4 (2001): 287–95.

Wilmers, Nathan. "Job Turf or Variety: Task Structure as a Source of Organizational Inequality." *Administrative Science Quarterly* 64, no. 4 (2020): 1018–57. https://doi.org/10.1177/0001839220909101.

Wilsdon, James. *The Metric Tide: Independent Review of the Role of Metrics in Research Assessment and Management*. Los Angeles: Sage, 2016.

Wouters, Paul. *The Citation Culture*. Amsterdam: University of Amsterdam, 1999.

Woolston, Chris. "Scientists' Salary Data Highlight US$18,000 Gender Pay Gap." *Nature* 565, no. 7740 (2019): 527. https://doi.org/10.1038/d41586 -019-00220-y.

Wright, Glen. "A Guide to the REF for the Shameless Academic." *The Guardian*, December 12 2014.

Wu, Jiang, and Xiu-Hao Ding. "Author Name Disambiguation in Scientific Collaboration and Mobility Cases." *Scientometrics* 96, no. 3 (2013): 683–97. https://doi.org/10.1007/s11192-013-0978-8.

Yuret, Tolga. "Tenure and Turnover of Academics in Six Undergraduate Programs in the United States." *Scientometrics* 116, no. 1 (2018): 101–24. https://doi.org/10.1007/s11192-018-2742-6.

Zambrana, Ruth Enid. *Toxic Ivory Towers: The Consequences of Work Stress on Underrepresented Minority Faculty.* New Brunswick, NJ: Rutgers University Press, 2018.

Zuckerman, Ezra W. "The Categorical Imperative: Securities Analysts and the Illegitimacy Discount." *American Journal of Sociology* 104, no. 5 (1999): 1398–1438.

——. "Optimal Distinctiveness Revisited." *The Oxford Handbook of Organizational Identity*, ed. Michael G. Pratt, Majken Schultz, Blake E. Ashforth, and Davide Ravasi, 183–99. Oxford: Oxford University Press, 2016.

INDEX

Christin, Angèle, 138–39, 141
citations: high-impact, 129; metrics
   of, 56
Clarivate's Web of Science, 198
Clark, Burton, 71
Clark, Gregory, 216n2
class, 78, 121–23; semantic shifts of,
   123, 123–24; study on, 216n2
classifications, 161, 184
Clemens, Elisabeth, 129
collaborations, scholarship, 80
colleagues: academic, 84, 145; as
   competitors, 177; evaluations of,
   149, 175
Collini, Steffan, 29
community: ethics of, 166;
   intellectual, 96
community membership, 105
Companion Species Manifesto
   (Haraway), 100
competitiveness, 45–46, 180
competitors, colleagues as, 177
computational models, 107
computational techniques, 198
conferences, 178
connections, academic, 178
contributions to service, 54–55
control: disciplinary, 24; of labor,
   24, 57
convergence: assessment of, 115;
   epistemic, 212; thematic, 112
conversations, difficult, 151
corpus, 211–12
costs, of research evaluation, 43
cost units, 37–38
Cottom, Tressie McMillan, 170,
   178–79
counted, being, 88–89
counting, 170
counting careers, 63–68
counting hierarchies, 138–44
counting techniques, 57–58

courses, academic, 174
COVID-19 pandemic, 188–89
credit score, social, 140–41
criteria, performance, 157
criticism, 41, 176
cultural intersections, 122–23
cultural taste, 115
cultures: academic, 104, 125; audit,
   25, 126; of evaluation, 57, 64,
   66, 162, 165; material, 163; of
   quantification, 166
Cummins, Neil, 216n2

data, 70, 70–71, 197; affiliation,
   199; bibliometric, 200–201;
   longitudinal panel, 205; oral
   history, 209
data sets, 72–77
death, of scientist superstars, 63
deindustrialization, 122
demographics, 74
demography, entropy in, 106
demotion, 182
departmental organization, 124
Departmental_Topics, 204
departmental typicality, 107–9, 208
Department_Author_Topics, 204
departments, 93; bureaucracy in,
   160–61; distance between, 110–11,
   111; economics, 155; homogeneity
   of, 111–12, 118–19; measuring, 45;
   scholars and, 87–88; scoring of,
   164–65; of sociology, 112–13
descriptive statistics, 201, *201*
developments, professional, 54
devotion, trajectories of, 13–21
digital humanities scholars, 83
disambiguation, 200
disciplinary change, 104–14, 179
disciplinary control, 24
disciplinary convergence, 163
disciplinary identity, 152

favors, 161
financial inequities, 188
financial resources, 27
"fit" in scholars, 95–96
fixed-effects logistic model, 220n27
fixed-effects negative binomial
    regression, 220n29
Fourcade, Marion, 23, 131
de Fraja, Gianni, 45, 187
funding, 38, 144; allocating, 56–57;
    REF, 51–52, 218n39, 224n15;
    scientific career, 62; for scoring,
    50–51; state, 4, 32, 161–62; student
    enrollment and, 34; in U.S., 64
funding councils, UK, 51
future habits, predicting, 115–16

games, research assessments as, 163
Gargiulo, Floriana, 198
Gelber, Scott, 17–18
gender, 60–61, 78, 220n27; of authors,
    208; in British social sciences, 75;
    mobility and, 80–81; productivity
    and, 73–74, 90
gender gaps, 76–77
gender privilege, 173–74
Gensim, skip-gram, 211
Gensim library, 203
geometry, 116
goals, setting, 21
Goffman, Erwin, 14
"golden age," of scholarship, 43
Goldthorpe, John, 122
Goodwin, Craufurd, 175
governance, shared, 182
grade point average (GPA), 50, 88,
    163–64
grading, 50–51, 149
Grading the College (Gelber), 17–18
Graeber, David, 190
grants, prestigious, 62
Griffen, Zack, 217n28

Hacking, Ian, 8, 137
Hall, Stuart, 99
Halsey, A. H., 44
handbooks, 56
Haraway, Donna, 100
von Hayek, Frederick, 27
Heads of Department, 149
health sciences, 48
Hellen (political scientist), 157–59
heterodox economists, 130, 132
hierarchies, 17, 18, 20; administrative,
    142–43; counting, 138–44;
    domesticated, 167–69; in
    economics, 21–22; of placement,
    220n31; of prestige, 152–53, 153,
    156–57, 168, 177–78; of status, 143;
    of value, 127; vocation and, 191–92;
    of worth, 169
higher education, 30–31, 34; British,
    65, 187; in U.S., 64
Higher Education Funding Councils
    of England, Wales, and Scotland, 48
Higher Education Standards
    Authority, UK, 74
high-impact citations, 129
h-index, 19–20
histories, oral, 198, 208–10
Hoggart, Richard, 112
homogeneity: of departments, 111–12,
    118–19; thematic, 209
How Institutions Think (Douglas),
    182–83
How Professors Think (Lamont), 215n37
humanities, arts and, 48
human suffering, 192
Husbands, Christopher, 113, 114
hydra, 43–47
hypothesis, of language, 211

identifying excellence, 42
identity, 20–21; disciplinary, 152
impact, societal, 170

Sayer, Derek, 224n12
scarcity, 34
scholarly excellence, 4
scholarly labor, 134–35
scholarly landscape, academic work
  and, 104–5
scholarly quantification, 12, 98
scholars, 10–11, 53–54, 181; career
  strategies and, 127; departments
  and, 87–88; digital humanities, 83;
  early-career, 66; as employees, 142;
  established, 91; evaluations and,
  68–69; "fit" in, 95–96; grants and,
  62; influences on, 57; interviews
  with, 209; job change and, 78;
  at Liverpool, 173; metrics and,
  57–58; mobility and, 91–92, 102;
  positions and, 61–62; pressure
  on, 125; publications by, 150–51;
  science policy, 58; similarity of, *85*;
  submitted, 50
scholarship, 16–17, 185; collaborations
  and, 80; "golden age" of, 43;
  sociological, 152
science: counting, 7–8; political, 22, *87*,
  159; prestige in, 90; sociology of,
  61. *See also* British social sciences
science of science, 196, 197
science policy scholars, 58
Science Research Council, 33
scientific career funding, 62
scientific careers, 59–60
scientific change, 63, 195–96
scientific fields, power and, 139
scientific knowledge, 195
scientific labor, 190–91
scientists, 7, 17; deaths of, 63; social, 9,
  55–56, 107–8, 195–98
scientometrics, 8
score: intensity, 164; power, 164–66;
  typicality and, 109, *109*

scoring, 49–51
Scott, John, 112
security, employment, 27
selective affinities, 33–37
selectivity, 47; exercise for, 43;
  research, 36
self-awareness, 22
semantic convergences, 133
semantic shifts, 118; of class, *123*,
  123–24
semantic similarity, among
  institutions, 118, *118*
service, contributions to, 54–55
Shapin, Steven, 16, 17
shared governance, 182
Shattock, Michael, 30–31
shifts: epistemic, 198; lexical, 119
Shore, Cris, 183
similarity, 83–84, 87, 95, *205*;
  between departments, *86*;
  across disciplines, *87*; of scholars,
  85
simulating value, 145–51
single-institution careers, 27
skip-gram Gensim, 211
Smith, Adam, 6
social credit score, 140–41
social life, 185
Social Science Citation Index
  (SSCI), 69, 73, 76, 197–98, 199
social scientists, 9, 55–56, 107–8;
  studying, 195–98
sociological scholarship, 152
sociology, 22, *86*, *87*, 111, 120, 181;
  class and, 121–22; departments
  of, 112–13; LSE, 113–14, 148;
  of quantification, 137–38; of
  science, 61; topic models and,
  203; urban, 2
solidarity, 6, 169; anthropologist, 183–
  84; disciplinary, 183; productive,

Printed and bound by CPI Group (UK) Ltd, Croydon, CR0 4YY
25/08/2022
03143861-0001